Discard

Fishing Giants

Other Books by Robert H. Boyle:

Bass Boss

Dead Heat, The Race Against the Green House Effect,
with Michael Oppenheimer

At the Top of Their Game

Acid Rain, with R. Alexander Boyle

Stoneflies for the Angler, with Eric Leiser

Bass, with photographs by Elgin Ciampi

Malignant Neglect, with the Environmental Defense Fund

The Fly-Tyer's Almanac, edited with Dave Whitlock

The Second Fly-Tyer's Almanac, edited with Dave Whitlock

The Water Hustlers, with John Graves and T. H. Watkins

The Hudson River, A Natural and Unnatural History

Sport, Mirror of American Life

Fishing
Giants

and Other Men of Derring-Do

Robert H. Boyle

The Lyons Press
Guilford, Connecticut
An imprint of The Globe Pequot Press

The author thanks Lilly Golden for her editing and Kathryn Belous-Boyle, as always, for everything.

Photo of Preston Jennings on page 196 courtesy of the American Museum of Fly Fishing. Photo of James Joyce by Gisèle Freund.

The Lyons Press is an imprint of The Globe Pequot Press.

Printed in the United States of America

10 9 8 7 6 5 4 3 2 1

Design by Compset, Inc.

The Library of Congress Cataloging-in-Publication Data is available on file.

FOR RIA

With heartfelt thanks for широкуюдушу
beyond human comprehension

Lives of great men all remind us
We can make our lives sublime,
And, departing, leave behind us
Footprints on the sands of time.

—Longfellow, "A Psalm of Life"

Fishing Giants

Contents

Foreword

All the men in this book are obsessed with the outdoors, nature if you will, be it fishing, tying flies, studying aquatic insects, hunting, collecting butterflies, or populating a fictional watery world with myriad species of fish.

With the exception of James Joyce, who died in 1941, I met and wrote about all of them for *Sports Illustrated*. They intrigued me, and I wanted to know what drove them and how they came to be driven. Sometimes I'd spend up to several weeks following a subject around, interviewing him as well as family and friends, and, when needed, critics. Then sometimes I'd get an idea for a piece about someone I'd known for years because I had suddenly seen a new side to him.

A prime example is the late Cus D'Amato, the fight manager and trainer. I'd written about Cus and his fighters for almost ten years, and I knew that he was eccentric. In fact, I once wrote that "for D'Amato every night has a full moon," but it wasn't until I had to spend a month in Las Vegas waiting for the second Liston-Patterson heavyweight title fight to begin and doing background research that I discovered that Cus was crazy, absolutely crazy, about fishing. Yes, a month in Vegas for a fight that lasted only two minutes and seventeen seconds with Patterson flat on the canvas, but a month that was not totally wasted because I went fishing with Cus for largemouth bass in Lake Mead and rainbow trout in the Colorado River.

Looking back almost seventy years, I can see that I was programmed to write about the men here; I was imprinted as a boy. When I was four I caught my first fish, a sunny, in a lake in Connecticut. When I was ten I was shooting a .22 for record at summer camp in New Hampshire. When I was twelve I went duck hunting on the Chesapeake. But don't think that I was raised in the country; I grew up in the heart of Manhattan.

I spent summers in the New England countryside, either visiting cousins or at camp. Although I loved baseball, boxing, running races, and other sports, I spent many hours fishing, turning over rocks in brooks to collect whatever I could find—contrary to common belief, some of the most beautiful things in the world live underneath rocks—and catching chipmunks, squirrels, and porcupines in live traps. Some sixty years later I still bear a scar from a chipmunk that sank its teeth into my right index finger as I yelled, futilely, to a friend, "Brophy! Brophy! Close the other end of the trap!" In late August I would arrive back in Grand Central Station with tin cans containing frogs and salamanders that, alas, failed to thrive as apartment dwellers.

I survived city life in good part by immersing myself in the outdoor magazines, especially the classified ads, particularly those about dogs: pointers, setters, hounds, retrievers. I was and still am wild about dogs. Before I discovered girls I lived my pre-teen dreams deep in the classified ads, and even after I discovered girls I still dreamed about the classified ads, well, at least part of the time.

My dog dream, or rather my dream dog, became reality, albeit all too briefly, with Jeff. Jeff was a "dropper," the term used for a pointer-setter cross, in his case an English pointer and an Irish setter. I was fourteen when I discovered him in, of all places, a cage, in which he could hardly turn around, in a Third Avenue pet shop. I learned that his owners, a French refugee couple—this was during

World War II—dropped him off in the morning, when they went to work, and picked him up in the evening. Jeff was still a puppy, only five months old, and they were afraid that he would chew their apartment to pieces if he were left alone.

Jeff was feathered like an Irish setter and looked like one, except for white stocking feet and a white face with freckles. Somehow or other I managed to persuade the French couple and my mother to let me have him. He cost $35. A sweet animal, a big galoot, he slept up at the foot of my bed, and, growing dog that he was, he loved to eat. Once he managed to sneak into the apartment next door where the family were expecting guests for dinner. They came out of the kitchen to find Jeff atop the dining room table finishing off the roast beef. But what a pointing instinct. I would take him to a vacant lot at Second Avenue and 35th Street, and there he would hold point on sparrows hopping about.

But Jeff reserved his greatest pointing performance for the fruit stalls outside Verdi's Market on Third Avenue. There, when he stiffened on point, my heart would swell with pride as I imagined us going on to win the Grand National. Indeed, passersby would gather to stare at this immobile, rock-hard animal, head forward, right front leg cocked at the elbow and tail lifted, frozen in absolutely classic point, his eyes transfixed on a fly crawling on a banana.

We never did get to the Grand National. When I was away at summer camp, Jeff suddenly died from what the vet said was meningitis. He was only two and a half years old.

Years later in the Marine Corps I had a platoon sergeant named Henderson who came from the South, Alabama I think, who told me that he used to run classified ads in the outdoor magazines offering coon hounds and squirrel dogs for sale. I asked how he trained them, and he said he never trained any of them. The little town where he lived—where guys went to their family reunions to meet girls—had loads of strays wandering around, and whenever he got an order for a dog all he had to do was whistle and ship off the first one that came his way. No one, he said, ever asked for his money back. In fact, he got letters saying, "Best damn coon dog, or best damn squirrel dog, I've ever had. Can you get my buddy one like him?"

In college at Trinity, in the middle of Hartford, I didn't do any fishing, but I once went rabbit hunting in Farmington with a friend, Winkie Bennett, and I disgusted my roommate by skinning and cleaning a couple of rabbits on top of my trunk. A year in graduate school at Yale commanded all my time, and besides the middle of New Haven was not conducive to outdoor activities. Called into the Marines with the outbreak of the Korean War, I wound up in an amphibian tractor battalion in the Fleet Marine Force, Atlantic, which is where I met the dog-dealing Henderson, who was also a bootlegger in civilian life. In fact, he removed the port engine in an amtrac and installed a still. I did some trolling for fish from an amtrac off the now-controversial island of Vieques, but sharks and barracudas seized upon whatever I caught and I was left with just fish heads.

When I returned home to Manhattan I got a job with the United Press, as that wire service was then known. I started out as a reporter on the city desk—local desk in UP parlance—and then moved on to writing radio news. That was a strange business: every story for "The World in Brief" had to be compressed into two sentences, and the sentences had to be in the present tense because listeners were getting "up to the minute" news. Moreover, you had to avoid using sibilants because "ess's" caused announcers with false teeth to whistle.

My career took a significant turn one day when the bureau manager asked me if I knew anything about sports. I said that I'd played a lot of sports and was a Dodger fan. With that he shifted me to an opening on the sports desk, and I began going out to do interviews. Six months later, I heard that Time Inc. was starting a sports magazine, code named *Muscles,* and I sold what became *Sports Illus-*

trated a piece about Henry Laskau, a national walking champion who was occasionally accused of running. Inasmuch as I got ten times as much for the piece as my weekly take-home pay from UP, I applied for a job at *SI,* and in September of 1954, when the magazine was only four issues old, I joined the staff. In 1956, *SI* sent me to Chicago as a correspondent for both *SI* and *Time,* and in 1959 I went to San Francisco for the two magazines. I was based there when I went to Arizona to accompany Vladimir Nabokov as he chased after butterflies. In 1960, at the request of André Laguerre, *SI's* new managing editor, I returned to New York as a senior writer. For a while I was even listed as a senior editor because André wanted writers to have parity with editors, which caused Roger Hewlett, who had come over from *Time* to edit at *SI,* to lament, "I used to be a writer on an editor's magazine, and now I'm an editor on a writer's magazine."

When *SI* began publication, the editorial mix was half spectator sport and half participant sport, and it remained pretty much that way until about 1986, the year I retired and became a "Special Contributor." Since then the magazine has become jock oriented, almost all elbows, armpits, and gold chains, pegged to events that millions of people watched on TV the previous weekend. Indeed, I doubt that *SI* would publish many, if any, of the pieces included here. As a matter of fact, *SI* originally bought and then returned "You Spigotty Anglease?" to me on the grounds it would be "over the heads of our readers," and thus it wound up in *The New York Times Book Review.*

I was lucky to have been on the magazine during the glory years. I had my share of duty assignments, but if I had an idea for a piece, I took it to Laguerre or his successors, Roy Terrell and Gil Rogin, gave a two-minute pitch, got their assent, and took off.

The following profiles span the years 1959 to 1996. Each of these men taught me something about what it is to be a fanatic, what it is to be a genius, and what it is to be a giant among both.

No Fly-by-Night Cabbie Is Jack

Jack Gartside

Jack Gartside is a tall, lean, 39-year-old Bostonian who looks like Fred Astaire (so people say) and speaks like a Boston Brahmin. He probably fishes more blue-ribbon trout streams than any millionaire alive. He spends the greater part of every summer fly-fishing in Montana, and on occasion he also fishes in England, Norway, Sweden and Japan. In the summer of 1981 he fished in New Zealand for a month. The Boston-Auckland round-trip plane ticket cost Gartside $1.79, which is about the same as he will charge you for a ride from the Ritz-Carlton Hotel to the Esplanade in his taxi.

That trip and that "fare" are fairly typical of Gartside's angling expeditions. One Sunday in late May a year ago, he had been lolling by the Charles River reading *The Boston Globe* when he came upon an ad announcing that, in order to publicize its new route from Boston to Denver, Continental Airlines was going to give away round-trip tickets to 225 people to anywhere in the world that the airline flew. They would be selected from among those who showed up at Logan International Airport the following morning dressed in costumes depicting the destinations of their choice. There was one major catch, and one minor catch: The minor one was a token charge of $1 plus tax; the major one was that those picked had to depart that day.

At 10 A.M. Monday, Gartside made his appearance at the airport decked out in an Aussie campaign hat and a bush jacket made in New Zealand. "I thought that thousands of people would be there," he says, "but there were only about 300. By noon there were 500. Still, I figured I had a 50–50 chance. At 2:30 I was picked, and I only had two hours to get my boarding pass, rush back to my apartment for my rod, my flies and my clothes, and then get back to the airport again. You bet I made it."

Gartside landed in Auckland with all the money he had in the world, $200, but he calculated that would hold him for a while, given the way he travels. One of the people he first met, Bob Sullivan, a tackle dealer at Lake Taupo on the North Island, lent him a pair of waders, and Gartside then hitchhiked around the island by thumbing with his right hand while using his left to hold the waders and his rod aloft. The ploy worked beyond Gartside's expectations. A motorist who stopped to pick him up was going fishing himself, and he took Gartside along, for a *week,* and showed him all his secret spots. Later, a husband and wife Gartside met after he cadged a cigarette from them in a theater lobby and started telling how he had flown from Boston for only $1.79, put him up on their farm for a while and even loaned him their car to get around in.

Gartside held out in New Zealand for a month. When he arrived back in Boston, he had exactly $1.35 in change left in his pockets— "I always just make it under the wire"—and had to drive a cab for three weeks before he and his cat, Tobermory, named after a talking cat in a story by Saki, could drive out to West Yellowstone, Mont. in his battered 1965 Volvo sedan. The Volvo, which Gartside bought for $300 five years ago, currently has 397,000 miles on it, and it serves as his home away from home. The car is registered in Montana, and the license plates say FLYTYER, a self-advertisement for Gartside, who makes his living tying flies as well as driving a cab.

When short of cash in the boondocks, Gartside will drive to a spot by a river where fishermen park and sell flies tied to order.

To describe Gartside simply as a hawker of stream-side flies would be like calling Nathan's Famous frankfurters mere hot dogs. Along with John Betts, who ties with synthetic materials, Gartside, who ties almost exclusively with natural materials, is in the front rank nationally, which means the world. "I'd put him at the top," says Bud Lilly of West Yellowstone, who views flytiers with an experienced businessman's eye and whose mail-order catalog has featured Gartside's flies ever since the cabbie ambled into Lilly's shop one day in 1976 with a Pheasant Hopper stuck on his vest. "Jack's flies are superb," Lilly says. "His Pheasant Hopper is a real thing. When I first met Jack, he was kind of a drifter, but he has established direction, and if he continues in that direction, he's going to make an impression on the fly-fishing world. He has a lot of integrity, a lot of principle and a lot of feeling for what the sport is. He's an *artist*. He has a feeling for natural materials, a feeling for an idea, and he's not greedy. By not greedy, I mean he's not 'commercial' the way some flytyers can be."

Robert Rifchin, editor of *The Roundtable,* a magazine published by United Fly Tyers, Inc., confirms Gartside's credentials. "Oh, absolutely," he says. "Little known, but very talented. In terms of skill and ability, he's on a par with Betts. Jack can tie a conventional pattern with anyone in the United States, but he's an innovator, mostly because he didn't have money. He found ways to use materials that everyone has thrown away for years. He isn't a speedy commercial tyer, but I've never seen anyone who has consistently produced better flies. There's no junk at all. He wouldn't let it go out with his name on the box. He'd fish it himself."

Back in Boston, Gartside often whiles away the time spent in taxi queues by tying flies in a vise attached to the steering wheel. Indeed, he originated his Hacklehead streamers while waiting at Logan. "I was tying some large marabou streamers," he says, "and as the sun was lying low, I needed a way to finish a head neatly under poor lighting conditions and hit upon this method." Recently a man got in the cab, saw what Gartside was doing and bought a dozen streamers.

When not tying flies in the cab, Gartside reads voraciously. His apartment is stuffed with thousands of books, in addition to a half dozen deer hides, a moose hide, pheasant skins, chicken necks and other fly-tying materials. At present, he's rereading Shakespeare's tragedies, and he has named a new fly Hamlet's Cloud. "Act Three, Scene Two," he says. "Hamlet asks, 'Do you see yonder cloud that's almost in shape of a camel?' Polonius: 'By the mass, and 'tis like a camel, indeed.' Hamlet: 'Methinks it is like a weasel.' Polonius: 'It is backed like a weasel.' Hamlet: 'Or like a whale?' Polonius: 'Very like a whale.' Most fish are like Polonius. They see what they want to see, and this fly can be anything."

Gartside, who leases his cab by the mile from the Boston Cab Company, usually waits for fares in front of the Ritz, the Sheraton Boston or the new Marriott on the waterfront. His fares have included Laurence Olivier, Rudolph Nureyev, Seiji Ozawa, Joan Kennedy, William Buckley, Annie's dog, Sandy, Sarah Caldwell and Red Sox Pitcher Bruce Hurst. "The actors are usually very short jobs," he says. "They're playing at the Colonial, the Shubert or the Wilbur, and they stay at the Ritz."

On occasion a fare will prove to be an adventure. "A girl got into my cab one evening," says Gartside, "and she told me she wanted to stake out a Japanese restaurant. Her name was Jodie, and she suspected that her boyfriend was having an affair with her roommate, a Japanese girl who was a waitress in the restaurant. I parked across the street from the restaurant, and after a while the boyfriend showed up and met the Japanese girl. They got into his car. 'Follow them,' Jodie said. We must have gone 15 miles trailing them before they finally drew up in front of her house. Jodie said to me, 'Why don't you go to the door of the apartment and pretend you're a

Western Union messenger, and I'll hide in an alcove and when they come to the door I'll surprise them.' It was a dull night, so I said, 'O.K., but pay me now.' She did, and I went into the house and knocked at the door. 'Who is it?' asked the Japanese girl. 'Western Union,' I said. The Japanese girl opened the door, and behind her I could see the boyfriend, both in scanty costumes. 'What is it?' she asked. 'I have a message from Jodie,' I said. 'What is it?' she asked. I said, 'I think you should ask her yourself.' At which point I thought it wise to depart as Jodie came out from the alcove."

If Gartside seems unusually well-spoken and well-read for a cab-driver, it should be noted that until seven years ago he was a high school English teacher in Boston. He quit the day some students set fire to a desk and the classroom went up in smoke. "It's safer driving a cab at night in Boston than it is teaching in a Boston school during the day," he says.

Gartside and his sister, Gladys, are the only Gartsides in the Boston area phone books. The name is English (it literally means by the side of an enclosed garden), and all the Gartsides in his family came from Lancashire. Grandfather Gartside was a machinist on his way to Australia who passed through Boston and never got any farther. Instead, he married a young English girl who was working as a domestic servant in Newton and raised a family. Jack's father, John, was also a machinist, and life was always a struggle. To make ends meet, he worked as a part-time cop, while his wife worked as a secretary and telephone solicitor. She also played the organ in St. Anne's Episcopal Church in Revere, Mass., where her husband served as a lay reader. "My father was a great reader," Gartside says. "He had a wonderful speaking voice, a High Church voice. He always talked about the church and never about his work, although he never missed a day."

When Jack was born, his mother gave him the middle name of Clarence after her uncle, Clarence Wheeler, a general manager of the National Biscuit Company. "She hoped he would remember us in the will," Gartside says. "My mother named my sister after Uncle Clarence's only daughter, Gladys. When Uncle Clarence died, he didn't remember us at all but left everything to his daughter."

As a boy Gartside read every book he could get his hands on. "I read *King Solomon's Mines, She,* all of Rider Haggard. Arthur Conan Doyle, all the Holmes stories. I reread them every other year. Ghost stories—M.R. James, Algernon Blackwood, John Collier, Roald Dahl. I've always been very strong on story and plot. That's why I read and why I fish and why I live and why I play poker and why I drive a cab—for the surprise ending. Think of that passage in the Bible, 'O Lord, let me know the number of my days.' Wouldn't it be awful to know that? My father always told me stories, too, and he encouraged me to travel. He was always poring over maps, and we would make imaginary trips together. But he never did make any trips. He couldn't even drive a car. Failed every driver's test he ever took."

The younger Gartside also had a vivid imagination; he would see himself as a character in whatever book he happened to be reading. "I went to a neighborhood reunion in Revere the other day and saw kids I used to hang around with when I was 10 or 11," Gartside says. "One fellow remembered me as a boy Tarzan. The mayor remembered that I went around with a lasso for two or three years roping everyone I saw, including him. Almost broke his neck. When I was in the seventh grade I held the school record for truancy and tardiness, and I guess I haven't stopped yet. I'm still late for everything.

"The first time I was ever arrested was when I was 12, but I impressed the police with my reading knowledge. I had gone to Filene's Basement with a friend whose mother had given him money for a pair of shoes. My friend lost the money, and he didn't dare go home. 'I'll pinch a pair for you,' I said. I did, and I was caught. The police took me in a paddy wagon to the station, where I was locked up behind a grill near the sergeant's desk. The cop and the sergeant, both Irish, were talking about politics, and the sergeant asked, 'Who wrote that book, *The Last Hurrah?*' The cop didn't know, but I called out, 'Edwin O'Connor,' and the sergeant said, 'Can't be such a bad kid if he knows that.' The second time I was arrested was in Norway for trespassing on a salmon river, a river that costs a fortune to fish. I didn't think anyone would see me. I pleaded ignorance. I said I was hiking when I came across this river, and I just happened to have my rod with me. Since I had my town license and a Norwegian girlfriend testified on my behalf, they let me off."

It wasn't so easy with the pinched shoes from Filene's Basement. "I had to go to juvenile court," Gartside recalls. "I was given a suspended sentence and told to stay out of trouble for six months."

Gartside's father, who was mightily upset by the incident, sought to channel Jack's energies into fishing. The senior Gartside didn't fish himself, but there was a long breakwater at Revere that was exposed at low tide, and Gartside would go there to fish for pollack, mackerel and striped bass. "I was often stranded out there when the tide rose, and the Coast Guard had to rescue me several times," he says. "Once I got my picture in the paper. I was a Red Sox fan, still am, and at the Sportsman's Show I saw my idol, Ted Williams, tying flies. I don't think I'd thought much about trout then, but I said to myself, 'Boy, if Ted Williams is doing this, it must be good.' I went home, took two of my grandfather's micrometers and used one to clamp the other one down while I used it as a vice. My grandfather wasn't pleased at all when he found out. The calibrations were off ever after. I tied flies with fur from the cat and pigeon feathers. I started fishing for trout, and with the first streamer I tied I caught a trout in Fish Brook, a tributary of the Ipswich River. I had a fishing friend, Henry Lightbody, a misnomer if there ever was one because he was one of the fattest kids I've ever known. We'd sit behind one another in class, desks half-open, reading Ray Bergman and Joe Brooks in *Outdoor Life*. Bergman wrote about trout fishing in the East, Brooks about Montana, and that's why I later went out there."

When Gartside was 18, he enlisted in the Air Force. "I joined to see the world," he says. "Where did I first end up? Cape Cod. Later on, I did get to Okinawa and Japan. Fly fishing appeals to the Japanese. It's very graceful and contemplative."

Gartside got out of the Air Force in 1966, went home and found that his father was dying. "All he did was raise a family, work hard, have all these dreams about traveling and never went anywhere," Gartside says. "And then one day when he was 53 he found himself flat on his back with cancer. He spent almost a year in dying, and a few weeks before he died he told me never to end up like that, full of regret for all the things he never did. I do what I do, I am what I am, I take from my father's death."

Gartside worked his way through the University of Massachusetts in Boston, where he majored in English and minored in German. He graduated in 1969, went to work as a teacher and spent the summers fishing. In 1975, he quit teaching to drive a cab.

To support himself on his jaunts abroad, Gartside has served as an extra in a Norwegian movie about Vikings (he played a peasant), has worked as a waiter in Sweden and Japan, has unloaded Argentine beef on the docks of Lübeck in West Germany and has swept African tobacco off the floors of an Amsterdam cigarette factory. Everything he swept, including dust and dead snakes found in the bales, accompanied the tobacco on the conveyor belt, and he soon was promoted to blender. In that capacity he added chocolate, mint and other flavoring to cigarettes for the European market that were supposed to have an American taste. "I worked in a stainless steel vat filled with mint from China," he says. "Ever been in a mint vat? A great smell."

In this country, Gartside takes odd jobs whenever his car breaks down as he drives back and forth between Boston and the trout streams of Montana. Once after he ran into a moose with a Ford van, he spent a week in Minneapolis putting screws in caskets and another week degreasing skimobile runners in order to pay for the repairs. When really pressed for money, he'll skip eating. "I can imagine eating a meal, and then I won't eat because my imagination has fed me," he explains. "That's why I'm so skinny—6'2" and 153 pounds."

Gartside owns only two rods. One is nine feet long and made of graphite, the other, a seven-footer, of fiberglass. "I'm not a good fisherman because I don't know equipment," he says. "I just know how to catch fish. After a while you get to know where the fish are." Indeed, one fish he's very proud of is a four-pound brown trout he caught in England. That's a nice fish, but it hardly seems worth a brag, except for the fact that Gartside caught it in London in the moat of the Old Palace near Parliament. "There are some nice trout there," he says. "People feed them bread and popcorn, but if you get down there early enough you can get in a cast." His best fish was a 13½-pound brown trout that he took in the Gallatin River in Montana in 1979 on his first cast of the year out West. "Kind of spoiled the whole season for me," he says. "It was on August 1, a hot day when even mad dogs and Englishmen were hiding under bushes. A friend took pictures of it, and then I released it. I took that fish on a fly that's listed in Bud Lilly's catalog as the Filo Fly. It's also sold as the Gartside Pheasant Nymph, but it's most commonly called the Sparrow, at least in the East, after being so named by Pete Laszlo in *The Roundtable*. The Sparrow is by far my most successful subsurface, all-purpose fly. I use it in different sizes, color and hackle lengths for most of my nymph fishing. I also fish it as a streamer."

Filo feathers, or aftershafts, are the small, fluffy feathers found down toward the rump of a pheasant. Gartside started using them one day because he had little else to tie from a bird he had otherwise plucked bare. Along with the Sparrow, Gartside ties a number of ultrasoft flies, such as the Wet Mouse, which looks like a pussy willow bud. "I first tied up this pattern on a large, pointless hook as a plaything for Tobermory," he says. "It amused him for about two minutes." Trout apparently take it for a dragonfly nymph.

Another well known Gartside is the dry Pheasant Hopper that Bud Lilly spotted on Gartside's vest that day in 1976. He forms the wing by coating a pheasant feather with polyurethane spar varnish and stroking it into a V-shape that forms naturally. He then cups the wing over a body made of poly-yarn and an underwing made of deer hair. He has found that the most effective body colors are tan, gray, green and yellow, while an orangish body makes an excellent adult stonefly imitation. "The Pheasant Hopper is very durable and quite popular in the West," he says, "and it's been written up in a few books and magazines. Unfortunately, everyone who has written about it has, for some reason, gotten the pattern wrong. I don't use the 'church window' feathers on a pheasant for the wings but the feathers just below them on the back."

There is one inelegant, if spectacularly effective, fly that Gartside ties. It imitates a cigarette filter tip. He tied it one day after discovering that a number of trout in the Firehole River in Yellowstone had filter tips in their stomachs. Gartside has since learned that the trout probably strike at a filter-tip fly because it looks like a freshly molted nymph of an aquatic insect, especially one of the perlid stoneflies.

Besides selling to Lilly or to anglers who happen to jump into his cab, Gartside sells flies by mail. His flies cost from $1.35 to $2 each, and he maintains a year-round post office box in West Yellowstone (Box 853, zip code 59758) to receive orders; the postal service obligingly forwards the mail to Boston when he's in residence there.

"I think my flies are pretty good," Gartside says. "I have my strengths and my weaknesses. I work with what I have, and I've been very limited in money for materials. To me, fly tying really has very little to do with fishing. If all the rivers in the world dried up tomorrow, I'd still tie flies. I like looking at photographs of flies. I take pictures of them, and I have prints made from the slides. Maybe it's growing up with TV, but things look more real to me in a photograph."

Despite his love of fly tying, Gartside refuses to tie full time. "It's lonely work," he says, "and doing it full time would become monotonous. I can't stand focusing on a small space for long periods of time. I like to get out and see things and meet people. That's why I like driving a cab. Also, driving a cab is unpredictable. I like surprise endings."

Recently Gartside has been driving the cab more and tying flies less, in an effort to pay vet bills for his cat, Tobermory, who came down with a mysterious ailment. Though the cat recovered, the bills were so high that Gartside had to sell his piano for $600.

This summer, Gartside spent two free weeks in England (he was the guest of his sister, Gladys, who was left an inheritance by Uncle Clarence's spinster daughter, Gladys, when she died in 1980), and after returning he hacked for a month to raise cash for his annual trek to Montana. Alas, just as he and Tobermory were set to take off in the Volvo, the car blew its water pump and alternator. Gartside then took a bus to Montana, while the cat, which was refused passage on the bus, went in a crate by plane. They met in Bozeman and from there they hitched to West Yellowstone. Says Gartside, speaking for himself and Tobermory, "We'll be in Montana until the snows move in or the Red Sox win the pennant—whichever comes first."

—SEPTEMBER 13, 1982

Gotcha!
Hook, Line
and Lingerie
John Betts

A notice to managers and clerks in lingerie, secondhand clothing, wig, fabric, crafts and artists supply shops: If John Betts, age 43, 5'9", 165 pounds, blond hair, blue eyes, residing at 49 Gillespie Avenue, Fair Haven, N.J. 07701, enters your establishment, whips out a 10-power magnifying glass and begins to fondle a toupee, sigh over paintbrush bristles, or ooh and ah over nightgowns, peignoirs and other froufrou of the boudoir, be assured he is legit. Betts isn't a fetishist, he's a flytyer, and the flies he ties, usually concocted entirely from synthetic materials, bid fair to cause a revolution in fly-fishing.

In recent years an increasing number of flytyers have been turning to synthetics in place of the traditional fur and feathers, but no one is close to Betts in the range and creativity of his forays off the beaten path. He has devised a whole series of extraordinarily realistic and durable flies for fresh and salt water out of the new materials, and some of his "tying" techniques, such as using the flame of a cigarette lighter to make insect bodies from polypropylene yarn, are as novel as the far-out materials he employs. Compared to Betts, other tyers practicing with synthetics are at the "Chopsticks" level, while he is playing Bach. "Betts has a unique mind," says Ted

Niemeyer, the fly tying editor of *Fly Fisherman* magazine. "He can take synthetic materials and find multiple uses for them. He just doesn't develop a body or a wing, but a whole fly."

All of which leads to the question: How well do the wonder-fabric flies do on fish? "I caught more fish, and bigger fish, last year than I ever caught before," says Betts. "On my last cast on the last day of the '80 season, I caught a 4½-pound brown trout on one of my synthetic nymphs." Others who use Betts' flies agree that they are extraordinary. Dr. Heinz Meng, professor of biology at the State University of New York at New Paltz, says of Betts' mayflies, "They're the best. They *look* like a mayfly; they land like a mayfly; they float like a mayfly . . . fish go wild over them."

A couple of years ago Betts sent some of his first synthetic mayflies to Robert Rifchin in Natick, Mass. Rifchin is the editor of *The Roundtable,* a magazine published by United Fly Tyers, Inc., and he sees a lot of flies and hears a lot of claims about them. "I was very skeptical until I went to the pond at a local trout club," Rifchin says. "The fish really get pounded by the members, and as a result they become extremely selective. I went there in the fifth week of the season, and the trout were so wary no one could catch a thing. I tied on one of John's mayflies and cast it out. I caught a trout. I caught another trout. I caught another. I caught another. In fact, I caught 63 of them. Then I went to a local stream and caught more trout on the fly. His mayflies are exceptional."

The once skeptical Rifchin is just getting warmed up. Last year, he goes on, he and Betts fished the Delaware together to study the efficacy of a polypropylene minnow that Betts had devised. Rifchin says, "I was using a smelt imitation, a modified Grey Ghost streamer. John's polypropylene minnow was the same color. It was a fair comparison. We fished the same water, cast for cast. John had follow after follow, strike after strike, fish after fish. I only got two.

"Then there's John's spoon fly," Rifchin continues. "He makes a small loop of monofilament line and dips it into Pliobond cement to form a sticky membrane. He then dips this into powdered metal. You put the spoon fly, which has a small hole in it, on the leader just ahead of the hook so that it wobbles and flashes but won't catch on the point. John sent me one last year, and I took it along with me to Cape Cod when I went to fish a stream with sea-run browns. A friend was fishing a pool there and we could see fish over 25 inches long. My friend got nothing, and after he gave up, I fished the pool. I tried everything standard with little success. Then I tied the spoon fly. On my second pass a big female, 28½ inches long and weighing 7½ pounds, swam over and ate it. It was the biggest trout I'd ever caught, and this was right in the middle of a hot August day. I've since caught fish of 22, 23, 25 inches on that spoon fly."

Then there are Betts' caddis flies. Peter Dully of Englewood, N.J. uses the adult caddis patterns on landlocked salmon in Maine. "The most fantastic flies I've ever used," he says. "They're unbelievable. They'll turn fish on when nothing else will. In fact, I use them when you think you might have to use a stick of dynamite. And the flies are rugged. One caddis fly I used caught 14 landlocked salmon."

Like his flies, Betts is a bit far out. He considers himself "the most conservative and conforming person I know," yet at age 16 he wired his fingers apart so he could play octaves on the piano. He often ties flies while listening to classical music on hi-fi and watching commercials on TV at the same time. "TV is about commercials," he says. "I love trash." He is also a bird watcher ("I learned to read with a bird book"), and several years ago he was the first to spot a European widgeon that had been blown off course and wintered in the middle of Rumson, N.J. A graduate of Lawrenceville School in New Jersey, Betts flunked out of Washington & Lee his freshman year because he spent 10 to 14 hours a day practicing in the pool so he could make the swimming team: "I wanted to be recognized," he explains. "I wanted everyone at college to call me by my first name. The coach was delighted, I made the team, everyone learned my first name, but I wasn't around the second term to answer to it."

Betts enlisted in the Air Force and served four years in Texas as a medic. Upon his discharge, he returned to Washington & Lee for a semester and then dropped out because, among other reasons, he wasn't allowed to have a car. So Betts embarked upon a series of odd jobs. He worked as a laborer in a concrete-pipe factory in Cheyenne, Wyo. and then spent a year in England as a groundskeeper for Peter Scott, the noted ornithologist and artist, and the Wildfowl Trust in Slimbridge. Betts' principal task consisted of shooing cackling geese away from the house so Scott could paint and write a book about waterfowl without being disturbed.

Back in the U.S., Betts worked as a loan collector for a bank in Denver, but left to take a job in another concrete-pipe plant after he was thrown through a screen door by a pugnacious delinquent. He moved back East to work as a lathe operator for Johns-Manville in New Jersey and then was employed by the Orvis Company in Manchester, Vt., where he repaired reels, shipped parcels and clerked. He was fired after a year and a half. "I was never able to complete anything," he says. He worked for a vet and then for a silversmith at $1.45 an hour. The silversmith suggested that Betts go to college on the GI Bill. "I thought that was for poor people," Betts said. The silversmith looked at him. "What do you think *you* are?"

In 1967 Betts enrolled at the University of Vermont to study forestry. "I loved it," he says. "I did a 4½-year program in 3½ years and I never cut a class." After graduating, he worked a while for a landscaper in Vermont, and then, in 1973, went into that business on his own in New Jersey. One of his specialties is bonsai. He has a Scotch pine 35 to 40 years old that is 19 inches high, with tiny needles, and azaleas that are probably 40 years old and only eight inches high.

A flytyer since he was eight, Betts began tying orthodox ones professionally six years ago, and in 1977 he began to fiddle around with synthetics. He did so because of philosophical and economic considerations. "I couldn't afford to fish with bamboo rods, silk lines and gut leaders," he says. "Like most other fishermen I use fiberglass rods, plastic-coated fly lines and nylon leaders, and synthetic flies seem appropriate. I'm also not putting any demands on animal populations for feathers and fur for flies. I used to hunt a lot and I kept every fish I caught. Now I release every fish I catch, and I don't hunt. I don't want to sound soapy, but killing for sport was no longer necessary for me."

Betts' first all-synthetic fly was made of polypropylene. Called Poly-Fly, it had two looped wings that looked like ears, four fuzzy legs, a floppy detached body and tails. Although the fly floated well in rough water and took fish, Betts was dismayed by Poly's slovenly appearance, and that winter he descended into his freezing basement to redesign the fly and make it "socially acceptable," as he writes in *Synthetic Flies,* a 68-page hand-lettered book he recently wrote and published on his own. The following spring, Betts emerged from his basement with a realistic mayfly with upright synthetic wings and immediately headed for a local pond, confident that, like the Gossamer Condor, he was destined for a "flight into fame and immortality."

The fly proved a clunker; its rigid wings twisted the leader and caused the fly to land upside down on the water. Betts decided he would try blow-line fishing, an old Irish technique in which the wind blows the fly and light line over the surface of the water. He made a 13½-foot telescoping rod from two fiberglass blanks, inserted one-pound-test line inside the hollow rod, returned to the pond, tied on the fly and held the rod up in the air. Static electricity in the rod's walls bound the line to the fiber glass. Tenderly he pulled 60-odd feet of spidery line out from the rod on the lawn bordering the pond. With that, he let the wind launch his fly and line. "Once in the air the effect was truly amazing," Betts writes in *Synthetic Flies.* "At 80 feet the line billowed and blew, and the fly sailed and skimmed over the water. A sudden dead spot put the fly down for an instant; in that space a tiny perch grabbed it. With his strike he parted the line instantly.

"Soon I had another fly in the air at 80 feet, but against light reflecting from the water's surface, the fly was hard to see. I had to keep waving this long rod around to make the fly move enough to make itself visible. After a bit I found that no amount of waving made anything visible. I couldn't figure out what was wrong—until I noticed that the line itself was missing. My fly and over 80 feet of line were wafting off on their own."

Never one to give up, Betts corrected the aerodynamics of the wings and devised a mayfly that would cast easily and land right side up on the water. For wings, he likes to use either white organza, a nylon monofilament used for bridal gowns, or plastic bags. To give the wing a veined effect, he holds a sheet of plastic against his leg and gently buffs it with sandpaper. Legs are often composed of synthetic White Sable paintbrush fibers tapered at the tips. Using these and other materials, he has tied nymphs and dry flies to hooks as small as a minuscule size 28. His minnows can be used with effect in either fresh or salt water; his shrimp and crab patterns are for salt water. The crab is an ingenious pattern. It is tied backward on the hook, claws extended. When the crab fly settles on the bottom and is retrieved, it scuttles backward, the hook point plowing up sand or mud and the claws waving in a threatening fashion, very similar to a real-life crab on the run.

As a general rule, Betts uses white synthetics. If he wants, say, a green drake mayfly, a blue-claw crab or a black-nosed dace minnow, he colors the white fly with waterproof marking pens. Should a different-colored species of any of these be what the fish are really after, Betts simply dips the fly into Carbona to turn it white again. Then he marks it anew in the appropriate colors. When occasion demands, Betts will use a material already colored, such as a vibrant creamy yellow see-through vest ("I guess it's what you'd call a vest," he says) that he got at Frederick's of Hollywood. "It has a fleshy and luscious look," he says. "When you color it with a brown marking pen, you get olive, and I've used this for caddis wings."

Betts charges $2.50 to $3 for each of his flies, more than double the going rate for standard flies. If the customers like the flies, they can easily learn to tie their own with materials that are readily available, thanks to modern technology. "I'm not interested in keeping any of this to myself," Betts says. "I've no desire to patent my flies, and I don't want a captive audience. I want all these synthetic flies and techniques to belong to the world. Why? Because synthetic flies will make fly-fishing more popular, just as fiberglass rods did. And the more people who fly-fish, the more people will join the Trout Unlimited or the Theodore Gordon Flyfishers and see to it that we have wise stewardship of our natural resources. If I can help do that by devising synthetic flies, I'll feel as though I've made my contribution to the world."

—MAY 1, 1981

He Deftly Ties the World's Fanciest Flies

Harry Darbee

If it were possible to cross a Henry David Thoreau with an H. L. Mencken, the result probably would be someone very much like Harry Darbee of Roscoe, N.Y. To the informed public, Darbee is known for the conservation battle he is waging to prevent two Catskill trout streams, the Willowemoc and the Beaver Hill, from being destroyed by the New York State Department of Public Works. To fishermen, Darbee is celebrated, even venerated, for any number of other reasons as well.

For one, Darbee is a superb flytyer. Darbee's tying, done in partnership with his wife, Elsie, is unusually imaginative, and his work has been hailed in more than 30 books, ranging from James Leisenring's *The Art of Tying the Wet Fly* to Roderick Haig-Brown's *Fisherman's Summer*. Among Darbee's creations are Darbee's Green Egg Sac, Darbee's Spate and a large imitation of a mayfly that is a cross between a bass bug and a trout fly and is thus known as the Beaver Kill Bastard. With the late Percy Jennings, an amateur tier, Darbee created a trout fly that is not an imitation of anything and is called, for no reason other than the fact that a girl just happened to name it so, the Rat-Faced MacDougall. He has established a unique fan club. Among the users of Darbee flies are or have been Vannevar Bush, the scientist, who used to try to get a discount on new flies by trading in old ones he found hanging from trees; C. R. Smith, the chairman of the board of American Airlines and an ardent salmon fisherman; Lord Portal, a friend of Smith's who tried some Darbee flies and pronounced them wizard; Sparse Grey Hackle, the angling writer; C. Otto v. Kienbusch, the angling book collector who discovered the volume proving that Izaak Walton was a plagiarist; John J. McCloy, the banker; and the late Edward Ringwood Hewitt, a marvelously dotty soul who occasionally used to make believe that he himself was a trout.

The Darbee home, a cozy seven-room house that is cluttered with feathers, fur, hair, hooks and other appurtenances of the trade, is only a long cast from the Willowemoc. It serves as a gathering point, in or out of season, for anglers, local characters, fishery biologists, curious tourists and wandering oddballs who come to hear Darbee hold forth on all sorts of subjects, often until dawn. The atmosphere is Cannery Row out of Abercrombie & Fitch.

Darbee's conversational range takes in the entire field of natural history. He is a first-rate entomologist with, as befits a flytyer, a deep interest in aquatic insects. He has done a great deal of stream-improvement work and has a fund of information about the changes caused in streams by fluctuations of flow and variations in temperature. Indeed, his limnological knowledge is so impressive that he has appeared as an expert witness at more than 200 hearings before the New York State Riparian Commission.

Darbee is interested in the genetics of fowl. He has raised his own crossbred blue chickens for hackle, and his preoccupation with chicken breeding has been so sufficiently rare and successful as to have excited inquiries from European poultrymen. He is also a botanist with a marked fondness for edible nettles, and, as a practicing mycologist, he has eaten his way through 35 species of mushrooms lurking in local forests. In his years as a trapper—and he was one of the most successful in the Catskills, taking as many as 100 foxes a winter in the days when a good pelt fetched $25—he used to dine on such gamy fare as infant porcupine, parboiled raccoon, fried muskrat, boiled crayfish and sautéed gray squirrel.

Intellectually alert, Darbee is one of the lay members of the Resources Board of the American Fisheries Society. He possesses a well-chosen library of ichthyological studies and general literature. His favorite author is Mencken, and he has a great stack of old *American Mercurys* to which he repairs for laughs when no visitors are about. Once when Darbee was in Baltimore, Mencken's home town, and down to his last five dollars, he did as the master would have done and blew the fin on a good feed and a gallery ticket to *Lysistrata*. The next morning, dead broke, Darbee went to work as a door-to-door magazine salesman, one of the few square jobs he ever had. "Harry," says his wife, "is very unpredictable."

Darbee is trim and of medium height. He has a snub nose, a high forehead and a white pompadour that gives him the look of a prosperous Russian playwright, circa 1903. On both sides, he is Connecticut Yankee stock. Now 58, he was born in Roscoe, the eldest of five children. He passed the formative years of his childhood near West Park on the Hudson, where his father worked for the West Shore Railroad. When he was 10 years old the family moved back to Roscoe, and except for a year spent in Wisconsin laying track and fishing and a hitch in the Navy as a hospital corpsman in World War II, Darbee always has lived in the Catskills. He originally derived his approach to nature (which may be best summed up as leaving it the hell alone) from John Burroughs, the bearded sage who was a neighbor in West Park. Burroughs was then in his 70s, and young Darbee used to accompany him through the woods in search of bird nests.

A chronic truant from school, Darbee started fishing seriously when he was 10 years old. By 12, he was tying his own flies and guiding anglers. Upon leaving high school, he immersed himself in the outdoors. He spent an entire summer hunting ginseng root.

"After I got out, I had, oh, cleared about $10," he says, "but I had lived in the woods all summer."

Ever since 1928 Darbee has been tying flies professionally. He and Elsie, whom he married in 1933 after she came to work as an assistant, weathered the Depression easily since the Big Rich tightened their budgets by fishing instead of larking off to Europe for vacations. Still, there were some customers who wondered how the Darbees could manage. One of them, the late J. P. Knapp, chairman of the board of Publication Corp., felt such pity that he gave Darbee a standing order to tie flies whenever he hit a slack period. At one time Knapp had some 250,000 flies in the house. "Knapp," explains Darbee, "used to say, 'When I get a good fly, I like to keep it around.' "

The Darbees do their tying at adjoining desks in the front parlor. It is generally impossible to tell their work apart—they have even argued between themselves as to who tied what—but there are some purists who say that, while Harry is the better talker, Elsie is the better tyer. Such remarks do not in the least bother Darbee, who is only too glad to show anyone how to tie. "I have no jealousy," he recently told a budding tyer. "If you could beat me to hell tying flies, I'd swell up with pride."

Considering the cost of materials and the work, knowledge and skill involved, Darbee flies are inexpensive enough. Regular dry flies, for instance, are $7.20 a dozen, and fancy salmon streamers, which take up to half an hour to tie, $1 to $3 each. The flies most in demand are Light Cahills (named after a 19th century Dublin flytier who used to hold the fly up to a customer's ear and inquire if he heard it buzz); Hairwing Royal Coachmans (so called because the first was tied by Tom Bosworth, coachman to Queen Victoria); Quill Gordons (tied by Theodore Gordon, the father of American dry-fly fishing, to imitate any number of early-season mayflies that are a pale blue-gray); Irresistibles (invented by Joe Messinger, and imitating nothing at all in nature); and Rat-Faced MacDougalls (which one

Darbee customer absentmindedly referred to as "the fly with the horrible name, the Scar-Face McCarthy, I believe").

The materials used are varied: maribou, peacock, golden pheasant, Impeyean pheasant, toucan and mallard feathers, Greenland baby seal, Australian opossum, hares' ears, and pelts of deer, mink, fisher, polar bear, brown bear and other exotica. The prescribed dressings for one salmon fly, the Jock Scott, for instance, call for dressings from 12 different parts of the world.

Nowadays Darbee sometimes must make do with substitutes, since he is hampered by what he calls "the great horsefeathers law," an act of Congress prohibiting or restricting the importation of certain rare plumages. Although Darbee is an avowed "forever wilder," he can never forgive the Audubon Society for backing the law. "The law hasn't prevented birds from being shot," he says. "Hell, they're food to some people, and the feathers are just a byproduct. I don't know any flytyer who isn't a conservationist. Now I have to have a license, and write to the Government telling how many jungle cock or mandarin I want and where I'm going to buy them. Sometimes I have to wait three, four or five years for an order."

Despite having to use substitutes, Darbee remains a finicky tyer. He concocts his own wax, which is used to make the silk tying thread tacky, from bleached beeswax, resin and castor oil, and at work he sets his own pace. Once, when pressed for an extraordinarily large order of trout flies, he tied eight dozen a day for 30 days straight, a feat he vows he will never repeat. The effort left him completely worn out. One friend, who has been waiting more than two years for two dozen special-pattern flies, says, "It's a good thing Harry doesn't run a restaurant. If you ordered a fried-egg sandwich, he'd go out to tell the hen to lay a few eggs, then he'd start grinding his own flour."

The idea that he is an artist makes Darbee choleric. "The flytier is an artisan 98% of the time and perhaps an artist the other 2%," he once wrote. "When creating a pattern or inventing a style or type of fly not heretofore known or maybe in adapting new techniques to old fly-tying problems, a tier could be called, temporarily at least, an artist. But to place an artistic label on the humdrum process of repeating a pattern day after day, as any professional tyer must to earn his dinner, is stretching the word artist beyond its meaning."

Still, if Darbee does not consider a tyer an artist, "I can," he says, "certainly proclaim him an individualist in the full sense of the term. To me, fly tying represents a way of life quite as much as a means of livelihood. Tying flies along the banks of a beloved stream, away from the bustle and stench of a city, is my idea of the ultimate in occupations. Tying flies for a living has enabled me to enjoy a certain independence of action and thought not easily come by in these days of mass production and time-clock-dominated lives."

In recent years Darbee has given much of this time toward trying to save the Willowemoc and Beaver Kill from the ravages of a proposed superhighway. For his efforts, the Theodore Gordon Fly-Fishers gave him the Salmo Award last spring. The award was nice to get, but it did not make Darbee any happier about the future. "I'm far from complacent about America's natural resources," he says. "I think we're balanced on a fine line, and it's just possible we can lose our resources faster than anyone thought. But when you say that, people think you're a nut. I'm not. I was, I think, brought up with some ideals."

—AUGUST 21, 1963

Spare the Rod(s), Spoil the Cast

Lefty Kreh

When a stubby, bald, fifty-five-year-old man named Bernard (Lefty) Kreh shows up at a fishing-club meeting or sporting-goods show, fishermen gather like sunnies around a worm. Elderly Wall Street brokers, oil tycoons and blue-collar workers alike shout, "Lefty! Remember me? Hey, Lefty!"

At home in both fresh- and saltwater, Kreh is one of the best light-tackle fishermen ever and a master caster with fly, plug or spinning rod. Ambidextrous, he can cast a spinning rod and a plug rod, one in each hand, simultaneously, or, dispensing with a rod, he can easily cast the whole length of a ninety-foot fly line with just his bare hands. He can hold a crowd around a fly-tying bench in thrall as he ties everything from a huge saltwater streamer known as Lefty's Deceiver to a *Caenis* mayfly on a teensy-weensy No. 24 hook. He also makes his own jigs, plugs, spoons and "the best carp doughballs anyone ever made." He designs new rods, reels, fly lines, anchors and tackle boxes, and he knows as much about knots as anyone in the world. Professionally, he is the outdoor columnist for the *Sun* in Baltimore, and he is the author of three books, one of which, *Fly Casting with Lefty Kreh,* has been translated into Japanese, German and Swedish. Lefty once held sixteen world saltwater-fishing records, but as he says, "I never deliberately tried to catch a record fish. I think that's the wrong approach. I simply caught sixteen fish that were world records. I don't want to compete with anyone but myself."

A camera bug, Kreh has taught advanced nature photography for the National Wildlife Federation for the past ten years. Perfectionist that he is, he develops his own color film when he has the time, and he keeps 10,000 slides filed so neatly that he can locate any one slide in fifty seconds. "You got to be organized," he says. His luggage and tackle are color coded, and he can take off instantly from his Cockeysville, Maryland, home on a trip for smallmouth or tarpon or trout, or to give a lecture on the West Coast. Although Kreh defines an expert as "any SOB more than 150 miles from home with a slide show," he travels extensively each year, showing slides and lecturing on such topics as "Why We Fish," "Fly Casting and Its Problems," and "Light Tackle in Saltwater." On the road, Kreh always makes it a point to get in a day or two of fishing with the best fishermen in each area. "The main reason I lecture is that it allows me to travel on someone else's money to gain the latest information," he says. "That's how I keep on top of everything."

Filled to the gills with fishing expertise, gifted with gab and equipped with a seemingly limitless repertoire of jokes, putdowns and one-liners, Kreh comes across to his audiences like a cross between Jack Nicklaus and Don Rickles. When his slide projector broke down and had to be fixed during a talk at a Trout Unlimited meeting in Linden, New Jersey, Kreh announced he would fill in the time with a few Polish jokes. There was a stir when three men stood up and one said, "We want you to know we're Polish."

"That's all right, fellas," said Kreh. "I'll tell them nice and slow so you can understand."

Everyone, including the three men, laughed, but Poul Jorgensen, a flytyer who was on the program with Kreh, says, "Anyone but

Lefty would have had his head punched in." Kreh says, "Everybody ought to be able to laugh at himself. When you stop laughing at yourself, you're in trouble. People take things too damn serious."

Kreh himself had a hardscrabble life as a youngster in Frederick, Maryland. The oldest of four children, he was six when his father, a brick mason, died and his mother had to go on relief. "There were no toys," Kreh says, "but I had a good time." The North Bench Street neighborhood was tough, and he responded to the challenge. After Joe Louis won the heavyweight title, Kreh, billed as the White Bomber, fought a kid from the black neighborhood, Jimmy Hill, who was the Brown Bomber. "A white kid stole a beautiful rug from a store and rope from a trucking company, and the kids put up a ring in a neighbor's backyard," Kreh recalls. "They charged kids to see the fight. I hit Jimmy with a lucky punch on the chin and knocked him out. I had beat up a lot of kids before, but I had never knocked anyone out. I thought I had killed him, and we all ran off leaving Jimmy on the stolen rug. The lady who owned the house saw him unconscious, and she called the cops, who identified the rug, and a couple of us almost wound up in jail. The kid who stole the rug was never even questioned, but later he was killed pulling a holdup. I might have wound up in jail or getting killed myself, but when I was eleven I was told that I could go to a Boy Scout camp if I would wash dishes. I did, and I joined the Scouts. The Scouts gave me a moral base, and that really helped save my life."

On his way to becoming an Eagle Scout, Kreh won the first angling merit badge in his part of Maryland. In his spare time he earned money trapping muskrats and mink and catching catfish in the Monocacy River, which he sold to local stores. "The river was only a two or three-mile walk away," he says, "and I'd go there to bush bob. I'd take strands of mason twine, put hooks on them, bait them with freshwater mussels and tie the twine on branches overhanging the river. In those days there were a lot of freshwater mussels to be found. You could take half a bushel on any sandbar. The catfish would roam the banks at night and grab the bait, and the limb would set the hook and fight the fish. The average catfish was ten to fifteen inches long, and I got ten cents a pound, cleaned. Ten cents was a lot of money, and frequently we'd get catfish up to six pounds."

In high school Kreh was a basketball guard despite his lack of height. He got the nickname Lefty because he would dribble down-court with his right hand and then suddenly change to dribble, pass or shoot with his left hand. When he graduated in 1942, he joined the Army and served as a forward observer with the 69th Division in France, Belgium and Germany. While in the Army, he became a Roman Catholic. "In Frederick I'd gone to the Baptist church, and as a poor kid I saw that poor people were kind of looked down upon," he says. "I looked at all religions, including Judaism, but Catholicism seemed to answer what I wanted more than any other."

Discharged as a corporal with five battle stars, Kreh returned to Frederick and got a job with the old Army Biological Warfare Laboratories at nearby Fort Detrick. He soon became the night foreman in the main production building, raising bubonic plague, anthrax, tularemia and a host of other deadly infectious cultures.

In 1947 Kreh married Evelyn Mask, whom he met in a bowling alley. They went fishing on their honeymoon, but they no longer fish together because Kreh regards fishing as his work, and "I don't want to bring my wife to the office." The Krehs get along famously—"If he was any sweeter, I couldn't stand it," says Ev. As a cook, Ev finds "no challenge" in Kreh since his tastes run from peanut butter to overcooked meat. Once at a friend's house, Kreh set off the smoke alarm after he went back into the kitchen to rebroil a steak he thought too rare. When he orders steak in a restaurant, he tells the waiter, "Cremate it."

At Fort Detrick, Kreh worked nights so he could hunt and fish all day. An expert shot, he doubled on grouse, tripled on quail and nailed pheasants with a bow and arrow. He kept his eye sharp by shooting crows at an immense roost near his home. During one two-and-a-half year period he calculated that he had fired 7,000 shells at them. His favorite call for crows in the early summer sounded like that made by a baby crow falling from a nest. "A deadly way to attract crows," he says. He also called ducks, geese, hawks, foxes and bobcats. His call for foxes and bobcats, Kreh says, "sounds like a screaming rabbit."

Kreh's proficiency in calling crows and his ability in taking smallmouth bass on small plugs he had carved brought him to the attention of two outdoor writers, Tom McNally and Joe Brooks, who became his friends. They got him started fly casting with a fifteen-minute lesson. "After that, I was on my own," Kreh says. "I developed my own style. I think I was fortunate that there were so few good flycasters in Maryland because I would have wound up copying them. I fished fourteen hours a day, mostly for smallmouth bass in the Potomac, and even though I could cast with either hand, I got pretty tired if I didn't do things right. So I began breaking down the parts of a fly cast. There was no one to talk to, lucky for me, and I found that if I lowered my rod at the beginning of a cast and raised it quickly, I lifted all the line from the water. Then I could make an effortless back cast and not put shock waves into the line. The average guy spends more energy getting line off the water than he does getting the line behind him for the cast.

"The most important thing in fly casting is that the fly is not going to move until the line is tight, so it becomes very important to remove all slack, shock waves or sag before you make your power stroke in either direction. A lot of the techniques I developed on my own were considered near heresy, but I cast effortlessly. Basically, a good flycaster is a guy who can do it without work, and you don't see many of them around.

"I think I know more about casting and about different kinds of casts than anyone else, and the reason is that I am always fishing under different conditions. Take saltwater fly-fishing. To be a good saltwater fly-fisherman you have to be a better fisherman than a freshwater flycaster. In freshwater, presentation is the main thing, but in saltwater you have to contend with larger tackle, winds, know more casts and then spot and whip a bigger and tougher fish than you'd find in freshwater. The average saltwater fish can tow a freshwater fish of the same size, around by the tail. In saltwater flyfishing, when you see a fish, you've got five to seven seconds to make the cast. In that time you have to determine the direction in which the fish is traveling, the depth and its speed, and then make your cast. George Harvey, of State College, Pennsylvania, is by far the best trout fisherman I've ever fished with, but George would have trouble with three-pound bonefish."

For all this, saltwater fish are not necessarily the hardest to catch. "There are too many variables to say that," Kreh says. "If I were to list the three most difficult fish to catch, they would be these: First of all, largemouth bass in sandpits or quarries with clear water. They are the toughest of all. Second, taking really big tarpon on a twelve-pound-test fly tippet. Third, big brown trout in spring creeks."

In the early 1950s Kreh began to branch out while continuing to work at Fort Detrick. He began writing an outdoors column for the local *Frederick Post* and the *News,* and then for other papers in the area. He also began going on the road to give fly-, plug-, and spin-casting exhibitions at boat shows and state fairs. He would cast flies into a cup, knock a cigarette from a girl's mouth and cast four fly rods at the same time, two in each hand. "But that was just entertainment," he says. "Then I'd start to do things that a fisherman could use in the field, such as changing the direction of a cast in midair."

Except for an occasional casting clinic, Kreh no longer gives exhibitions, but he gives private lessons for one hundred dollars an hour. "I'm the best teacher of fly casting there is," he says. "I can spot what a fisherman's doing wrong and correct it right away, no matter whether he's left-handed or right-handed, because I'm the only casting instructor I know who can make all the bad casts with either hand." The tuition fee of one hundred dollars is obviously worth it to some anglers. Recently, a couple from Texas flew to Baltimore in their private plane for a two-hour lesson.

As Kreh sees it, his biggest break came in 1964, when Joe Brooks suggested he apply for the job of director of the Metropolitan South Florida Fishing Tournament. Now sponsored by the *Miami Herald* and Coca-Cola, the tournament, which runs from mid-December to late April, draws hundreds of thousands of contestants. There are divisions for fly, plug and spin fishing, and entrants are encouraged to release their catches after they have been witnessed. The only awards are trophies.

Kreh got the job and quit Fort Detrick. "The Met tournament is one of the finest training grounds in the world," he says. "It has set the standards for light-tackle fishing. The whole south Florida social system is based on fishing and boats, and the guy who runs the tournament, as Joe said, 'is like being the mayor of south Florida fishing.' You are in contact with all the charter skippers and guides in the Everglades, the Keys and the western Bahamas. A large percentage of the guides know that the Met tournament director recommends people to them. When I got the job, guides and charter skippers immediately invited me to go fishing. I learned the favorite spots of the best guides.

"The finest cadre of light-tackle fishermen live in south Florida, and they're fishing twelve months a year. South Florida is the only place in the country where fishermen are judged by their tackle. Down there it's almost a stigma to catch a fish on bait. Twelve-pound-test is about the heaviest spinning line anyone will use, and anything over a fifteen-pound-test leader isn't regarded as fly-fishing. As a result, the area has the best light-tackle fishermen in the world. A good south Florida light-tackle fisherman can take fish anywhere. Why, he can even take a 300-pound grouper on twelve-pound-test line."

Kreh worked as the Met tournament director for nine years. On his four-month vacation every summer, he would fish for trout in

Montana and then for carp, with his doughballs, in Maryland.
"Hardly anyone in this country fishes for carp, but I'll tell you this,
carp are one of the premier gamefish around," Kreh says. "I go carp
fishing eight or ten times a year." On rare occasions he has taken
carp on wet flies, but his standby bait is his own doughball concoc-
tion. The recipe is as follows:

DOUGHBALLS À LA KREH

2 cups cornmeal	1 tbs. vanilla extract
1 cup flour	1 tbs. sugar
½ 3-oz. pkg. strawberry Jell-O	1 quart water
Yield: 30 doughballs.	

In a two-quart saucepan, bring the water to a boil and add Jell-
O, vanilla and sugar. Stir for a minute and then reduce heat so that
mixture barely boils. In a bowl combine cornmeal and flour by
mixing well with a wooden spoon. Sprinkle the cornmeal and
flour mixture on the surface of the water. The bubbles will make
little volcano-like eruptions through the cornmeal-flour mixture.
As the eruptions occur, cover them with the mixture until it has all
been used, then stir for 20 or 30 seconds. Remove from stove and
let cool. Mold the dough into balls one inch in diameter. Use immediately or store in refrigerator for as long as three days. Serve
on a No. 2 hook.

"I make my doughballs about two-thirds the size of a golf ball,"
Kreh says, "and they sink right to the bottom. They are gummy
enough to stay around the hook but soft enough so I can easily set
the hook."

In 1972 Kreh became the outdoor columnist for the *St. Peters-
burg Times* and a year later moved to Baltimore when he got a better
offer from the *Sun*. In his columns Kreh writes about a variety of
subjects besides fishing and hunting: why leaves change color in the
fall, wild flowers, bird feeders, conservation, the aerial transport of

seeds. He is always giving his readers sound advice: "If you want to be a good fisherman, question everything, especially the absolute," he says. Freshwater fly-fishermen using wet flies, nymphs and streamers ordinarily employ a five- to ten-foot leader, but Kreh, going against convention, often uses a leader no more than eighteen inches long with a sinking line. "I don't use it in tiny brooks where the impact of the line might spook the fish, but otherwise I use it all the time," he says. "You have more control, and you get down faster. I've taken wild rainbows with a leader so short, maybe two inches at most, that I couldn't tie another knot in it."

According to Kreh, hunting is changing rapidly in this country, and fishing is about to follow. "I pretty much gave up hunting fifteen years ago," he says. "Attitudes about hunting have changed. It used to be that you were proud to know a good hunter. Nowadays a good hunter keeps to himself. Also the land that's left is being closed off. The farmers aren't the old sons of the soil they used to be. They've been off to college, and they have a different view of life. They're sure as hell not going to let you on their land to shoot pretty little birds, rabbits or deer. They aren't even going to let their own children shoot them. They regard animals as part of the family.

"What you're going to see is a lot of hunters turning to fishing, and attitudes in fishing are going to change. Right now offshore fishing is dying. Going out from Ocean City, Maryland for white marlin and making a 180- to 200-mile trip in a day is not only going to be expensive, it's going to be unpopular. The macho guy who likes to go offshore is going to be looked on like some guy who's driving around in a big gas guzzler, and he's going to feel ashamed. The trend in fishing will be back to the 1940s, when people fished close to home. With the pressure on trout streams and bass lakes, we will become like the English, who fish for roach or carp. I personally think carp have a big future.

"Our concepts are going to change, and I think that may be to the good. The one thing wrong with most fishermen in this country now is that they have restricted themselves to several species, or one type of fishing. You meet a guy who fishes only for trout or for bass, or you meet someone who says, 'I only use a fly rod.' That's wrong. I can tell you, they miss out on a lot of fun."

—APRIL 7, 1980

Shhh! It's the Black Ghost

Art Broadie

When the Black Ghost can't get off a shot at a squirrel hiding on the opposite side of a tree, he takes off his jacket, drapes it over a bush, ties a piece of string to the branches and walks to the other side of the tree as the squirrel scampers to the jacket side. The Black Ghost sits still for five minutes, then jerks the string, moving the jacket. Bang! Another squirrel for the pot when it runs to the Black Ghost's side of the tree.

Sometimes when the trout are not hitting, the Black Ghost will wade down a stream, sending waves into both banks. Then he gets out, walks back upstream to where he entered, has a leisurely smoke, picks up his rod and starts catching trout. "Got to wake 'em up," he says.

To those who know him, the Black Ghost is the best hunter and trout fisherman around. Doubtless there are other outdoorsmen as good as he is living in small towns throughout the country, but the Black Ghost, who can stand for all of them, certainly is an original.

The Black Ghost is Arthur T. Broadie, a cadaverous, sixty-year-old boiler-plant operator at the Franklin D. Roosevelt Veteran's Administration Hospital in Montrose, New York. Tufts of hair spring out of both ears, and he usually wears a grin that gives the impression that he knows something no one else does. That is often the case. He is called the Black Ghost because he drives a pickup truck with a homemade camper on the back that has Black Ghost streamer flies painted front and rear.

"The idea of the Black Ghost came to me suddenly one night down on the job," Broadie says. "I was looking at the doggone truck, and I thought I ought to decorate the thing. Pretty near every day I fish for trout, I'll use the Black Ghost sometime or other, and then I wanted a CB handle that no one else had. I checked the paint locker, and I had all the colors I needed. I made a template, drew the streamers on in pencil and painted them. Everything seemed to fit together."

The Black Ghost's old camper, which he stripped down this year for parts for a new camper, had the words "Black Ghost" spelled out beneath the painted flies, but he left off the lettering on the new camper because the old one used to inspire all kinds of exclamations when he drove past Bunch's Place, a favorite black hangout in Peekskill, New York, Broadie's hometown.

It may seem odd that the Black Ghost—a sort of contemporary Daniel Boone on wheels—would choose to live barely thirty-five miles north of New York City, but then Broadie spent most of his life practicing his hunting and fishing skills on estates in the area, wherever and whenever he pleased, regardless of the no-trespassing signs and the fish and game laws. Indeed, poaching—hunting and fishing on posted property—was, is and probably always will be a Broadie family custom. "I've never been a game hog," Broadie says, "but I do believe that if there is a chunk of ground out there and some guy says it's his, that doesn't mean those critters on it are his."

For the Black Ghost the thrill of the chase is not just pursuing game but being pursued by an angry landowner after he has bagged his quarry. "Got to find me a little hidey-hole," he will say when scouting some fresh territory that might offer sport. The hidey-hole is usually a brier patch into which the Black Ghost will hurl himself like Peter Rabbit with Mr. McGregor in hot pursuit. "People don't like to mess with brier patches," says Broadie, who has poached some land so often that he knows each and every hidey-hole by heart.

Years ago, the whole Broadie clan—Grandpa, Pop, Uncle Will, Art and his two younger brothers—used to fish Forbes Pond in the small town of Croton. "I loved Forbesie's," says Broadie, and his love only increased when a stern gentleman bought the pond and the surrounding acreage for his estate. Broadie came to know the new landowner's habits well, and although the landowner had no such knowledge of Broadie or even his name, he became determined to catch the poacher. It was a game in which Broadie took great delight. "One day I'm up there fishing the pond, and here comes the new owner with a state trooper," Broadie recalls. "That turkey yells, 'There he is!' like he was sure he was going to catch me. I took off through the woods with the two of them after me. There was no way I was going to beat them out of there, but I knew this hidey-hole, a big rock with a slope underneath it that was covered by blackberry bushes. I headed right for it. I was no sooner in my hidey-hole than I heard the trooper jump on the rock. Then the owner got there. 'What happened?' he asks the trooper. The trooper says, 'He must be to the road by now.' I was tempted to grab his ankle and say, 'Nope, I'm right down here in my hidey-hole.' After they left, I skeedaddled out of there, and I didn't go back . . . for a week."

The Black Ghost was seven years old when he first went poaching. Dusk was falling as Grandpa and Pop led him quietly through the woods to the edge of a lake. There Pop stripped down, waded out into the water and began lifting what seemed like rock after rock off the bottom. Suddenly a rowboat bobbed up, Pop and Grandpa bailed it out, and all three got in and went fishing. "Ain't nobody to mess with you at this time of night," Grandpa said.

Knowledge of the best hunting and fishing on estates—such as that of Dr. Edward L. Thorndike of Columbia University, "that fellow who wrote the dictionary"—was "handed down in the family," Broadie says. "I figured those estates were all my territory. Don't forget that this was the Depression. Pop was a railroad man, and he was only working two or three days a week. Everything was a meal. Even the game warden didn't pay attention to the season most of the time."

Broadie attended Hendrick Hudson High School and, although he played hooky to fish or hunt, he graduated in three years with an 89.6 average. "Latin knocked the hell out of it," he says, "but I've always been glad I took it because I can break down words to figure out what they mean." Most of the time, Broadie talks like a rustic, but when he gets serious he will start using words and phrases such as "indigenous," "cogitating" and "my poaching proclivities." "Sometimes you got to go along with the crowd," he says.

College was out of the question, so Broadie worked for an auto mechanic and then in the New York Central Railroad repair shops at Harmon—when he wasn't loose in the field. Deer were then protected by a closed season, and Broadie learned that the warden was out to nail whoever was hunting at DeRham's Brook where it flowed into Constitution Marsh across the Hudson from West Point. "One morning the warden shows up at the brook at four o'clock," Broadie recalls. "He looks around, no one else is there, and so he hides in some bushes. He waits and waits. Five o'clock goes by, and no one has shown up. Six o'clock. Still no one. Then this nice big fat buck comes down to the brook. The warden looks around. He doesn't see anyone. He pulls out his .38 caliber revolver, shoots the buck and packs it out of there. A couple of days later I met the warden in a place where he hung out, and I just casually said to him, 'How does the venison taste?' That was the end of the conversation, and after that he never did run me into the woods."

When he's out hunting, Broadie chews on black birch twigs to keep himself from getting thirsty, and he habitually moves with stealth, even when entering a room. "People who grew up in the city can't be quiet in the woods," he says. "They walk with their feet out because they grew up on pavement." The only man Broadie ever knew who was quieter than he is in the woods was the late Nelse Kingsley. "I'd be stock-still waiting for a squirrel," Broadie says, "and all of a sudden I'd hear Kingsley's voice right behind me, asking, 'Seen anything, Art?' "

The New York Central found Broadie to be a quick learner. With the skills he acquired in the Central's shops, he is able to do all his own truck and car maintenance and repairs, plumbing and electrical work and carpentry. "I can put in the footings, lay up the foundation and completely build a house and put every damn thing in it," he says. He also ties his own Black Ghosts and other flies and jigs, does decorative leatherwork, makes knives, carves decoys and designs and builds his own duck boats. In the days when he hunted Constitution Marsh in winter, he built an air boat that could hit sixty miles an hour skimming across the ice. When he cuts down a Christmas tree, he always cuts two, the extra one for spare branches which he inserts into holes drilled in the trunk of the first tree to make it absolutely symmetrical. "I'm learnin' all the time," he says. "How many guys would look at a picture of something in a book and say, 'I'm going to make me one of those,' and then make it? I do."

In 1943, Broadie married his wife, Alice, and then spent, by his own recollection, "exactly three years, one month and nineteen days" in the Army. When he returned home, he worked as a welder and pipe fitter until he landed a job with the Veterans Administration in 1963. Of course, he also returned to poaching. What else could a man like Broadie do with the 2,000-acre Camp Smith Military Reservation at his disposal? Broadie's activities so incensed the colonel in charge, whose children had a pet deer with a red ribbon around its neck, that he took to patrolling the roads himself at night in a Jeep. As Broadie learned, after one narrow escape, the colonel would park the Jeep at the crest of a steep hill with the lights out. When he heard a noise on the road below, he would release the brake and zoom downhill, aiming for the intruder. Broadie was after ducks, not deer—he hasn't hunted deer in twenty-five years because that season conflicts with the bird season—and to avoid the colonel he clambered up the back side of a mountain, Anthony's Nose, before sunrise one morning. By eight o'clock he had worked his way down the other side into some prime duck country. Suddenly he heard an explosion, the whine of a shell overhead and another explosion behind him as the shell landed. He had arrived just in time for artillery practice. He ducked into a hidey-hole behind some rocks and waited out the bombardment for three hours. The next time Broadie hunted ducks at Camp Smith was between six and seven-thirty in the morning. "Nobody gets up at six to start firing artillery in the peacetime Army," is the way Broadie figured it.

Art and Alice raised four sons. The oldest is thirty-five, the youngest twenty-six, and Broadie took them all hunting and fishing. "Set them down anywhere, and they can make a dent," he says. "All fishermen and hunters and all law-abidin' citizens."

The Black Ghost has used a fly rod ever since his sixteenth birthday. His father gave it to him shortly after his mother died. "It was a three-piece, nine-foot el cheapo club," he says. "No one had any money. It had an old skeleton reel that cost twenty-nine cents, and I used to buy fly lines, mill ends twenty-five- to thirty-feet long, in a stationery store for twenty-five cents. I didn't even know anyone who owned a fly rod. In those days the only thing I knew about fly-fishing was what I read in magazines. I had the whole month of June to practice with cork-bodied bass bugs. Everybody used big plugs for bass, and they all laughed at me when I showed up with little bugs—until I started taking four to five fish for every one they were taking.

"Then I started to use the fly rod to fish for trout. First I used bait, worms and shiners, and it wasn't too long before I'd get my limit. Then I'd switch to flies. Eventually I started going without bait. I went to flies because I realized I could turn fish loose without injuring them. After I started releasing more fish, I started catching more fish. Maybe it's because I was more relaxed. This was the '30s, and guys used to climb up and down my back for releasing fish. Some guys still feel that they have to prove themselves by bringing home a fish."

Broadie remembers the days on which he caught certain fish the way other people remember where they were when Pearl Harbor was bombed or when Bobby Thomson hit the shot heard 'round the world. "The memory bank up there in my head tells me what to do when I want to go fishing," he says. "Different streams have different rhythms, and you have to know what the trout want. For instance, on some water the fish like a fairly long retrieve of a streamer, and on others they like short twitches. Even the same stream changes from spring to late spring, with water temperature and water flow. When the water's high and the temperature's low, you can't rip a streamer in front of a trout's snoot. You have to tease him out. When the water gets real low and warm, that's high-speed fishing. You got to startle them into grabbing aholt.

"It all depends on the stream. Up on the Ausable, you want to use several flies at once, tied on about thirty inches apart. The flies should be a brown, a gray and a black. The idea behind it is this: if I get a fish right away, I know what color I caught him on. If it's on the brown fly, I put on another brown fly but with a little different pattern. Then I may take a fish a little faster. My theory is that I'm coming closer to whatever natural insect they're feeding on, what's indigenous to the stream. You can take two streams just six or seven miles apart, both with the same species of insects, yet those insects will differ slightly from one another in color or markings.

"Now if you want your heart to jump right out of your mouth, get on a stretch of the Beaverkill, tie on a size-four streamer, then six feet up the leader tie on a six-inch dropper and a dry fly. Overall, the leader is eighteen feet long. Flip that streamer twenty or twenty-five feet downstream, and hold the rod up so that the dry fly is hanging up in the air. You make the dry fly dance up and down. Then you just dap the water with it. I mean a trout will *smash* it. But where your heart jumps out of your mouth is when a twenty-inch brown decides to eat the streamer that you've forgotten all about. That jars your turnips!"

Nearly every spring the Black Ghost manages to dredge up at least one brown trout of three to four pounds from the turbulent lower Croton River when water thunders downstream from a reservoir that serves New York City. "I can tell you about this because I know no one is going to go down there to catch these fish," he says. "Conditions have to be just right, and there were just five days last spring when I had proper conditions. I need a rising water level on a dark, dismal, rainy day when herring are being washed downriver. They got nitrogenosis [*sic*] and their eyes are blowed out. Last spring, in all those five days, I got just one hit, and I took a twenty-two-inch fish. How many guys will fish five days to get one fish? But then I know I'm going to get a good fish or not get anything."

Last summer, before driving to Montana to fish during his vacation, Broadie was invited to fish Cedar Pond Brook, across the Hudson from Peekskill. Little known to the public, it is an historic stream that was fished in the late nineteenth century by Theodore Gordon, the father of dry-fly fishing in the United States, and later by Ray Bergman, whose book, *Trout,* first put Broadie on to the Black Ghost streamer. Unknown to Broadie, an expert for a local water company seeking to dam the stream had testified at a state hearing, shortly before, that no trout existed in the lower reaches of Cedar Pond Brook. However, in only two hours of fishing, Broadie, who had never been on this water before, landed and released seven brook and brown trout. Using a Black Ghost, he did not so much fish the brook as attack it. Standing ankle-deep in fast water, he would whip the streamer upstream and retrieve it quickly in and around the rocks. He ignored the pools and seemingly defied every other convention as he sloshed around the brook, which was only twenty feet wide. One would have thought that the trout would have fled in panic, but on several occasions Broadie took fish almost right at his feet. "Got you, turkey!" he would exult.

As he explained later, "During the bright part of the day, few trout are in the pools, but that's where most of your fishermen will spend their time. The few fish in the pools are only six to seven inches, and they have no brains, anyway. The good trout are behind the rocks where the water is broken. And they're there for several reasons: they have a better chance of picking up food, the white water gives them more cover, they get more oxygen and there's always a backwash so they can just hold there without wearing themselves out. A lot of people don't think that fish can hang out in that water, but they're the easiest to catch because they've got to make a snap decision when they spot something that might be lunch floating by. Yet when it gets dark, a pool might contain fifteen to twenty fish. Where do they come from? They drop down from the fast water."

Broadie prefers to fish alone—"Why should I waste fishing time telling some turkey what I'm doing and why I'm doing it?" he says—but his reputation is such that other fishermen, including those who consider themselves truly expert, will try to see what he's up to when they spot his camper near a stream. Bill Elliott, the wildlife artist who illustrated the new edition of Joe Bates's *Streamers & Bucktails: The Big Fish Flies,* all but swaggers when he talks of his own fishing exploits, but the mere mention of Broadie's name causes him to fall on the ground like Dracula before a cross. "You've never seen anyone fish until you've seen Art fish," Elliott says. "I had heard about him, and whenever I saw that camper with the big Black Ghosts painted on it, I would park and try to sneak up on him and watch to see if I could learn something. The first time I watched him, he was fishing a run with a big Black Ghost streamer, and I've never seen a man cover as much water as he did. I saw him make six casts and take six fish. He can put life into a fly better than any man I've seen. After I sneaked up on him the third and fourth time, he finally turned around and said, 'For God's sake, if you want to see what I'm doing, c'mon over here.'"

"He's extremely opinionated," Elliott continues, "but I like that because he knows what he's talking about. He's a guy who watches a lot and notices things that other people let pass by. He's very unorthodox. One time on the East Branch of the Croton River, there was a pouring rainstorm. The water was getting roiled and cloudy. Wanting something that the fish could see, I was using big nymphs, and I took six fish over fifteen inches. I was very proud of myself. When I got about 150 feet above the Phoebe Hole, I noticed a guy in a yellow slicker and a cowboy hat. It turned out to be Art, and he was doing quite well, but the crazy thing was that he was using a big Royal Coachman, a dry fly, and he was catching two fish for my one. No fish were rising for a hatch, and most guys wouldn't consider dry flies at all, but Art was bringing them up. He's capable of making fish show themselves."

Asked about the incident, Broadie figures he wasn't at all unorthodox. He was doing what his memory bank told him to do. "First of all," he says, "the fly was a *fanwing* Royal Coachman, and that's important. Second, it was September, we'd had our first cold weather, it was raining and everything correlated just so. You see, these fish know they're not going to get any succulent dry flies anymore, the good fly hatches are over. They think these fanwings are the last, and they want them. They're a delicacy. That morning on the East Branch, that memory bank just clicked up there, and I said to myself, 'Hey, this is the last day they'll be suckers for dry flies.' And that fanwing is a devastating fly, though I've never seen anything on a stream that looks like it. But the fanwing has to be tied just right with the wings spread quite a ways apart so that if you drew a line around the whole fly it would form a perfect circle. Then you want to use a leader that'll twist casting, but be strong enough to unwind so that the fly goes flip-flop, flip-flop, flip-flop, as it rolls on the water. Float that past a rock with twelve to fourteen inches of water and a little hidey-hole underneath, and it looks like that fly is alive, flip-flop, flip-flop."

In the fall, the Black Ghost either goes bird hunting or fishes the Hudson for stripers and carp. A few weeks ago he was fishing from the railroad trestle north of Garrison where Constitution Marsh empties into the river on the ebb tide. Broadie's youngest son, Eugene, was with him. Eugene has a big, bushy mustache, looks like an NFL linebacker and says little. Another man, a local landowner, was also fishing from the trestle. "Pop," said Eugene, "I'm going to see if I can get some ducks, heh, heh, heh." "You do that, Gene," said the Black Ghost.

After Eugene had gone back to the camper, got a shotgun and ambled off down the tracks, the landowner started to chivvy Broadie. "I've heard you've poached in your time," he said.

"Where did you ever hear such talk?" asked Broadie.

"Around," the man said.

"Around?" asked Broadie. "Lots of things are said 'around.' "

"You can level with me," the man said.

"Level with you?" said Broadie. "I don't have to level with anyone."

"Level with me," said the landowner.

"Mister," said Broadie, "I like to hunt grouse. So does Gene. Where you live, there are grouse. As Gene says, and you can ask him when he comes back, those are a couple of nice dogs you've got at your place. They don't bark when Gene comes around."

As the landowner's jaw started to go slack, Broadie had a hit. It was a striper. "Got you, you turkey!" he shouted. Then the Black Ghost turned to the landowner and said, "One other thing. I've always said I'm the biggest liar in forty-eight states."

—DECEMBER 8, 1980

The Man Who Lived Two Lives in One

Zane Grey

There never has been anyone quite like Zane Grey. Famed as the author of *Riders of the Purple Sage* and fifty-seven other Westerns tinged with purple prose, Grey ranks as the greatest bestselling novelist of his time. For years the total sales of his books fell behind only the Holy Bible and McGuffey Readers. At his death in 1939 his novels had sold more than 15 million copies in the United States alone, and they are still selling at the rate of 750,000 to a million books a year. Magazines paid Grey as much as $85,000 for the serial rights to a single work, and Hollywood transferred epic after epic to the silver screen. Gary Cooper, Cary Grant, Warner Baxter, Warner Oland, Richard Arlen, Richard Dix, Randolph Scott, Wallace Beery, Roscoe Karns, Harry Carey, William Powell, Jack Holt, Jack LaRue, Billie Dove, Lili Damita, Fay Wray, Jean Arthur and Buster Crabbe are among the stars who got their start in Zane Grey movies.

On film or in print Grey's Westerns enthralled the public. The books were stilted, awkward and stuffed with painful dialogue ("If you think I'm wonderful and if I think you're wonderful—it's all really very wonderful, isn't it?"), but they throbbed with the narrative drive of a true storyteller and the fervor of a moralist who made certain that virtue triumphed over evil on the range. "Never lay down your pen, Zane Grey," John Wanamaker, the white-haired merchant prince, once advised, putting a friendly hand on the novelist's shoulder. "I have given away thousands of your books and have sold hundreds of thousands. You are distinctively and genuinely American. You have borrowed none of the decadence of foreign writers. . . . The good you are doing is incalculable."

Grey received acclaim and money (and some critical brickbats) for his writings, but in another field his distinction was almost beyond compare—he was one of the finest fishermen the world has ever known. In the words of Ed Zern, who edited the anthology *Zane Grey's Adventures in Fishing,* "It is reasonable to assume that no one will ever challenge his right to be known as the greatest fisherman America has ever produced." It has been said that the dream of many American males is to have $1 million and go fishing. "Well," writes Zern, "Zane Grey had $1 million, and he really went fishing."

Grey is the classic case of the compulsive angler. He was truly obsessed by fish. "Not many anglers, perhaps, care for the beauty of a fish," Grey wrote in *Tales of Fishes,* one of his eight books on angling, "but I do." He would rhapsodize on the beauty of a huge tuna that "blazed like the sword of Achilles" or marvel over the shimmering colors of a dolphin, only to feel a pang because the dolphin was dying and he was "the cause of the death of so beautiful a thing." The leaping of fish absolutely fascinated him, and even fish fins and fishtails had what he called, with a flourish, "a compelling power to thrill and excite me."

From black bass to blue marlin, Grey pursued fish the world over with unmatched avidity. He explored and established new fishing grounds and techniques in Florida, California, Nova Scotia, New Zealand and Australia. He took great delight in fishing where no one had ever fished before, and his sense of anticipation was so keen that even arranging tackle for a trip gave him exquisite pleasure. He was the first man to catch a fish weighing more than 1,000 pounds on rod and reel. In his day he held most world records: 582-pound broadbill swordfish; 171-pound Pacific sailfish; 758-pound bluefin tuna; 318-pound yellowfin tuna; 1,040-pound striped marlin; 1,036-pound tiger shark; 618-pound silver marlin; 111-pound yellowtail; and a 63-pound dolphin. The record for the yellowtail and the yellowfin tuna have not been beaten since the International Game Fish Association began keeping records in 1938. Grey was held in such high regard that the Pacific sailfish was named for him, *Istiophorus greyi*. Hardy's in England manufactured a Zane Grey reel, while in the United States there was a Zane Grey bass bug, a Zane Grey steelhead fly and a Zane Grey teaser.

Grey had his bad days fishing—he once passed 88 days without a strike—but he remained enthusiastic. "The enchantment never palls," he wrote. "Years on end I have been trying to tell why, but that has been futile. Fishing is like Jason's quest for the Golden Fleece. . . . Something evermore is about to happen." When something did, Grey wrote about it exuberantly. If he made an unusual catch he would wire *The New York Times*. There were some critics who thought him guilty of exaggeration. A friend, Robert H. Davis, the editor of *Mumsey's Magazine,* wrote Grey, "If you went out with a mosquito net to catch a mess of minnows your story would read like Roman gladiators seining the Tigris for whales." David added, "You say, 'the hard diving fight of a tuna liberates the brute instinct in a man.' Well, Zane, it also liberates the qualities of a liar!" Grey cheerfully reported these comments himself in *Tales of Fishes.* Such criticisms did not bother him. But he was vexed and angered when his sportsmanship was called into question, as it was on a couple of occasions.

Zane Grey's passion for fishing, which, by his own admission, grew stronger through the years, started in his childhood. "Ever since I was a little tad I have loved to chase things in the water," he wrote. He was born in Zanesville, Ohio, on January 31, 1872. His Christian name was actually Pearl, and the family name was spelled Gray. After college he dropped Pearl in favor of his middle name of

Zane, and he changed the spelling of Gray to Grey. He also shaved three years off his age, according to Norris F. Schneider, the foremost authority on Grey, and upon his death obituaries reported he had been born in 1875.

Grey came from pioneer stock. His great grandfather, Colonel Ebenezer Zane, settled what is now Wheeling, West Virginia, in 1770 and moved into Ohio after the Revolution. Zanesville is named for him. Zane Grey's father, Dr. Lewis Gray, was a farmer and a preacher who eventually became a dentist with a practice in the Terrace section of Zanesville.

The oldest of five children, young Pearl was so mischievous that he was known as "the terror of the Terrace." On one occasion he destroyed a bed of imported tulips planted in front of the Zanesville Historical and Art Institute. The name Pearl, especially in conjunction with the name Gray, apparently bothered him considerably. The only time he ever liked it was during his adolescent years, when he strove to dramatize himself by dressing in pearl-gray suits.

He was six when he saw his first fish. "Looking down from my high perch into the clear pool directly under me, I saw something that transfixed me with a strange rapture. Against the sunlit amber depths of the little pool shone a wondrous fish creature that came to the surface and snapped at a bug. It flashed silver and rose." The experience stayed with him. In school and church Pearl Gray was a dreamer. "I dreamed, mostly of fields, hills and streams. . . . As I grew older, and learned the joys of angling, I used to run away on Sunday afternoons. Many a time have I come home late, wet and weary after a thrilling time along the river or stream, to meet with severe punishment from my outraged father. But it never cured me. I always went fishing on Sunday. It seemed the luckiest day." Dr. Gray told Pearl the only good fishermen who had ever lived were Christ's disciples, but the boy paid no heed, and he became the admirer of a local bum named Muddy Mizer who was always fishing on the Muskingum River.

Besides fishing, Pearl's other love was baseball, a sport at which he and his brother Romer, called R.C., excelled. Pearl was a pitcher, and he and R.C. played semipro ball around Ohio. Dr. Gray wanted Pearl to become a dentist, and he had him start by polishing sets of false teeth on a lathe. His pitching arm stood him in good stead. When the family moved to Columbus, Pearl unofficially went into practice on his own, pulling teeth in Frazeysburg until the Ohio Dental Association compelled him to stop. He continued playing baseball, and after one game a scout from the University of Pennsylvania offered him a scholarship. His father allowed him to accept it on the condition that he major in dentistry.

At Penn, Grey was at first highly unpopular. Ignorant of student traditions, he accidentally entered the upper class section of a lecture hall one day and triggered a riot in which his clothes were torn off and the room wrecked. After another contretemps he was chased by sophomores into a stairwell, where he managed to hold them off by hurling potatoes. His name and his refusal to go along with the crowd, to smoke, to drink or to gamble, made him the butt of jokes, and he escaped by spending most of his time reading in the library and playing baseball. He proved to be so good a ballplayer that, as he wrote later, "The bitter loneliness of my college days seemed to change. Wilborn, captain of the track team, took me up; Danny Coogan, the great varsity catcher, made me a member of Sigma Nu; Al Bull, the center on the famous football team that beat Yale and Princeton and Harvard, took me as a roommate."

Grey played left field for Penn. His one lapse came in a game against Harvard, when he accidentally stepped into a hole and a fly ball hit him on the head, allowing the winning run to score. Ordinarily his fielding was excellent. He once made a catch that helped Penn beat the Giants at the Polo Grounds. In his senior year he came to bat in the ninth inning against the University of Virginia with Penn trailing by a run. There were two out and a man on second. A verbose professor shouted, "Grey, the honor of the University of Pennsylvania rests with you!" Grey homered to win the game.

Grey was graduated with a diploma in dentistry in 1896. He opened an office in Manhattan on the West Side, and there he languished. He did not like the city, and he got away whenever possible. He played baseball for the Orange Athletic Club in New Jersey, and he became the youngest member of the Camp Fire Club. There a fellow member suggested that Grey write a story about his bass fishing on the Delaware. He did, and the story—his first effort—was published in *Recreation* in May 1902. The appearance of the article gave him direction, and he began writing an historical novel about his ancestor, Betty Zane, who carried gunpowder to her brother, Colonel Zane, during the siege of Fort Henry in the Revolution. All winter Grey labored over the book in a dingy flat. Upon completing it he drew the cover and inside illustrations. No publisher would accept *Betty Zane,* and, after a wealthy patient offered to back it, Grey had it printed privately. Sales were nil, but in a visit to Zanesville in 1904, Grey grandly announced that he had given up dentistry to devote himself "exclusively to literature."

In 1905 Grey married Lina Roth of New York, whom he had met a few years earlier while he was canoeing down the Delaware in one of his escapes from dentistry. She had faith in her husband and a bit of money to boot, and he gave up his practice to write while living in a house overlooking the Delaware in Lackawaxen, Pennsylvania. There he wrote, hunted, fished and savored "the happiness that dwells in wilderness alone." R.C., by now a professional ballplayer, chipped in with an occasional dollar, and Zane later repaid him by making him his official secretary and constant fishing companion.

Grey followed up *Betty Zane* by writing a couple of other books about the Ohio frontier, *The Spirit of the Border* and *The Last Trail,* which the A. L. Burt Company eventually published. They were flops. But Grey hung on, and in 1907 he went west with one Buffalo Jones, visiting the wilder parts of Utah and Arizona. Jones had a ranch on the rim of the Grand Canyon, where he was hybridizing black Galloway cattle with buffalo and calling the offspring cattalo. In his spare time he liked to lasso mountain lions. Grey loved it all, and, upon returning to the East, he wrote a book about Jones, *The Last of the Plainsmen,* which he took to Harper, a firm that had rebuffed him previously. Eagerly he awaited word and, hearing none, he visited the publishing house, where an editor coldly informed him, "I don't see anything in this to convince me that you can write either narrative or fiction." It was the bleakest moment in Grey's life. He was 36 years old, he had abandoned dentistry, his wife was pregnant with their first child and he had failed again. "When I staggered down the old stairway and out into Pearl Street I could not see," he later recalled. "I had to hold on to an iron post at the corner, and there I hung fighting such misery as I had never known. Something came to me there. They had all missed it. They did not know . . . and I went back to Lackawaxen to the smile and encouragement that never failed me."

He promptly wrote his first Western novel, *The Heritage of the Desert.* Harper yielded and published it in 1910—the year of the birth of his first son, Romer—and Grey thought he was at last on his way. Quickly he wrote *Riders of the Purple Sage,* but Harper rejected it as too "bulgy." Grey asked a vice-president of the firm to read the manuscript. He liked the novel, and so did his wife, who stayed up until three in the morning to finish it. The book was published, and Grey was permanently established. In fifteen years *Riders of the Purple Sage* sold two million copies. Grey also turned out half a dozen juveniles, many of them dealing with his baseball experiences. In *The Young Pitcher* he wrote of the potato episode at Penn and drew himself as Ken Ward, the hero. His brother, R.C., also called Reddy, was Reddy Ray, spark plug of the team. In *The Shortstop,* Grey named the hero after Chase Alloway, a professional player he had known in Ohio. (In the Western *The Lone Star Ranger* Grey named one of the villains Chess Alloway.)

Although comfortably off, Grey continued to write feverishly. He could not abide waste of time. As a writer and as an angler Grey was a finisher, and he followed both callings to the hilt. "It is so easy to start anything, a fishing jaunt or a career," he wrote, "but it is an entirely different matter to finish. The men who fail to finish in any walk of life, men who have had every opportunity . . . can be numbered by the millions." At top speed, Grey found he could write 100,000 words a month. He would pen himself up in his study, where he would sit in a Morris chair, writing in longhand on a lapboard, furiously chewing the top of a soft No. 1 pencil when a sentence failed him. He compiled notebooks of vivid phrases and expressions, and he often thumbed a worn copy of a book, *Materials and Methods of Fiction,* by Clayton Hamilton. Grey's son Romer, now president of Zane Grey, Inc., says, "That was Father's bible. It had a greater influence on his writing than any other work." Grey wrote only one draft of a book; he left the finishing of the manuscript to his wife. When not writing he fished. He knew a long stretch of the Delaware by memory. "I own nearly a thousand acres of land on it," he wrote. "I have fished it for ten years. I know every rapid, every eddy, almost, I might say, every stone from Callicoon to Port Jervis. This fifty-mile stretch of fast water I consider the finest bass ground I have ever fished." In July, when the river was low, he would scout the water for big bass by going upstream and drifting face down on a raft. "I see the bottom everywhere, except in rough water. I see the rocks, the shelves, the caverns. I see where the big bass live. And I remember." When the time came to fish, Grey became part of the landscape; he trod the slippery stones "as if I were a stalking Indian. I knew that a glimpse of me, or a faint jar vibrating under the water, or an unnatural ripple on its surface, would be fatal to my enterprise." Not every visiting angler exalted the fishing; some referred to Lackawaxen Creek as the Lackanothing or Lackarotten.

With money coming in, Grey and R.C. began fishing in Florida. They went after bonefish, snook and tarpon. Grey was among the first to go after sailfish, and he did so well that other fishermen flocked to the Gulf Stream. He was intrigued by wahoo, then seldom caught, reasoning that they could be taken because "all fish have to eat." He caught wahoo, and he helped put the Keys on the map. Wherever he went, he fished. On a trip to Mexico to gather material for a novel, his train chanced to pass by a jungle river, the Santa Rosa. Immediately Grey wondered, "Where did that river go? How many waterfalls and rapids hastened its journey to the Gulf? What teeming life inhabited its rich banks? How wild was the prospect! It haunted me!" In time he made the trip in a flat-bottom boat. On a trip to Yucatán, he happened to hear of "the wild and lonely Alacranes Reef where lighthouse keepers went insane from solitude, and where wonderful fishes inhabited the lagoons. That was enough for me. Forthwith I meant to go to Alacranes." Forthwith he did. There he met a little Englishman, Lord L., and "it was from him I got my type for Castleton, the Englishman, in *The Light of the Western Stars.* I have been told that never was there an Englishman on earth like the one I portrayed in my novel. But my critics never fished with Lord L."

Grey never lost any time. On a fishing trip he was up before everyone at four in the morning, transcribing the adventures of the previous day. If fishing was slack, he worked on a book until breakfast. He wrote much of *The Drift Fence* and *Robbers' Roost* at sea, and he piled up such a backlog of books that *Boulder Dam,* which he wrote while off on a trip in the 1930s, was not published by Harper until 1963.

In 1914 Grey started going west to Catalina each summer, where he tried swordfishing. In his first year he spent over three weeks at sea, trolling a total of 1,500 miles. Grey saw nineteen swordfish but did not get one strike. Instead of becoming discouraged, he was pleased. "By this time," he wrote, "I had realized something of the difficult nature of the game, and I had begun to have an inkling of what sport it might be." On the twenty-fifth day Grey sighted a swordfish, which he hooked. But the fish broke away, and Grey was sick at heart. The following summer found him back in Catalina. "I was crazy on swordfish," he admitted. To get his arms, hands and back into fighting trim, he rowed a boat for weeks on end. His patience and training were rewarded—he set a record by catching four swordfish in one day.

Between gathering material for novels and advising on movies and fishing, Grey began to visit Southern California so frequently that he moved his family to Los Angeles in 1918. Two years later he bought the small estate in Altadena that now serves as the headquarters of Zane Grey, Inc. Once established on the West Coast, Grey took up steelhead fishing in Oregon, and on a trip down the Rogue River he ran into a prospector who offered to sell his shack and land. Grey bought the place at Winkle Bar as offhandedly as he would buy a dozen new rods. He also owned some land and a small hunting lodge in Arizona. He shuttled from one place to another, writing, fishing, hunting, and gathering material. "[The year] 1923 was typical of what I do in the way of work and play," he replied to an admirer who had asked what a typical year was like.

> The pleasant paradox, however, is that my play turns out to be valuable work. January and February I spent at Long Key, Florida, where I wrote, read, fished and wandered along the beach. The spring I spent with my family in Altadena, California, where I wrote and studied, and played with my family. Tennis is my favorite game. During this season I motored with Mrs. Grey down to San Diego and across the mountains to El Centro and Yuma, through the wonderful desert land of Southern California. June found me at Avalon, Catalina Island, a place I have found as in-

spiring as Long Key, and infinitely different. Here I finished a novel, and then began my sword-fishing on the Pacific. My brother, R.C., and I roamed the sea searching for
giant swordfish. Sometimes we ran a hundred miles in a
day. The sea presents a marvelous contrast to the desert. It
inspires, teaches, subdues, uplifts, appalls and remakes
me. There I learned more of nature than on land. Birds and
fishes, strange sea creatures, are always in evidence. In
September I took Mr. [Jesse] Lasky and his [Paramount]
staff to Arizona to pick out locations for the motion picture, *The Vanishing American.* Upon the return I parted
with the Lasky outfit at the foot of Navajo Mountains. . . .
I, with my guide Wetherill, with selected cowboys and
horses, tried for the third time to reach Wild Horse Mesa.
In October I went to my hunting lodge in the Tonto Basin,
where the magnificent forests of green pine and silver
spruce and golden aspen soothed my eyes after the long
weeks on sea and desert. Here I hunted and rode the lonely
leaf-covered trails, lay for hours on the Rim, listening to
the bay of hounds, and spent many a pleasant evening
round the camp-fire, listening to my men, the gaunt long-
legged and lead-faced backwoodsmen of the Tonto Basin.
November and December found me back again at Altadena, hard as nails, brown as an Indian, happy to be
home with my family, keen for my study with its books
and pictures, and for the long spell of writing calling me
to its fulfillment.

Grey always had some new adventure going. A Norwegian
named Sievert Nielsen, a sailor turned prospector, read Grey's
novel *Desert Gold* and wrote to him under the misapprehension
that the story of the lost treasure in the farfetched plot was true.
Grey was so charmed with the letter that he invited Nielsen to see

him. They became friends and together hiked across Death Valley for the thrill of it.

Grey's success at landing big fish prompted a correspondence with Captain Laurie Mitchell of Liverpool, Nova Scotia. Mitchell, who was to become one of Grey's fishing companions, was enthusiastic about giant bluefin tuna off Nova Scotia. He himself had landed only one—it happened to be a world-record 710 pounds— and had lost between fifty and sixty of the big fish. Other anglers had caught perhaps a total of ten. The fish were simply too tough for ordinary tackle. This was just the sort of challenge that appealed to Grey, who promptly began laying plans to fish in Nova Scotia. He reasoned that his swordfish tackle would be adequate for the tuna, provided that the boat from which he was fishing was fast and maneuverable. He had two light skiffs built in Nova Scotia, and from Florida he ordered a special launch, twenty-five feet long and equipped with two engines capable of doing eighteen miles an hour. The launch was so designed that at full speed it could turn on its own length. Grey installed Catalina fighting chairs in each boat.

Within a couple of weeks Grey proved his strategy to be right. He hooked three tuna and landed two, one of which was a world-record 758 pounds and the largest fish of any species ever caught on rod and reel.

Before leaving Nova Scotia, Grey fulfilled a boyhood dream of buying "a beautiful white ship with sails like wings to sail into tropic seas." The three-masted schooner, which he called *Fisherman,* held the record for the run from Halifax to New York City. Grey scrupulously made certain she never had been used as a rum-runner; ever the teetotaler, he would not have a bootlegger's boat as a gift. He had *Fisherman* outfitted with all the tackle that "money could buy and ingenuity devise," and, with R.C. and Romer, he set sail for Galápagos, Cocos Island, the Gulf of Panama and the Pacific coast of Mexico. On this trip he caught a 135-pound Pacific sailfish, the first known to science, but otherwise fishing conditions were not good because of an abundance of sharks.

Broadbill swordfish remained Grey's great love. In 1926 at Catalina, he and his brother caught a total of 10, including Zane's world-record 582-pounder. In that same year R.C. caught five marlin, all weighing more than 300 pounds. No other angler had then caught more than one 300-pound fish, and the 354-pounder taken by R.C. was a world record. It was a great year for the brothers, and, as Grey wrote, "Not the least pleasure in our success was to run back to Avalon with the red flag flying at the masthead, to blow a clarion blast from the boat's whistle, and to see the pier filled with excited spectators. Sometimes thousands of visitors massed at the end of the pier to see the swordfish weighed and photographed. On these occasions R.C. and I would have to stand the battery of hundreds of cameras and shake hands until we broke away from the pier."

Not everyone cheered Grey. He and R.C. broke early with members of the Catalina Tuna Club over Grey's choice of tackle. Although a light-tackle man in freshwater, Grey used very heavy tackle for big-game fish. He argued that fish that broke off light tackle either became prey to sharks or died.

Grey accepted the invitation of the New Zealand government to investigate the big-game fishing possibilities in that country. Captain Mitchell and R.C. went with him. They revolutionized local practices; instead of fishing with bait deep down, they took fish by trolling. Grey caught a world-record 450-pound striped marlin and a record 111-pound yellowtail, while Captain Mitchell set a record with a 976-pound black marlin. Grey's greatest pleasure, however, was finding copies of his Westerns in even the remotest homes he visited. "This was surely the sweetest and most moving of all the experiences I had; and it faced me again with the appalling responsibility of a novelist who in these modern days of materialism dares to foster idealism and love of nature, chivalry in men and chastity in women."

Back home, Grey had difficulties in Arizona. In 1930 the state passed game laws and established seasons, and Grey, accustomed to hunting bears whenever the mood was on him, was angered. He felt that he was entitled to hunt year round, because he had put Arizona on the map. When a warden refused to issue him a resident license Grey was "grossly insulted," and he gave up his lodge in the Tonto Basin. "In twelve years my whole bag of game has been five bears, three bucks and a few turkeys," he said. "I have written fifteen novels with Arizona background. Personally it cost me $30,000 to get material for one book alone, *To the Last Man.* My many trips all over the state have cost me $100,000. So in every way I have not been exactly an undesirable visitor." He was so indignant he said he would never return and, as a parting shot, he said that the game commission and the Forest Service had sold out to "the commercial interest." As a case in point, he cited the north rim of the Grand Canyon as nothing more than a "tin-can gasoline joint." Grey felt strongly about the Grand Canyon, so much so that he could not bring himself to write about it. It was simply too marvelous to describe.

Fishing in the Pacific lured him more and more. He revisited New Zealand and Tahiti, where he caught his record 1,040-pound striped marlin. The fish was mutilated by sharks; had it not been, it would have weighed 200 pounds more. When the Australian government asked him to explore big-game fishing there, Grey went to Australia and landed his record tiger shark off Sydney Heads. Always the unknown beckoned. He spent $40,000 for a steel-hulled schooner originally built for the Kaiser, and another $270,000 went into refurbishing the ship, which he named *Fisherman II.* His dream of dreams was to fish the waters of Christmas Island off Madagascar, where there were reports of sailfish twenty-two feet long. Equipped with six launches, *Fisherman II* embarked for Christmas Island on a round-the-world cruise. The ship was 195 feet long, but she had a narrow twenty-eight-foot beam and she rolled, even in a calm sea. Even Grey got sick. "We had so much trouble it was unbelievable," says his younger son, Loren. "We got as far as Totoya in the Fijis. The captain was ill. The chief engineer had appendicitis. We were there for over a month or more with costly repairs. Father finally called the trip off because of a pressing business matter with his publisher." Eventually Grey gave up on the ship, and she ended her days as a cannery tender for a West Coast tuna fleet.

While steelhead fishing in Oregon in 1937 Grey suffered a stroke. Romer and a guide carried him to a car and got him home, where he recuperated. Within a year he seemed recovered. He went to Australia to fish and then back to Altadena to write, before going on to Oregon for steelhead. There he insisted that Loren and three friends fish "not only all day, but every day in the week," says Loren, now a professor of education at San Fernando Valley State College. "We finally had a big fight with him and said we wanted to go home. If he wouldn't let us go home, would he at least let us go into town on weekends and live it up a little bit? He finally gave in, so we'd fish just five days a week."

Determined to make a complete recovery, Grey worked out with a rod in a fighting chair set on the porch of the west wing of his house. Every day Grey would battle imaginary fish, pumping the rod perhaps 200 times before calling it quits. He was getting ready for the next expedition. It never came. On October 23, 1939 Zane Grey died. His workouts in the fighting chair apparently had been too much for him. He once wrote, in his younger days, "There is only one thing wrong with a fishing day—its staggering brevity. If a man spent all his days fishing, life would seem to be a swift dream." For Zane Grey, compulsive angler, the swift dream was over.

—APRIL 29, 1968

He's Got a Very Fishy Look

Charles E. Brooks

The sign at the precipitous edge of the Black Canyon on the Yellowstone River warned that this was grizzly-bear country. It was also Friday the thirteenth, but Charles E. Brooks, former secret agent turned angling writer, paid no heed. "Come on," he said. "Those salmonflies are hatching down there." When a companion asked what they would do if they ran into a grizzly, Brooks, a bear of a man himself, said, "I'll sing. They don't like noise."

Five hours and seven miles later, Brooks clambered out of the canyon. There had been no grizzlies, but plenty of plump cutthroat and rainbow trout—all released. Brooks had gone down into the canyon because he was interested in checking on the salmonfly hatch and seeing what his deerhair-and-hackle imitation of the adult would do. It outfished all other ties. Salmonflies, as they are called in Montana, are actually huge stone flies, insects that grow to two inches in length, and Brooks has been studying them for years. Indeed, ever since he retired as an Air Force major in 1964, he has been examining almost everything that creeps, crawls, swims or flies in the trout country of southwestern Montana in an effort to make himself a better fisherman. As a friend once put it, "Charlie's trying to climb into a trout's head."

Brooks's books, notably *Larger Trout for the Western Fly Fisher-man, The Trout and the Stream, Nymph Fishing for Larger Trout,* have won him a growing reputation as an angling author and au-thority, and his latest book, *The Living River,* his intimate account of the Madison River, is destined to secure it. In all likelihood, Brooks is ready to join the ranks of the "holy three," namely George LaBranche, Edward Ringwood Hewitt and Sparse Grey Hackle, as a sainted American angling author. He is an original. His style is clear, direct and without pretense, and his works are packed with telling detail gleaned not only from scientific studies but also from the thousands of hours he has spent creeping, crawling and swim-ming—often underwater—to get a trout's or salmonfly's view of the world.

Brooks, now sixty, is not a trout fisherman to the fly rod born. He was a hillbilly raised in the Missouri Ozarks during the worst years of the Depression. His father was badly hurt in an industrial acci-dent in 1929, and the family, which included his mother and six brothers and sisters, lived in a succession of shacks. The Brookses kept body and soul together by chopping cotton. When Charlie was nine, he traded a bagful of deer tails to a local flytyer for two dollars and fifty cents in cash, a big box of materials, one hundred hooks and an hour-and-a-half lesson in tying—"the greatest bargain I ever made in my life." Fishing the Current River with his own flies, cane pole, chalk line doused with linseed oil and horsehair leaders, Brooks "caught fish like nobody's business, and they were always welcome at home because we ate everything."

After he graduated from grammar school in 1933, Brooks be-came a migrant farm worker. He sent all his wages home to support his family, except for the five cents a day he kept to buy bread and buttermilk. "I had that for supper," he says. "The farmers usually provided some kind of dinner, and I never did eat breakfast until I was twenty-five or twenty-six."

After his father died in 1936, Brooks joined the Civilian Conservation Corps and worked in the West. Impressed by the mountain streams of Montana and Wyoming, he promised himself he would live there one day and write about fishing. Eager for a high-school education, he left the CCC in 1939 when the football coach of the high-school team in Milan, Missouri, promised him a job if he would play. Brooks was the outstanding defensive player in the history of the school, led the conference in punting and scoring and also lettered in baseball, basketball and track. He completed high school in three years with a straight-A average. All the while, he held down two jobs, rising at five in the morning and going to bed at eleven each night. The first month he was there, several teachers complained about his whistling and singing in the halls, and when a teacher asked him why he did it, he said, "I'm so happy to be here. But I'll stop. I can be just as happy inside."

In 1942, Brooks joined the Army Air Corps as an aviation cadet. In time he was commissioned as a bombardier. He flew fifty missions over Europe. His pilot, Richard Witkin, now transportation reporter for *The New York Times,* says, "Charlie's the only man I ever met in my life who enjoyed war. I don't mean he liked to kill people, but when I was going through flak and enemy fighters, I was scared witless. To Charlie it was a thrill. To him, flak and enemy fighters were exciting. He's the last of the great adventurers."

Released from active duty in 1945, Brooks got temporary work as a park ranger at Yosemite but was turned down for a regular job because he lacked a college degree. He thought of going to Stanford, but he felt he could not learn any more there than he could from books or life. By now, married and knowing that he wanted to write, Brooks decided that the best thing he could do was to reenlist in the Air Force, put in his twenty years and then retire to explore and write.

Brooks was assigned to counterintelligence. One of his favorite assignments turned out to be scouting possible invasion sites along the Alaskan coast. He quickly discovered that the tide went out too far to allow an amphibious landing, but his superiors were slow in digesting this information, so he spent several months fishing trout and salmon streams under the guise of being a wealthy sportsman. When Brooks left the Air Force for good, in 1964, he and his wife, Grace, set out for West Yellowstone, where they built a house.

Brooks soon began his research in Montana by observing the nymphs and larvae of insects that serve as food for trout in the Firehole, Gibbon and Madison rivers. "My aim is to fish the nymph imitation at the right place with the right motion," he says. "I wanted to find out what nymphs were in the water, and what action I should impart to the imitation." In one hundred-yard stretch of the Madison, he observed Mayfly nymphs of the species *Siphlonurus occidentalis,* the gray drake, as it is known to anglers. "I found that the gray drake has to have a silt bottom around weeds, a current speed of not more than one and three-fourths miles per hour and a depth of about twenty inches," he says. "The nymph is slow-moving and clambers around weeds. It moves about in the early morning or late afternoon. It doesn't like bright sunlight." While Grace fished an imitation gray drake so that it either swam along the bottom or seemed to climb the weeds, Brooks watched the reaction of the trout underwater. As a result of this type of investigation, Brooks ties his nymph imitations without a wing case on the back so that if it should be turned over by the current, a fish won't wonder why it's upside down. "A live nymph never turns upside down in the water," he says. "A nymph imitation has to have color and form and life, and the more signs of life the better." The ultimate in life simulation is Brooks's imitation of any of a number of large dragonfly nymphs. It is basically a one-eighth-inch-wide strip of natural brown seal fur, left on the skin, wrapped around the hook shank. In the water it pumps and breathes enticingly. "It's a rough, scraggly fly, but so is the natural," says Brooks.

To study the nymph of the giant salmonfly, *Pteronarcys californica,* he spent time down in Hole No. 2 of the Madison, breathing through a hose. "I found that the *Pteronarcys* nymphs feed twice every twenty-four hours," Brooks says. 'I'd see them come out from under the rocks where they live to feed on algae on top of the rocks. First the smaller nymphs would come out, then the bigger ones and, finally, the biggest. The fish weren't interested until all the rocks were covered with nymphs of all sizes. Then I tried to find out why the nymphs were feeding when they did. I finally pinned it on temperature. In the summer they like to feed at fifty-eight degrees and generally knock off when it reaches sixty-two degrees. In the fall, when the water cools, fifty-two degrees will bring them out to feed."

At times, when a nymph would get washed away from the rocks by the current a trout would glom onto it. To simulate the nymph in the current, Brooks began fishing what is now known as the Brooks Method. Using a short leader and a high-density sink-belly line, he casts way upstream and, holding his arms high, allows the nymph to bounce along the bottom in a dead drift.

One autumn several years ago, when the well-known dry-fly fisherman Art Flick visited Brooks to fish the Madison, a cold snap hit. Brooks took the water temperature. It was forty-six degrees, and he announced that the fishing would not be good until about 11:30 A.M. Meanwhile he would show Flick how to fish the heavy water with the Brooks Method. Flick got a few strikes, but Brooks explained that these were smaller fish that always began feeding before the bigger fish in much the same way that the small *Petronarcys* nymphs began feeding before the bigger ones did.

At 11:30 Brooks took the temperature, found it was fifty-two degrees and told Flick the trout would start hitting. They did, right on schedule.

Brooks has been active as the permanent secretary of the Southwestern Montana Fly Fishers, a club he helped found in 1969. Though it has never had more than twenty-four members, its accomplishments are noteworthy. Its sole objective is to protect, maintain and improve the trout streams of the region. Among the club's achievements is that of putting an end to the stocking of hatchery trout of catchable size in streams with naturally producing populations. "When you dump thousands of living units into any area not totally a desert or wilderness, you create an immediate shortage of shelter, *and* you create an intolerable sociological pressure on those biological units already there," Brooks says. "It does not matter whether we are talking of fish, rats, monkeys or humans. The result is precisely the same—chaos."

Public support for the Southwestern Montana Fly Fishers' goals has become significant. Indeed, last year's closing of the middle Madison to fishing for an undetermined period so that biologists can study the stream won wide public approval. "The swing is our way," says Brooks. "The people here see that they can prosper because people come from all over the country, even the world, to find what they don't have at home, quality fishing in an unspoiled environment." Then he adds, "My energies in life are expended on a narrow plane. I'm involved in studying, writing about, protecting and improving the ecology of trout streams in southwestern Montana. That's it. I'm not out to save the whole world. People who are out to save the whole world don't save anything. But I can say with certainty that the trout fishing we've got, as good as it is, is going to improve even more."

—SEPTEMBER 3, 1979

A Warm Spot for a Very Cold Sport

Kenneth Gerhardt

When Kenneth Gerhardt of Peekskill, N.Y., a manufacturer's representative who sells pollution control and efficiency equipment to power plants, was asked last winter to include the frozen tundra of upstate New York as part of his sales territory, he was overjoyed. Gerhardt could hardly wait to get up to Oneida Lake, 10 miles northeast of Syracuse, where the average temperature in January and February is 18 degrees and where the average snowfall each winter is 112.3 inches. A dedicated ice fisherman, Gerhardt was well aware that Oneida has the reputation of being the finest walleye lake in the East and perhaps the entire country. "Walleyes might fight with all the dash and abandon of a wet cardboard box," Gerhardt says, "but they are delicious."

Fishermen who know Gerhardt consider him the best ice fisherman they have ever met. Christopher Letts, a 46-year-old naturalist and educator who now lives in Cortland, N.Y., says, "I grew up in Illinois and Michigan, the heart of ice fishing country, and by the time I was 16, I thought I knew it all. But Ken has changed me. He has influenced me more than anyone else ever has. He's showing the way in ice fishing. He's the driving force."

Not everyone is so impressed. Gerhardt laughs and admits that when his three daughters were younger and still living at home, they and his wife, Janet, would send him off on his midwinter angling expeditions with comments like "You're insane. You're a sick man."

Gerhardt's specialty is going after panfish—yellow perch, white perch, crappies and sunnies. "Contrary to what many people think, ice fishing for panfish is more effective than summer fishing by a factor of 10," says Gerhardt, who averages two to three dozen fish a trip. "The fish school tighter in the winter, you can hold right over them, they don't move around much, and once you find them, they stay in the same general area for three or four days. And for eating, there's nothing like panfish from an icy pond. In the summer I wouldn't walk across the street for a yellow perch, a crappie or a bluegill, but in the winter I pursue them with devotion."

Gerhardt is the kind of fisherman who attracts a crowd even on a day when the wind-chill factor is -20 degrees. Not surprisingly for a salesman, he is a talker; stories, quips, jokes, limericks and fishing tips pour out of him nonstop. Gerhardt isn't just interested in entertaining or instructing the crowds that gather around him, he wants to have company, because ice fishing can be extra productive when other fishermen are nearby. The panfish down below often go into a feeding frenzy, Gerhardt theorizes, because all the lures simulate a school of bait.

Gerhardt also fishes through ice for trout. One winter afternoon a few years ago, a news producer at WNET-TV, the PBS station serving metropolitan New York, decided to send a crew up to the West Branch Reservoir, 15 miles northeast of Peekskill, to videotape all the dopey ice fishermen suffering in the subzero cold. The producer figured the footage would be good for a lot of laughs. No sooner had the crew arrived at the reservoir than fishermen began gathering at a hole and shouting. The crew scampered across the ice and taped the episode, which began with Gerhardt playing a fish as other anglers frantically chopped away at the hole to enlarge it. Finally Gerhardt pulled the fish through the hole and plopped it onto the ice. It was a 14-pound, 6-ounce brown trout.

That night the tape was shown, but if there were any laughs, they were at the expense of WNET. In the rush to get the tape on the air, technicians did not have time to edit the soundtrack, which came on laden with admiring but unbleeped obscenities from the crowd.

Gerhardt, 62, took up ice fishing 45 years ago, before winning seven battle stars while serving with the Army in Europe during World War II. He also took up fly-fishing to occupy himself during the warmer months. Though he was a superb flytyer and a graceful caster—he could effortlessly send a heavy lead-core line 100 feet across a stream—he abruptly abandoned fly-fishing 15 years ago. He had become smitten with deep-sea fishing for cod, pollock and the occasional halibut 25 to 40 miles out in the Atlantic off Cape Cod. His trout-fishing friends were aghast. When one of them, Colonel Henry A. Siegel, chided him for giving up trout in favor of "coarse fish," Gerhardt replied, "Hey, Henry, the fish I catch are wider between the eyes than yours are long."

Gerhardt, who earned a degree in mechanical engineering from Brooklyn Polytechnic Institute, says, "My approach to fishing is that of an engineer. When I go fishing I define the problem, and then I solve it." Ultraprecise and systematic, he makes (and occasionally invents) his own lures, rigs and rods, and he keeps detailed fishing logs that note even the stomach contents of fish he has caught. For the record, bluegills taken through the ice often have wads of daphnia—water fleas—in their stomachs, while yellow perch prefer to gorge themselves on dime-sized baby bluegills instead of minnows. Says Letts, "Ken will empty out a stomach, put the contents in a glass of water and then swirl the glass around and inspect it as though it were Don Perignon."

Gerhardt often writes about his findings in *The Fisherman Magazine,* a weekly regional that caters to hard-core anglers from Virginia to Maine. "Gerhardt has an incredible following," says Harold Berkowitz, the proprietor of Midland Tackle in Sloatsburg, N.Y., one of the busiest mail-order operations in the nation. "If he writes a story recommending this rod blank or that reel, I'll have at least a hundred orders within a week. And I'm talking about $150 items. Fishermen believe in him."

According to Gerhardt's records, the time of day is very important in ice fishing. "The best time is from first light to about eight or nine o'clock in the morning," he says. "The second-best time is from 3 or 3:30 until dark. Where to fish is important. In most cases, panfish will be in water 10 feet deep or less, except for New York City reservoirs, where huge perch, 16 inches or more, are taken in 60 to 70 feet of water."

When exploring a frozen pond that he does not yet know well, Gerhardt drills a five- to eight-inch-diameter hole 10 to 15 feet offshore, preferably off a point of land. He used to make his holes the traditional way, with an ax or a big hand auger, but nowadays he uses a power auger, not unlike the kind that phone company workmen use to install telephone poles. The machine goes for $250, but it can bore through 24-inch-thick ice in 30 seconds. Gerhardt doesn't fish a hole immediately, but instead works his way along the ice, drilling nine or 10 more holes every 10 yards. "Fish are very sensitive to sound," he says. "When I've finished drilling all the holes, I go back to the first one and start fishing there because the fish near it have had time to calm down."

Gerhardt uses a three-foot graphite jigging rod of his own make and design. The guides are extra large so they don't ice over, and at the tip is a spring "strike indicator." Essentially it is a sensitive metal spring that will flex at the slightest nibble by a fish, which is important because winter panfish, especially crappies and yellow perch, generally have a very soft strike. To make certain that he can see the softest of strikes in dim light, Gerhardt paints the eye on the tip fluorescent orange.

Almost inevitably, the first lure Gerhardt clips on—he uses quick clips so he doesn't have to tie knots in frigid temperatures—is a small ball-head jig with a gold-plated hook and a soft plastic grub. "The gold adds a little flash," Gerhardt says, "and before I add on the grub I put a drop of Krazy Glue behind the head of the jig and push the tail into it. Bluegills have a nasty habit of stripping the tail off, and there's a certain cost in comfort in putting a new tail on in the cold. This way there's no problem. Finally, I add a moussee— the larva of a fly—to the hook point, just for scent. The motion of the jig attracts the fish, but the moussee triggers the biting.

"This whole system has been years in the making. It is based on utility and efficiency in catching fish, even on very cold and windy days. I fish the jig at three levels: first just off the bottom, then 18 inches above the bottom and finally 36 inches above the bottom, or three reel turns. The motion I use with the jig is just a slight jiggle, jiggle, jiggle. I do six jiggles, pause 10 seconds, do six more jiggles and then give the jig a slow lift-up before letting it descend to the bottom again. I let it sit for about 10 seconds and then repeat all the jiggles. I do this about 8 or 10 times at each level. After I've gone through one cycle, I'll repeat the whole cycle once, maybe twice. If I catch a fish at the hole, I'll keep fishing there until there are no more bites. Then I'll move to the next hole out from shore. A lot of fishermen make the mistake of drilling just one hole and staying there even if they don't catch fish."

Gerhardt has found that in small ponds, panfish feed in pulses. The fish will feed avidly for five or six days and then stop for 14 to 18 days. Gerhardt keeps years' worth of detailed records on four such ponds, and says, "The fish feed and stop feeding at the same time, almost to the day, year after year." He knows this because he has purposely fished those ponds on days when his records said the fish wouldn't hit, and he was delighted to come up empty. "Ken can catch a lot of fish," says Letts, "but he really is more interested in finding out about fish behavior. He's always probing."

Gerhardt reasons that in a small pond, panfish feed the way they do because of population booms of daphnia and other organisms. Then, after gorging themselves, they spend 14 to 18 days digesting their food because cold water temperatures have slowed their metabolisms.

When Gerhardt's logs tell him that the panfishing will be poor, he often switches technique and goes for trout. "Jigging for trout is a different story," Gerhardt says. "You should be fishing in 30 to 50 feet of water, and you need a rod with a bit more backbone. The lure is a flat silver jig with a treble hook and a half-inch to three-quarter-inch-long piece of minnow tail hooked on one of the prongs. I let the lure down until it hits the bottom, I lower the rod tip to almost the water surface, then I snap the rod up four feet and let the lure flutter down. I do this 10 or 15 times. Then I take in four feet of line and repeat this until I've worked all the way to the top. Trout can be anywhere in that column of water, although 90 percent of the ones I've caught have been within 18 inches of the bottom. The 14½-pounder that I took in the West Branch was 40 feet down, on the bottom. Just two minutes before I hooked that fish, I had landed a 2½-pound trout."

Gerhardt employs a similar technique when he is fishing for walleye. But instead of a solid jig he prefers a lightweight spoon about two inches long that he will jig just off the bottom in 10 to 20 feet of water. He also has found that painting his spoons fluorescent green or orange is an improvement over their standard metallic finish.

In looking at his fishing objectively, Gerhardt says, "My ice fishing and my deep-jigging for cod are under 95 percent control. Every time I go out it's a learning experience. No one can ever say they know everything about anything, especially fishing. I'm constantly changing. Not everything comes up roses. But I always keep trying to find a better way." Which is hardly good news for the walleyes of Oneida Lake.

—FEBRUARY 15, 1988

The Strange Fish and Stranger Times of Dr. Herbert R. Axelrod

Dr. Herbert R. Axelrod

Dr. Herbert R. Axelrod is the great panjandrum of the tropical-fish world. Dr. Herbert R. Axelrod—the title and the full name are always run together by admirers as though they were one word—is without rival in the burgeoning world of tropical fish. Dr. Axelrod is an intrepid ichthyologist and explorer who has made more than forty expeditions to South America, Africa, Australia, the Fijis, Indonesia, Thailand, India and the Malay Archipelago. He can, he says, recognize more than 7,000 species of fish on sight, and he has discovered hundreds of species that were lost to science for years or, better yet, were never seen before by man. More than two dozen species of fish have been named after him, and one of these, *Cheirodon axelrodi,* the cardinal tetra, is the biggest-selling tropical fish in the world.

Besides being an incredible discoverer of fish, Dr. Axelrod is a remarkably prolific writer. He has written more than half a dozen major books on fish, all bestsellers. His first book, *Tropical Fish as a Hobby,* is in its ninth printing and has sold more than 80,000 copies. Dr. Axelrod has also churned out more than one hundred smaller books and pamphlets on fish, and several hundred articles, as well. His typewriter is always busy. Once on a Friday, Doubleday, the publishers, asked the doctor for a book on fish. On Saturday morning he sat down to write and, by the time he stood up on Sunday evening, the manuscript was completed. On Monday it was accepted and published as *Tropical Aquarium Fishes.* It sold 450,000 copies. As if to show this was no trick, Dr. Axelrod recently turned out a substantial paperback for Fawcett, *Axelrod's Tropical Fish Book,* over another weekend. The book is lavishly illustrated with hundreds of photographs, most of them taken by the doctor, who, with some justification, regards himself as the finest photographer of tropical fish in the world.

When not traveling up some Amazon tributary by dugout canoe or sitting before a smoking typewriter, Dr. Axelrod is kept busy presiding over the seemingly limitless destinies and rapidly multiplying fortunes of T.F.H. Publications, Inc., of which he owns seventy-five percent of the stock. T.F.H. Publications, Inc., or TFH as it is known in the trade, is the General Motors of the pet world, and its offices are in, of all places, Jersey City. Here, in a yellow three-story building of his own design, the doctor publishes *All-Pets* magazine, a monthly given over to such articles as "The Four-Toed Tortoise" and "Peafowl, from a Hobby to a Business." It is here that he also publishes his own very special baby, *Tropical Fish Hobbyist,* which not only has the largest circulation of any aquarium magazine but is, as the cover has proclaimed, THE ONLY AQUARIUM MAGAZINE IN THE WORLD ILLUSTRATED INSIDE WITH COLOR PHOTOGRAPHS!!! Invariably, these photographs have been taken by Dr. Axelrod to illustrate one of his own articles about an expedition he headed, net in one hand, rifle in the other, into some obscure backwater in search of a spotted *Corydoras* catfish. Among the subscribers who have thrilled to the doctor's accounts of rare adventure was the late Winston Churchill, who carried on a correspondence with him about fancy goldfish. Churchill, however, was merely one of a number of world figures enthralled by the doctor. He has been on intimate terms with Emperor Hirohito of Japan, a renowned seaslug specialist; the former King of the Belgians, Leopold III; and the President of Brazil, Humberto Castelo Branco, who asked Dr. Axelrod to draw up a conservation program for the Amazon.

In addition to magazines, Dr. Axelrod also publishes thousands of booklets dealing with all aspects of the pet world. Among those he has published are such bestsellers as *Modern American Mouse, Colorful Egglayers, Trick Training Cats, Your Terrarium, Horned Toads Pets, Monkey Business, Snakes as Pets* and *Rats as Pets*. For some time now Ernest Walker, former assistant director of the Washington Zoo, has been after TFH to publish a companion volume, *Bats as Pets,* but Dr. Axelrod has resisted his friend on the grounds that there are no pet shops selling bats. Walker keeps several free-flying bats in his Washington apartment, and whenever Dr. Axelrod comes to call, Walker, fearful lest his pets escape, opens the door a crack and whispers, "Come in quickly."

At least once a month Dr. Axelrod makes a trip to Florida, where TFH owns five tropical-fish farms near Tampa. TFH is the biggest breeder of tropical fish in the world; at last count there were approximately six million fish down on the farms. All in all, TFH so dominates the field of fish that a couple of cosmetics companies, seeking to diversify, recently offered the doctor $7 million to sell out. He refused, because he was making piles of money, and he has used part of the substantial profits of TFH to further the study of fish. Two years ago he reprinted Jordan and Evermann's four-volume classic on systematic ichthyology, *The Fishes of North and Middle America,* which had long been out of print, and presented 2,000 sets to the Smithsonian Institution free of charge. The Smithsonian has been selling the volumes at twenty-five dollars a set, and all the proceeds go toward tropical-fish research and expeditions. On occasion Dr. Axelrod has dug deep into his own pocket to finance expeditions by others when he has been tied down by affairs in Jersey City. He dispatched Dr. Jacques Gery of the Laboratoire Arago of the University of Paris to Gabon to search for exotic fish, and Dr. Martin

Brittan of Sacramento State College has taken a couple of treks into unexplored Brazil in quest of an elusive blood-red tetra, thanks to the doctor's largess.

In his own spare hours, infrequent though they may be, Dr. Axelrod is fond of playing Bach sonatas on the violin and reading extensively about the sciences. He holds degrees in mathematics, chemistry, physics and biology and, since he is fluent in French, Spanish, Portugese, German, Hebrew and Japanese, can get along in Russian and Polish and grasp the essentials in Hungarian and Swedish, his range of reading matter is wide as well as deep. The doctor has been a crack golfer, bowler and swimmer (when only ten he swam fifteen miles, from the American shore to the Canadian shore of Lake Ontario), but his favorite sports nowadays are racing pigeons and fishing. He is one of a handful of anglers who have caught an Atlantic sailfish on a fly rod, and when he made his first million dollars he celebrated by building four of the most luxurious pigeon coops in existence on the roof of his Jersey City emporium. At noontime he often clambers up to the roof and sends the pigeons flying while he munches on a sandwich. When in residence in Jersey City the doctor always lunches on a double liverwurst on rye sent in from Bauer's Delicatessen, but on the road he is a far more adventurous gourmet. As one might expect, his favorite dish is fish, any kind of fish, but in the jungle he sometimes gluts himself on howler-monkey stew. A good meal counts for a lot with the doctor. In fact, he once broke a trip from an aquarium in Frankfurt am Main to Cairo where he was to inspect fish carvings inside a pyramid, just to stop off in Rome for a highly touted plate of spaghetti.

This man of enormous energies and myriad talents is also a man of mystery. Rumors abound about Axelrod. One rumor, essentially true, has it that he dwells in splendor in an opulent bomb shelter and fortress tucked into the Jersey coast. Another story goes that, though the doctor is well into his seventies, he does not look a day over forty-five. In point of fact, Dr. Herbert R. Axelrod, ichthyologist, explorer, author, linguist, tycoon and sportsman, is only thirty-seven years of age. Meeting him for the first time is somewhat like discovering the real identity of the Wizard of Oz.

Dr. Axelrod, a burly six-footer, purposely keeps himself from public view for several reasons. For one, he believes that his private life is his own business. For another, he has no desire to be called at any hour of the night by an aquarist in Oklahoma City whose swordtails have fallen prey, say, to a mild case of *Ichthyopthirius*. For still another reason, Dr. Axelrod finds most people are bores. He once refused to meet Jacques Cousteau; he thought Cousteau was a bore. Indeed, Dr. Axelrod has been known to interrupt conversations with close friends by yawning in their faces and telling them to leave because he was bored. "I'm not rude for rudeness' sake," says the doctor. "I just don't have time to beat around the bush." When he was younger he worried that he had a personality problem, and he consulted a psychiatrist. The psychiatrist dismissed him at once on the grounds that Dr. Axelrod was the happiest man he had ever met, because he had no inhibitions. Possibly as a result of his complete lack of inhibitions, Dr. Axelrod is tremendously fond of quarrels and litigation. In recent years he has been sued fourteen times, and the filing of each suit gave him as much joy as the discovery of a new species of fish. Several cases arose out of denunciations Dr. Axelrod made of certain fish dealers in *Tropical Fish Hobbyist*, but inasmuch as he considers himself the world's ranking expert on tropical fish, he has no doubt that he will win them all. As a matter of fact, he has so far won thirteen of the lawsuits, with the other one pending. "I like to match wits," says the doctor. "A lawsuit is a chess game. When there's no challenge, I'm not interested."

Dr. Axelrod grew up in Bayonne, New Jersey, just to the south of Jersey City. Bayonne, a grimy oil-refinery town fronting Upper New York Bay, is an unlikely place to spawn a naturalist of Dr. Axelrod's stature, but in the days of his youth it still possessed marshlands and creeks not befouled by refinery wastes. The family had little money—Axelrod's father, Dr. Aaron Axelrod, now vice-president of TFH, taught mathematics in a local high school—but young Herbert earned pocket money by pressing pants, with characteristic gusto, for an overwhelmed tailor and by catching blue crabs, which he sold to Chinese laundrymen. For a dime he purchased a nondescript pair of pigeons from a fellow urchin, and he housed them in a sawed-off orange crate he kept hidden wherever he could down alleys and under stoops. Despite his best efforts, the pigeons made their mark on neighborhood porches and roofs, and protesting landlords forced the family to move several times. "I was crazy about the pigeons!" Dr. Axelrod recalls in a typical burst of enthusiasm. "I took them to school and hid them there. I used to take them into my room at night. I couldn't leave them. I didn't know it, but I actually developed the first mobile pigeon loft. It took the Army years to do that, and I did it as a kid!"

In high school Axelrod's passion for knowledge was such that he asked his father to send him to a Jesuit prep school in Jersey City. But since Dr. Axelrod *père* was teaching in the high school that his son was attending, he refused, because he did not want to denigrate the teaching abilities of his colleagues. Undaunted, Axelrod *fils* took to cutting school two or three times a week to attend Brooklyn Tech on the sly, because the teachers there were stimulating. Whatever Axelrod did, he did to the hilt. He had an IQ of 181, but he was nagged by doubts that spurred him to further efforts. "I guess I always wanted to show off," he says. "I was an ugly kid, with pimples all over my face. I weighed 110 pounds, and no girl would go out with me. I was obsessed with sex."

At sixteen Axelrod was graduated from high school, and at seventeen he enlisted in an Army officer college training program. He was sent to study engineering at the City College of New York and the University of Delaware. When the Germans almost broke through American lines in the Battle of the Bulge in 1944, all the students were rushed overseas, except Axelrod, who was too young for combat. He was apprehended at the gangplank and sent to Fort Lewis, Washington, while his clothes and equipment sailed off to France. At Fort Lewis, Axelrod served out his Army career as a private in an engineering company and whiled away his idle hours as a violinist in the Tacoma Symphony.

Upon discharge from the Army, Axelrod resumed his studies at CCNY, then transferred to New York University when offered a scholarship. His major field was mathematics, and at nineteen, he wrote his first published paper, "The Lattice Theory in Boolean Algebra." He took generous helpings of elective courses in languages and the sciences. "The more you learn, the easier it gets to learn," he says. While working on his master's degree at NYU he taught an extension course in aquatic life that attracted great attention because of its novelty. On Saturdays he took his students out to Long Island, where they explored tidal flats and swamps. He made them eat almost everything they collected. On occasion his enthusiasm for nature became so unbounded that the faculty took alarm. He was once censured by a professor for performing a caesarian on a guppy.

For a time Axelrod worked as a laboratory assistant to Professor Myron Gordon. When Professor Gordon went on sabbatical, he recommended that Axelrod teach his course on experimental laboratory animals, most of which were tropical fish. The head of the department, Professor Charles Pieper, asked Axelrod to write out his lecture notes in advance. Axelrod did, and he left them in a pile on Professor Pieper's desk. Professor Pieper happened to be delayed in returning, and in the interim a McGraw-Hill book salesman entered, read through the notes and was entranced. As a result, McGraw-Hill asked to publish them as a book. Axelrod consented, and the subsequent book, *Tropical Fish as a Hobby,* published in 1952, was to make him the leading authority on the subject at the tender age of twenty-four.

In 1950, however, Axelrod, by then engaged in obtaining his doctorate at NYU, was called back into the Army at the start of the Korean war. This time he went in as an officer—a lieutenant—and was sent to Korea, where he studied epidemic hemorrhagic fever, a blood disease, as a member of a field medical laboratory. His work called for him to take blood samples to Japan for detailed analysis and, inasmuch as the plane returned to Korea with a cargo of empty blood containers, Axelrod began filling them up with whiskey. He traded the whiskey for cigarettes, which he stuffed between the filled blood containers on the flight to Japan. As his import-export business boomed, he also began working on a second manuscript, *Handbook of Tropical Aquarium Fishes.*

On one trip to Japan, Axelrod visited the Tokyo University library, where he pored over the books on fishes. While looking for a misplaced volume, he happened to meet an ichthyologist, Dr. Tokiharu Abe, who showed him a copy of a book, *The Ophistobranchia of Sagami Bay,* that had been written by Hirohito. Axelrod riffled through the pages, then stopped to point out an error in the scientific name of an ophistobranch. Dr. Abe was incredulous, but Axelrod cited the correct reference in an obscure scientific paper he had just finished reading. With that, he bade the doctor adieu, put the incident out of his mind and flew back to Korea with a load of choice six-month-old Scotch.

As Axelrod now recalls it, about a fortnight later he was ordered to appear before General Matthew Ridgway in full-dress uniform. Recalling that a case of whiskey had recently disappeared, Axelrod suspected that military police had seized it as evidence for a court-martial, and by the time he entered General Ridgway's office he was hoping for ten years instead of the death penalty. To his surprise, however, the general had summoned him because Hirohito wanted Axelrod as a house guest. Ridgway wanted to know why, since no American had been asked to see the Emperor since General MacArthur had been relieved of command. Axelrod, forgetting the incident in the library, said he had no idea why he had been invited. Ridgway told Axelrod to accept the invitation and to do his best to get an invitation for himself (General Ridgway), as well. Axelrod said he would see what he could do and went off to Japan, where he spent a week at the summer palace on Sagami Bay, collecting marine invertebrates with the Emperor. Hirohito, who was most grateful for having had the error in his book pointed out to him, listened to Axelrod's plea on behalf of General Ridgway and rejected it, explaining that he and the general really had nothing in common. Axelrod admits that he had to agree. Hirohito then presented him with a jar of preserved eels as a gift for Dr. Leonard Schultz, curator of fishes at the Smithsonian Institution.

Shortly afterward Axelrod was discharged, and he hastened to Washington, where he gave the eels to Dr. Schultz. He also showed Dr. Schultz a draft of the *Handbook of Tropical Aquarium Fishes,* and Dr. Schultz was so impressed with its potential that he agreed not only to collaborate on the work but to waive his years of seniority as well and appear as junior author. Not long after this Axelrod's first book, *Tropical Fish as a Hobby,* was published, and it was such an instant success that McGraw-Hill asked him to return a dozen complimentary copies in order to meet the demand. The book was successful because no one with a working scientific background had ever before written a book about tropical fish, and moreover, Axelrod, unlike previous authors, revealed breeding secrets. His description of spawning *Hyphessobrycon innessi,* the neon tetra, was of great moment to aquarists everywhere.

Since Axelrod had returned home in the middle of the academic year, he was unable to resume his doctoral studies and teaching position at NYU until the start of the 1952 fall term. As a returning serviceman, he was entitled to receive his salary anyway, and he used the money to finance trips to British Guiana and Malaya, where he bought tropical fish that he sold from a rented store in Manhattan.

By the time the fall term began, Axelrod was well established in business. He gave up selling fish for the nonce and started publishing *Tropical Fish Hobbyist.* Using mostly pseudonymns to protect his scholarly background, he also wrote, published and distributed inexpensive booklets on fish and other pets. Within three years T.F.H. Publications, Inc. owned its own printing plant and bindery, and Axelrod was doing so handsomely that he was able to buy out several Jersey City businessmen who had backed him. Meanwhile, he was also busy on his doctorate in biostatistics. The subject of his dissertation was *The Mathematical Solution of Certain Biometrical Problems,* and in it he demonstrated that the statistical procedures used in twenty-five medical and dental research papers were incorrect. "It was a very startling study," says Dr. Axelrod, who is so fond of figures that he multiplies license plate numbers he sees while driving around in his car.

Dr. Axelrod's main strength in business is his ruthlessness. A couple of years ago he decided to reprint *Stroud's Digest of the Diseases of Birds,* a solid research work by Robert Stroud, the so-called Birdman of Alcatraz, who spent more than forty years in solitary confinement for murder. Stroud's agent had published the book in 1943, but it had been done poorly. Stroud was eager to see a decent edition on the market but, before giving Dr. Axelrod publication rights, he asked the doctor to endorse his appeal for freedom. "You're a murderer!" Dr. Axelrod exclaimed. "If it were up to me, you'd cook!" Stroud angrily gave the rights to another publisher, but the doctor secured the book for TFH by buying out the other publisher. Convicts, incidentally, intrigue the doctor, who has been conducting a pen-palship with prisoners he met when lecturing on tropical fish at the Indiana State Prison. To his amazement, Axelrod found that some lifers had been keeping guppies for more than thirty years despite strict regulations against pets. They had hidden generation after generation of fish in vials strapped to their bodies, and the birth of a new batch was cause for a cell-block celebration.

In the interest of science, Dr. Axelrod asked the captive guppy fanciers to keep constant watch on their pets for an intensive around-the-clock study of fish behavior. "After all," says the doctor, "these guys have nothing but time on their hands." To his dismay, however, the prisoners seemed to get sadistic pleasure in keeping prisoners of their own in prison, so to speak, and instead of chronicling fish behavior, they began putting guppies into smaller and smaller containers to see how much confinement they could take before they died. Still, this was not a total loss to Dr. Axelrod, who learned that a guppy can survive in a stoppered inch-long pencil-sized test tube laid on its side.

If there was one turning point in the fortunes of Dr. Axelrod and TFH, it came in 1958, when he took his greatest gamble by publishing the *Encyclopedia of Tropical Fishes,* which he wrote with William Vorderwinkler, editor of *Tropical Fish Hobbyist.* "I did everything that other publishers said I shouldn't do," says the doctor. "We used big pictures. We used big type. They said everything was wrong, that it was a completely lousy book by their standards. They said I was going to ruin myself. I put every cent I had into it, and then I went off to Africa and I said to myself that I'd either come back a millionaire or a bum. The *Encyclopedia* was a success, and we sell 15,000 copies a year. We've been shooting craps in the publishing business for the last ten years, and we've been winning." In point of fact, Dr. Axelrod is a very lucky crap shooter. He remembers a night in Haiti when he rolled seventeen straight passes, then played twenty-one and beat the dealer. Astounded, the owner of the casino and the croupier, who had been following him around, ominously insisted he stay the rest of the night to play twenty-one with them. Dr. Axelrod did, and he cleaned them out, too. "They couldn't believe what I was doing," he says as a matter of course, "so I told them I was cheating."

More than anyone else in the world, Dr. Axelrod is responsible for the changing tastes in the aquarium hobby today. The hobby started in grim seriousness in Germany one hundred years ago, and for years goldfish were the rage. But then, in the 1920s and 1930s, tropicals began to edge in, and in the past few years goldfish have been all but discarded in favor of tropical after tropical, thanks, in good part, to the expeditions, discoveries and writings of Dr. Axelrod. In the last five years alone, TFH imported more species of fish than aquarists had seen in all history. Today Dr. Axelrod, TFH and the United States lead the world in tropical-fish expertise, and Germany, the onetime leader, is a distant second.

A living memorial to the doctor is *Cheirodon axelrodi,* the cardinal tetra, which he discovered lurking in a reach of the Upper Rio Negro, a tributary of the Amazon, in 1954. This discovery is regarded as the greatest ever made in tropical fish, but the doctor himself did not know for an entire year that he had happened upon a species wholly unknown to science. The cardinal tetra, an extremely colorful fish, bears a superficial resemblance to its cousin, *Hyphessobrycon innesi,* the neon tetra, and Dr. Axelrod, thinking he had found a race of giant neons, marketed them as such after bringing back a shipment to the United States. To his astonishment, they spawned differently from the neons, and he at once sent out several specimens to his old friend and collaborator, Dr. Schultz at the Smithsonian, for classification. Upon examination, Dr. Schultz rang up Dr. Axelrod to announce that the fish not only constituted a new species of tetra, but moreover, a close look at their teeth showed that they belonged to a new genus, as well. Dr. Schultz described the new fish in the February 20, 1956 issue of *Tropical Fish Hobbyist* and assigned it the name of *Cheirodon axelrodi* in honor of its discoverer. Then, on the very next day, in an issue of the *Stanford Ichthyological Bulletin,* Professors George Myers and Stanley Weitzman, outstanding taxonomists in their own right, described a specimen they happened to have, and they called it *Hyphessobrycon cardinalis.* The fight started. Debate raged for more than a year and a half until the International Commission on Zoological Nomenclature convened and gave the nod to *axelrodi*. This contretemps is merely one of a number the doctor has figured in with academic ichthyologists, and their asides about his being a pushy upstart rankle him. "I've been hated for years because I've combined science with business. The guys who criticized me initially for selling science for money are now the ones who try to sell me science for money, including some of my so-called best friends," says Dr. Axelrod, happily putting in the zing.

Dr. Axelrod's favorite collecting grounds are the Amazon and its tributaries, which support an extraordinarily large and varied number of fishes. "The Amazon River system, I would judge," says the doctor, "produces enough protein in one month to feed the world for a year." Most of his jaunts into the jungle are done with Harald Schultz, a specialist in Indian ethnology at the São Paulo museum, who is not to be confused with Dr. Leonard Schultz, much less Willie Schwartz, another Brazilian collecting crony. Harald Schultz has been macheted, blowgunned, pummeled, trampled upon and threatened in the course of his field investigations on the tribal rites of hostile Indians, and Dr. Axelrod considers him the bravest man he has ever met. Schultz, in turn, looks upon the doctor as a strong, powerful man, a tremendous genius with a strange personality and a range of accomplishments that can only be likened to those of Charlie Chaplin. He also looks upon the doctor as the most foolhardy man he has ever met. Schultz thinks Dr. Axelrod's penchant for swimming with piranhas is a ghastly business—the doctor believes piranhas are not at all vicious and that their bad reputation has its roots in exaggerated stories told by Teddy Roosevelt, who journeyed up the Amazon in 1913. Schultz was once so put out at Axelrod's grabbing a passing snake by the tail that he refused, on principle, to come to the doctor's aid even though his screams for help indicated that the snake was about to win out. Dr. Axelrod managed to escape unscathed, but Schultz did nothing more than lie in his hammock with a look of anguish. Considering Dr. Axelrod's foolhardiness, he has done reasonably well in the jungle. His only mishap occurred last November when, exhausted from netting rare fish, he settled down to sleep on top of several fire-ant hills that escaped his usually keen eye. He was bitten severely, and he had to spend a month in a hospital in Manaus getting mammoth injections of cortisone.

In Dr. Axelrod's absence, Schultz collects fishes on his own. Named after him is *Hyphessobrycon haraldschultzi,* commonly known as Harald Schultz's tetra, first cousin to *Hyphessobrycon herbertaxelrodi,* the black neon tetra. Not long ago Dr. Axelrod received a letter from Schultz announcing that he had at last found a fish beautiful enough to be named for Schultz's wife, Vilma, and the fish, which had a bright-red belly and two metallic blue spots, was subsequently called *Copella vilmae.* In addition to genus *Hyphessobrycon,* Schultz and Dr. Axelrod also have a double entry going for them in *Symphysodon aequifasciata haraldi,* the blue discus, and *Symphysodon aequifasciata axelrodi,* the brown discus. A species of goby, *Butis butis,* rediscovered by Lee Ching Eng, a renowned Jakarta fish exporter, is widely known as Axelrod's crazy fish. It so happens that when Dr. Axelrod entered Lee's establishment late one night in 1959, the proprietor shouted, "Dr. Axelrod! I've discovered a new fish!" The doctor looked at the fish, which likes to swim upside down, and remarked, "I doubt that it's new, but it sure is acting crazy." From then on, Lee called it Axelrod's crazy fish.

The honor of bestowing a scientific name on a new species of fish belongs to the taxonomist who describes it and not to the discoverer. Fish have been named after Dr. Axelrod largely in recognition of his forays into unknown areas, but the fact is that the doctor has the knack of finding new fish where others have looked long and hard. A prize example of this (and one that he likes to cite) occurred in Trinidad several years ago. The island of Trinidad has more fish collectors per capita than any other place in the world. It has been thoroughly combed, so much so that the government has imposed a closed season on collecting for fear that the island's fishes are in danger of extinction. One afternoon, net at the ready, Dr. Axelrod landed in Piarco airport and immediately seined a small pool at the edge of the runway. As onlookers gasped audibly—the doctor vividly remembers the chorus of sucked-in breaths—the net yielded hundreds of specimens of bright red fish that had never been seen before by any Trinidadian or any taxonomist in the world, for that matter. Flying on to Rio, Dr. Axelrod dropped off some specimens with Dr. Haraldo Travassos of the Museo Nacional, who classified them as belonging to the tetra family. He named the species *Aphyocharax axelrodi*. Ordinarily Dr. Axelrod does not boast about discovering a new species, but he is rather proud of this find, which is marketed widely as the red pristella. "It was like going to a high-school ball game and finding five Babe Ruths, four Lou Gehrigs, two Pee Wee Reeses and one Duke Snider," says the doctor.

Dr. Axelrod's knack for discovering the unusual is not confined to fish. While dining recently in the best restaurant in Bogota, he detected a bitter taste in his cup of Colombian coffee. Drinking it down, he discovered a cockroach, and instead of being dismayed he was elated. He took the cockroach back to his hotel room, popped it in a bottle of formalin and sent it to the Smithsonian in the hope that it might be a new species. If it is, the suggestion has been made that it be named after the restaurant.

The Axelrod knack also extends to people. While returning from the Brazilian jungle for a rest in Manaus, he met a fellow scientist in the elevator of the hotel. The scientist turned out to be Dr. Jean-Pierre Gosse, adviser to Leopold III, former King of the Belgians. Dr. Gosse refused to believe that Dr. Axelrod was *the* Dr. Axelrod—Gosse, too, had heard the rumor that the doctor was well into his seventies—but Dr. Axelrod was finally able to prove his identity by citing the name of a species of fish, *Neolebias axelrodi* (what else?), then under taxonomic dispute at the British Museum. Dr. Gosse introduced Dr. Axelrod to King Leopold, who was staying just down the hall, and Axelrod, in turn, had his doubts that King Leopold was really King Leopold. The King finally was able to confirm his identity to the doctor's satisfaction, and the two of them had a joyous week together on the Amazon spearing game fish, *Arapaima gigas* by day and *Osteoglossum bicirrhosum* by night. Dr. Axelrod, incidentally, was the first man to capture young *Osteoglossa,* which are carried in the mother's mouth. The fish always swallows her young when speared or netted, but the doctor showed Leopold how to obtain the young by severing the mother's head with a swift slice from a machete. Upon the King's departure for home, Dr. Axelrod presented him with a pet jaguar that had a nasty habit of biting the doctor's ankles, and Leopold, forewarned, gave the animal to the Brussels zoo. Since then the doctor and the King have exchanged visits in Belgium and Jersey City, and last year Leopold presented Dr. Axelrod with a brace of Belgian racing pigeons. They are now ensconced in the luxurious lofts atop TFH headquarters, but the doctor, a member in good standing of the Ideal Racing Pigeon Club, has not entered them against local competition on the grounds that it would be unfair, because Belgian pigeons are the fastest in the world.

In Brazil, Dr. Axelrod has also become very much involved with Willie Schwartz, an eccentric German-Jewish refugee who fled the perils of Nazism for the relative safety of Matto Grasso. Together they helped gather creatures for a couple of Walt Disney nature epics. One of Disney's more difficult orders was for a pair of rare black jaguars. Schwartz and Dr. Axelrod managed to capture one, but they were unable to come up with another. Finally, Dr. Axelrod suggested that they catch a run-of-the-mill jaguar and convert it. They did, Dr. Axelrod administered an anesthetic, and he and Schwartz trucked the beast to a hairdresser in Manaus, where it was bleached and dyed and shipped off to Hollywood.

Life in the wild still spells joy for Dr. Axelrod, but in recent months his thinking has turned more and more toward the booming business of TFH. "I'm really a deep thinker sailing far out into space," says the doctor. "I can sit in a chair for hours just thinking until I'm numb. I'm a great thinker. I go to sleep thinking, and I wake up thinking. I go to sleep with my hands folded behind my head. I have grandiose plans. I never think small!" A couple of years ago, after a bout of deep thinking, Dr. Axelrod seized upon the idea of the Fish-In-A-Flash kit. "It was the most successful flop I've ever been involved with!" he exults. He took the eggs of *Nothobranchius palmquisti*, an East African fish that lays eggs that can survive drought, to a toy trade show in New York and showed how they would hatch in a glass of water. Wholesalers and mail-order houses piled in with $8 million worth of orders. Dr. Axelrod started his own hatchery to produce eggs by the millions for kits, but he had to cease production because the initial customers were disappointed. The hatched fish were almost microscopic, and the customers had difficulty seeing them. "They expected—pop!—two-inch, beautifully colored fish," says the doctor. "It was a bust."

The doctor tried a new scheme last year with Quaker Oats, manufacturers of Cap'n Crunch breakfast food. TV commercials for the product feature a Cap'n Crunch, who skippers a ship called the *Guppy,* and the doctor thought that this looked like a natural. He made arrangements with Quaker Oats to supply a pair of guppies to any tot who wrote in, enclosing a Crunch box top and nineteen cents, but the deal fell through when the doctor refused to guarantee that the guppies would live. "Who knows what a kid is going to do to fish?" he asks.

The doctor's present grandiose plans fall into two categories. First of all, he aims to corner the entire tropical-fish market. "I have the total approach," he says. "The books, the livestock, the accessories." A couple of weeks ago he spent $1 million to acquire the second largest aquarium manufacturing company in the world, and he is rolling his eyes at the largest. He is also aiming to increase fish production on his Florida farms, because the size of the tropical-fish market is limited only by the number of fish available. Dr. Axelrod will go to any lengths to increase production. One day last winter he chanced to hear of a fisheries library for sale at $2,000, and, without inspecting a volume, he immediately offered to buy it. "Any one paper in it would be worth $2,000 to me if it gave a hint as to how I could get more fish production," he explains. "It may be that some little trick somebody found out a hundred years ago is just what I need." The doctor is always reading for clues and hints. Several years ago he was perusing an article on salt lakes and brine shrimp, *Artemia salina,* in a Russian fishery journal. The author noted that salt lakes having the right requirements for brine shrimp were found in Russia, Israel, California and Canada. At the mention of Canada, Dr. Axelrod leaped from his chair. He knew all about the lake in California; a fish-supply house in San Francisco had a monopoly on the brine-shrimp eggs, which are used as food for tropical fish. But Canada was something new. Discovery of brine-shrimp eggs there would be worth a fortune; the eggs bring more than caviar. The doctor ransacked reference literature, but he was unable to find the name of the salt lake. In fact, the best reference he could find mentioned one in Saskatchewan. He put in a call to a pet-shop owner in Winnipeg, who was an amateur pilot. The pet-shop owner agreed to fly up and down Saskatchewan looking for a lake with a white mark around the shore from salt. A month later he called the doctor. He had found not one lake but three, Manitou, Big Manitou and Little Manitou. Dr. Axelrod mushed north at once. The shores of the lakes were laden with brine-shrimp eggs. The doctor leased the lakes from the government, and then, in turn, he sold the lease to Wardley's, a tropical-fish supply house in New York, for a five-percent royalty.

For the past year Dr. Axelrod has been reading and rereading Alfred P. Sloan's autobiography, *My Years with General Motors.* The doctor feels that Sloan (assisted by John McDonald) has written one of the great books of the age, and he has underlined a number of sentences that have special meaning to him and the future of TFH. Among them are: "There is no resting place for an enterprise in a competitive economy," and 'The urge for competitive survival is the strongest of economic incentives." The doctor has been applying these maxims to TFH, because the capture of the entire tropical-fish market is only part one of his grandiose plans. Part two calls for TFH to take over the entire *pet* market within ten years. In that time Dr. Axelrod foresees the gross of TFH swelling from $3 million this year to $20 million by 1970 and $100 million by 1975. "But it's not the money," says the doctor. "It's the power! The pet business is going through a fantastic boom that doesn't look like it's going to stop. The pet business is great."

As part of his grandiose plan for cornering the pet market, Dr. Axelrod plans to introduce a new pet to supplant the hamster in public affection. The doctor is down on hamsters. "We need a small, hardy animal!" he exclaims, and he has that small, hardy animal all picked out. It is the Mongolian gerbil. "The trouble with the hamster is that it is nocturnal, it sometimes bites, and it stinks," says the doctor. "The Mongolian gerbil has a longer tail, softer fur, is not nocturnal, doesn't bite and doesn't stink. The only difficulty is getting them to breed. I'm going to work on that. Right now I'm trying to tie up all the Mongolian gerbils in the United States."

After getting all the Mongolian gerbils to breed, Dr. Axelrod plans to set up retail pet and hobby shops in department stores, five & tens and discount houses all across the country. This will give him complete control of the pet market. "The shops will do everything from selling model airplanes and fish tanks to living fish and birds and chameleons and what-have-you," he says. "It will have a garden center. It will sell books, plants, seeds and microscopes. Everything and anything!"

But for all the fish, all the Mongolian gerbils, and for all the money rolling in, Dr. Herbert R. Axelrod occasionally sinks into gloom. "I'd be happy to be a pauper," he says, "if I could play the fiddle as well as Jascha Heifetz."

—MAY 13, 1965

The Creature from the Aquarium

I forget why I overimbibed one night some 14 years ago, but I vividly remember the incident that occurred the next morning. I toddled downstairs somewhat the worse for wear, eased myself into a chair at the kitchen table and then suddenly shot into the air in horror as a creature about the size of a softball lurched toward me across the floor.

Was I imagining what I was seeing? No, this was no apparition. It was a real creature waving its antennae and claws in hostile fashion. Was I about to be killed in my own kitchen?

I backed away cautiously so that no sudden movement on my part would prompt an attack, and then, when the creature stopped moving, I slowly circled around to examine it from the rear. Its coat was both prodigious and peculiar. Thick tufts of multicolored fur sprouted from the body and from one of its claws, while covering the other claw was glistening black hair.

I wondered if this creature could be new to science. The house in which I then lived—I was a widower at the time—was a converted barn, built four feet into the earth on its back side. There was no cellar, so the interior of the first floor at the rear of the house was composed, in part, of a stone wall that was below ground level. In the past, I had seen salamanders peering at me from small holes in the wall. Perhaps this netherworld creature had likewise emerged from the inner earth.

Then I realized what the "thing" was. It was a five-inch-long crayfish, one of several that I had put in my 120-gallon aquarium in the living room, and it had undoubtedly escaped by clambering up an air hose with its claws. I picked up the crayfish by the tail to give the multicolored fur and hairs closer scrutiny. From my examination, I deduced that the crayfish had crawled into the kitchen via the connecting furnace and laundry rooms, and while on the trek its still-wet body and claws had picked up dust motes, lint balls and a clawful of hairs shed by my black Labrador retriever.

This incident comes to mind because, after a long lapse, I am again keeping crayfish in an aquarium. They will serve as live models for ultrarealistic fishing flies that I have in mind to tie for smallmouth bass. For most of the last 30 years I have been keeping freshwater fish and invertebrates in aquariums. Not for me, though, are the swordtails, kissing gouramis, neon tetras or other pet-shop exotics kidnapped from the tropics. Instead I revel in observing what I have brought back alive from lakes and streams near my home.

Frankly, I am puzzled that other anglers do not do the same. They could gain insights about their quarry: for example, why fish strike (or why they don't), or how best to stimulate the wiggle of, say, a mayfly nymph or a wounded dace when fishing with imitations of them.

Anyone interested in keeping native creatures alive in the living room would do well to consult *Dr. Axelrod's Mini Atlas of Freshwater Aquarium Fishes,* put out by TFH Publications. Despite its title and heft, this 992-page book by Dr. Axelrod and several colleagues contains a most helpful section on basic aquarium setup and maintenance.

Rule #1: Avoid overcrowding as well as overconfinement, because some species of fish are decidedly territorial in close quarters. This is especially true of largemouth bass. In an aquarium, they establish a pecking order within a couple of days. Almost inevitably, the biggest fish becomes the boss bass and claims absolute sovereignty over the tank. On only one occasion did another species of fish displace a boss bass, and that was a plump 10-inch brown trout I added to the tank toward the end of one season. After getting acclimated, this terrible-tempered trout went on the attack, harrying and nipping at the fins of any fish that crossed its path. Eventually it drove the boss bass—and the other bass, all bigger than the feisty trout—to one end of the aquarium. After four or five months of undergoing daily attack, all the bass had died.

A 120-gallon aquarium allows enough Lebensraum for five or six large mouths to live together in relative peace. Aside from their pugnacity, they are easy fish to keep. They are hardy, and there is no need to deal with aquarium heaters because they do well in water kept at room temperature. They thrive on a diet of live shiners and earthworms, and they quickly become conditioned to being fed. When I would appear with a minnow bucket, the largemouths would come to the front of the tank, face me, wave their tails like dogs and erect their spiny dorsal fins to mark all systems go. Their eyes would take on a bright reddish glow, as if they had been plugged into a power socket.

In time the bass were taking food from my hand. Naturally, that led to some less-than-scientific experimentation—specifically, how did the bass react to various hookless lures or flies I had tied (on hooks with the barbs snipped off). For the fun of it, I would sometimes dangle a plastic worm over them. A bass would seize it, and we would play tug-of-war until one of us let go. If I let a bass take the worm, it would spit it out. One time, however, a bass seized a purple worm and, to my astonishment, swallowed it. I kept checking the aquarium for the worm, and two weeks passed before I found it floating on the surface, bleached an albino white.

Freshwater sunfish, which belong to the same family as largemouth and smallmouth bass (Centrarchidae), are also quick learners. Dery Bennett, the executive director of the American Littoral Society, once caught a bluegill sunny, put it in an aquarium and started feeding it houseflies. "It got to the point where I'd just pick up a flyswatter and that sunny would get excited," Bennett says. "When people came over to the house, I'd say, 'Do you want to see my fish swim?' and I'd pick up the flyswatter."

Unlike largemouths or sunnies, smallmouths are difficult to keep. Simply turning on the aquarium lights can frighten them because they are photophobic and avoid light whenever possible. In an experiment that a couple of scientists conducted, smallmouths and largemouths were taught to control the light falling on their aquariums. The largemouths kept the light on 60% of the time, while the smallmouths kept it off 96% of the time, which helps to explain why largemouths will venture in a lake shallows on a sunny summer day while the smallmouths prefer to hang deep or in the shadows of rocks and ledges.

Only one smallmouth I kept in my aquarium wasn't skittish. A neighbor caught the fish and brought it to me stuffed headfirst in a pail. The fish was badly beat up about the flanks and mouth, where it had been hooked, but this smallmouth was well worth saving because it was huge. It weighed about seven pounds and had the deep-bellied sunfish silhouette that older bass assume. I wet my hands, gently picked up the fish and lowered it into the 120-gallon tank. The bass proved to be as placid as it was outsized during all the time I kept it, the better part of a year. It was so laid-back that it never even went after the half dozen blacknosed dace minnows that I added to the tank as food a few days after the bass revived. Instead, the smallmouth allowed the dace to clean its mouth and flanks of small growths of fungus where it had been injured, much as rhinos permit birds to perch on their backs and feed on the insects they find there. But whenever I dropped a crayfish into the aquarium, the smallmouth flashed over and inhaled it, tail first.

In the past, I also maintained aquariums with brackish water (a third the salinity of seawater) so that I could keep fish, shrimp and crabs from the tidal portion of the Hudson River, which flowed near my home. I never had much success with those fish. White perch were boring, first-year bluefish inevitably died of shock (the longest one lived was two days), a three-foot-long Atlantic sturgeon steadfastly refused to eat (I returned it to the river), and juvenile striped bass were easily stressed and rarely survived more than a month. Moreover, some of the stripers carried a parasite anchored like a small worm on their sides, and within a confined space, these worms soon infested other fish. I would then have to sterilize the aquarium, which meant removing every fish in the tank; hunkering down on the floor and, using a length of garden hose and my mouth, starting a gravity flow to siphon off 120 gallons of water into eight-gallon buckets; running and emptying the buckets outside; removing all the sand and rocks; scrubbing the inside of the tank with formalin (a lethal mixture of formaldehyde and water) to kill off any remaining parasites; rinsing the tank; refilling it; and, finally, catching new fish. I did this two or three times before I gave up on stripers.

I did have luck with juvenile jack crevalles, a beautiful semitropical species that sometimes enters the Hudson in late summer, when the water is at its warmest. One September, I netted half a dozen jacks. They proved to be real showstoppers. They never did stop swimming, and they schooled closely, as if trying out for a video on MTV. They also grunted like pigs, and they were as quick as sunnies at figuring out when it was feeding time. When I entered the living room to feed them grass shrimp, happy little oinks would come from the aquarium.

Alas, the jacks all died five months later during a prolonged power failure. I had foolishly failed to have a battery-powered aerator on hand as a backup.

Grass shrimp are fascinating. They are transparent (they're sometimes called "glass" shrimp) and can change color to adapt to the background. However, they must be kept in an aquarium by themselves because all fish love them and gobble them up. The shrimp will eat just about anything, from bits of an earthworm to fragments of canned tuna or sardines, and because they're transparent, it is easy to track what they eat. The stomach of the shrimp, which is located in the head, turns orange when the shrimp is fed smoked salmon.

Grass shrimp will also eat other shrimp when they are molting and have no hard exoskeleton. In October I usually put about 40 or 50 of them in a three-gallon aquarium to provide fish food through the winter. By spring, I'm usually left with two very large grass shrimp warily eyeing each other.

Lest you get the wrong idea, I should point out that maintaining an aquarium is not all mayhem and stupid pet tricks. In 17th-century England, another species of transparent shrimp proved to be of tremendous benefit to humanity because of research done by Dr. William Harvey. As a result of studying those shrimp, Harvey discovered that the heart is a muscular pump responsible for the circulation of blood in man and other animals.

I know only one other angler who seriously collects for his own aquariums, my pal, the one and only Seth Rosenbaum. He maintains 10 aquariums, from five to 160 gallons in capacity, in the spare bedroom of his Queens, N.Y., apartment, the floor of which he had tiled to stop his downstairs neighbors from worrying about leaks.

In my experience, when it comes to keeping saltwater fish, Rosenbaum is without peer. He has kept more than 40 species alive and well in his apartment, among them orange filefish (which swim upside down), remoras that he removed from white marlin (the remoras use their suckers to hold on to the glass and don't move except to feed), and moray eels, including one that Rosenbaum netted on the island of Culebra near Puerto Rico when the moray slithered up on a rock to attack him. Morays generally refuse to eat anything that is not alive and moving. When Rosenbaum has a moray, he takes no chances with its mouthful of wicked teeth. He feeds them cut shrimp impaled on needles, which, in turn, are lashed onto long sticks.

Similarly, Rosenbaum used a stick to feed a three-pound Ridley turtle and a like-sized loggerhead turtle. But they proved to be such messy eaters that their leavings polluted the tank, and he presented the turtles to the New York Aquarium. (See above, regarding tank-cleaning procedures.)

Of all the creatures that Rosenbaum has kept, his favorites are octopuses. They are highly intelligent animals, and Rosenbaum has had three so far. His alltime favorite was one he found inside an empty conch shell while fishing at Dry Tortugas, at the very tip of Florida. "I had my collecting gear and battery aerators with me," he recalls. "So I put the octopus in a bucket to bring him home. When I took him on the plane, he got out of the bucket and started going down the aisle. I had to retrieve him, and that was the most success I've ever had at socializing with stewardesses."

Back in his apartment, Rosenbaum placed the octopus in a 65-gallon tank. He rejected suggestions that he name it Octopussy—"been used"—or Octopus Rex, and he simply called it occupant octopus, no capitals. "After a few weeks," Rosenbaum says, "occupant octopus got into a pattern of being fed at night when I came home. He'd be just up at the waterline of the tank, holding on to the side with his suction disks. If I didn't feed him right away, he'd start turning colors. He was getting mad. And if I then didn't feed him soon, he'd squirt water at me with his jets. He could actually train the damn things like guns. You could see them move. I would say at least a half a cup of water would come out of him.

"Once that happened on a regular basis, I often made it a point to bring guests in at feeding time. Occupant octopus would be sitting there, and after a minute or two, these purple waves would start going through him, and he'd bring these two turrets to bear. He hit the targets every time. I got wet, too, but it was worth it for the surprise factor.

"Somewhere I read that octopuses like to eat hard-boiled eggs. I would peel a hard-boiled egg, close my fist over it, put my hand in the tank and occupant octopus would come over and try to open it. I could feel the pressure, but he couldn't open it because his head was about the size of my fist. Then he'd start pulsating colors, a sign of anger, and I'd let him have the egg. But what I could never figure out is how anyone ever figured out that octopuses like hard-boiled eggs. *Who* was the first person to discover that an octopus will eat a hard-boiled egg?"

Occupant octopus was just doing what comes naturally in Rosenbaum's aquarium, but he was to meet a most unnatural end. "I was doing a lot of out-of-town work, and I had a maid come in twice a week to clean," says Rosenbaum. "I always covered the octopus tank with glass and put a weight on top of it because he would come out of the tank on occasion. In nature, an octopus will actually run up on land to chase a crab, grab it and take it back into the water, so it's used to being out of water. I came home one weekend, and occupant octopus wasn't in the tank. I couldn't find him. On Monday when the maid came, I asked her if she had seen the octopus, and she said that when she went into the bedroom to clean up, she found occupant octopus on the floor. I asked her it he was alive or dead. She said that he was dead—at least he was after she hit him on the head with a broom."

To take Rosenbaum's mind off the loss of his alltime favorite, I told him that I was once again keeping crayfish. With that he brightened, and, recalling my encounter with the escaped crayfish from years before, Rosenbaum said, "Do yourself a favor and get a Mexican hairless instead of a Labrador."

—APRIL 22, 1991

With a Quack, Quack Here

Donal O'Brien

The flagpole sways, and the wind rips the small-craft warning into shreds. The sea is an insane lather of whitecaps. Far to the east of Long Island Sound, the red edge of the sun slides over the horizon, flashing bolts of fire on the windowpanes of houses along the coast. Four miles out lies the granite-block seawall, slick with onionskin ice. The temperature is below thirty degrees, and the forecast calls for continuing northwest winds. It is a time and place for normal persons to avoid, but Donal O'Brien, Jr. arrives at the launching ramp with his boat, peers at the distant seawall and exclaims, "Gee, I can hardly wait to get out there!"

O'Brien is a duck hunter, a fanatic duck hunter. He loves ducks with such passion that a nephew calls him Uncle Duck. His decoy collection is one of the best in the country, and he himself is a superb amateur decoy maker whose carvings have won a number of best-in-shows at national and world championships. He is an excellent shot, and he trains tough, willing retrievers. A black Labrador that he raised and sold, Whygin's Cork's Coot, has twice won the National Open Retriever Championship. For O'Brien, ducks have a magic that other creatures lack. When he shoots one, he does not toss it aside but smooths the feathers in admiration. When his wife and four children are asleep in their house in New Canaan, Connecticut and the snow lies thick on the ground, O'Brien likes to slip out of the house to look at the birds in the moonlight.

By profession, O'Brien is a lawyer, a partner in a Wall Street law firm. "It's great to be able to come home from the office on a Friday night and know that at 4:30 Saturday morning I'm going to be getting up to shoot on the Sound," he says. "Duck hunting is very physical and very basic to me. I like the whole thing, feeling the cold, picking up the decoys, and when I am home on Sunday and think about what I did on Saturday, I'm revitalized and prepared to go back to the office to be civilized for five days." For a good part of the season, O'Brien risks his life getting revitalized for the office.

Shooting from the seawalls in the Sound ranks among the most dangerous pastimes known to American sportsmen. Some hunters get badly frostbitten, and others just disappear. Shooting off the coast of Maine can be risky, but usually there is a lobsterman or fisherman around. In November, December and January, the Sound is a vast, blank piece of water exposed to the wind and waves with only ducks—and duck shooters—on the move; the sailors and fishermen have retired to the fireside. It is a hard trip out to the icy rocks, and one misstep into the chilling water can mean death, but for O'Brien the seawalls hold an unmatchable spell, although he admits, "I have a ball of fear in my stomach every time I go out."

A couple of years ago O'Brien and a friend, Bob Johnson, embarked at dawn for the four-mile run to one of the walls. The weather was rough, but they made the trip safely. With O'Brien bouncing up and down in the sixteen-foot outboard, Johnson clambered onto the rocks. He reached for an oar held by O'Brien to pull the boat in close, but a swell rocked the boat and Johnson slipped into water sixty feet deep. When he sputtered to the surface, O'Brien grabbed him by the scruff of his parka and pulled him into the boat. "It was freezing cold, about ten degrees," O'Brien recalls, "and I think Bob went into shock. He couldn't function. He was lying on the bottom of the boat. I told him to put his boots up in the air to drain the water. But he didn't have the strength."

O'Brien gunned the boat back to the ramp. He threw the anchor overboard, jumped out, ran ashore, got into his car and drove the trailer into the water. He climbed back into the boat, pulled in the anchor, started the engine and ran the boat straight up onto the trailer. He then got into the car and pulled the boat ashore. He got Johnson out of the boat and stripped him of his cold, wet clothing. "I took my clothes off and gave them to him," O'Brien says. "I was left with long johns and hip boots."

O'Brien took Johnson to a diner where he made him down four or five cups of coffee. "He was absolutely gray and shaking," says O'Brien. "At nine o'clock we went into a package store, me in my long johns and hip boots, and Bob all dressed up and walking like Frankenstein. The guy in the liquor store literally thought something was going to happen to him. He was scuttling along the walls, and I remember saying, 'Don't worry, we're not going to harm you, we're not going to rob your store, we're duck hunters, and this guy fell in.' We got a bottle of brandy, Bob drank it, and at twelve o'clock we were back on the wall, shooting."

Now thirty-seven, O'Brien was born in New York City. He became interested in ducks when he was five, and by the time he was ten and he began shooting with his father, he could identify every duck he saw. He even picked his prep school—Hotchkiss—and his colleges—Williams and the University of Virginia—for the hunting and fishing to be found around them. While in law school, O'Brien, who has a fondness for painting but no time, seriously started carving decoys because he could whittle away at a head between classes.

"The first thing I do in making a decoy is to draw the duck I have in mind," O'Brien says. "I'm working on a black duck now, and I decided I wanted a low head. I sketch to scale, and I may make twenty or thirty sketches, all free-hand, and usually without a model in front of me. When I get something that appeals to me, I'll cut it out for my pattern." When all goes well, it takes O'Brien about half a day to make a shooting decoy and two days for a contest bird.

In 1966 O'Brien entered his first contest, the U.S. National on Long Island. He won best-in-show in the amateur decorative miniature class, an award he has won on two subsequent occasions. He prefers, however, to concentrate on the working-decoy division, the division in which there is the most competition. He was the U.S. National amateur champion in working decoys in 1969 and regained the title this year. In addition, he has won best-in-shows in 1969 and 1970 in the Maine contest and, this past June, in the first world championship, he won best-in-show in the working-decoy class and in the class for working-decoy pairs. Decoy contests are like dog shows in which classes are judged and the winners compete for best-in-show, and along the line O'Brien has dozens of bests-in-class.

O'Brien also brings a most practiced eye to decoy collecting. The art of decoy making is uniquely American, which is one of the attractions to O'Brien. "I get hooked on the things that are purely American," he says.

The classic period of decoy making began in the mid-nineteenth century with the advent of the breech-loading shotgun. In those days there was a seemingly inexhaustible supply of waterfowl and an expanding and hungry populace. The period ended, says Historian William J. Mackey, Jr., a friend of O'Brien's and author of *American Bird Decoys,* with the passage in 1918 of the Migratory Bird Treaty, which put a stop to market hunting. Perhaps the finest decoys were carved by Albert Laing and his followers of the Stratford, Connecticut school. To O'Brien, Laing, who died in 1886, was "a Michelangelo," and O'Brien's collection includes a number of gems by Laing, among them a black, a canvasback, a sleeping broadbill and a drake whistler in a tuck-head position.

O'Brien also has a number of decoys by Benjamin Holmes, Shang Wheeler, who died in 1949, and other members of the Stratford school. "The Stratford decoy tends to be a little bit oversized," says O'Brien, "always hollow, except for the cork bird, with the head its finest feature. The head is very realistic, tends to be quite puffy in the cheek and always has considerable detail in the bill. It's a sleek bird, not cluttered up. There is no wing carving, no feather carving. There is usually a crease down the back separating the wings, and in the cork bird the tail is frequently inlaid. Stratford decoys catch the over-all impression of ducks. They're full-bodied, tapering to a flat bottom. They're not round like Jersey decoys. The Stratford birds had to take rough weather and big seas, and a dewdrop weight was normally used instead of a keel. I consider myself in the Stratford school, though a lot of my decoys are made with keels."

A friend, Tom Marshall, a former fieldman for Ducks Unlimited, admires O'Brien's carvings but deplores the keels as unnecessary. In turn, O'Brien is dismayed at Marshall's continued use of a number of original Shang Wheeler decoys in his working rig. In a voice somewhat reminiscent of Titus Moody's, Marshall says, "Shang made 'em to hunt over, not look at."

O'Brien's collection is very strong on New England shorebirds, especially decoys from Nantucket. "From a collecting standpoint, I enjoy the shorebirds more than the ducks," he says. The gem of the shorebird collection is a set of six Eskimo curlews that O'Brien acquired several years ago from a friend who is a seventh-generation Nantucketer. Now believed to be extinct, the Eskimo curlew was avidly hunted on Nantucket during the nineteenth century. All told, O'Brien's decoy collection, displayed in a special room built as an extension to his house, numbers about 600 birds. It includes decoys from Connecticut, Chesapeake Bay (some of these are by Lee Dudley—"one of the greats"), Cape Cod, Maine and Long Island. The collection is genuinely staggering to see. O'Brien first met Kenny Gleason, one of his hunting companions, when Gleason happened to come to the house to fix the phone. "When Gleason saw the decoys," O'Brien says, "we couldn't get him out of the house."

"There's a tremendous excitement in decoy collecting," O'Brien says. "There's a whole mystique to it. I never forget where good decoys are. Once I was on a trip up to Maine, and I stopped for gas. There was a sporting-goods dealer across the street, and in the window were a number of Maine decoys, including a couple of mergansers. They were just like Tiffany jewels. I went in to talk—I use a soft approach, and this may cost me at times—but the owner wouldn't sell. Last fall I put sixty decoys in my car, good decoys, and drove up to Maine. It took me twenty minutes to put all sixty on the floor, and after I finished I said to the owner, 'Now you suggest a trade.' He stepped back, looked, and finally said, 'Oh, you win.' We made a trade. I got the mergansers, and he got three very good birds in return."

O'Brien's year begins the first week in October when he goes to New Brunswick, to shoot black duck and teal. In mid-October the season opens in Connecticut, and he begins shooting surface feeders—blacks, mallards, teal and widgeon—in marshes and on the Sound. His working rig generally consists of thirty-seven absolutely stunning black ducks that he carved himself. Hunting inland marshes, he will use as few as two or three decoys because the clever blacks would be wary of a large rig in a small area. "I try to simulate the wild-duck situation," O'Brien says. "Also, more things can go wrong with a big set in the marshes."

"When the inland water freezes over," O'Brien continues, "the ducks start to use the open water. Then I work with a fairly large rig of two to three dozen. You're trying to attract the birds from a long distance. When we shoot from the seawalls where the birds feed on the rocks, I try to have a few decoys right close in. Some of these will be feeding decoys with the bills in the water. There will be other decoys twenty or thirty yards out, in a dew-drop shape. I try to leave something open in the middle, though that's not important for the black duck, which can land on a dime. Finally, I'll have some stringers or liners out of range. Three or four of my black ducks have high necks. They're watch ducks. Few of the commercial decoys have high necks, but you watch blacks. There will always be a few with high necks. That's an alert bird, and I'll usually have a couple out in the middle of the rig, and the last high-neck bird will have a comfortable low-neck bird in front of him."

To O'Brien, the black duck is a marvelous bird. "They're the wariest," he says, "and you have to be happier with fewer. They're very coordinated in the air and seem much more in control of what they're doing than the broadbill or canvasback."

When the first half of the split season closes in Connecticut in late October, O'Brien hunts for grouse and woodcock. In early December he begins duck hunting again. By now weather conditions have made the Sound perilous, and the best shooting is when the water is at its icy worst.

Late in January, O'Brien and his friends do most of their shooting from lieout boats anchored a few hundred yards from the lee shore where they try to hold steady in the calmer sea. "We'll put out a lot of broadbill decoys," he says. "The last day of last season, we put out about one hundred. Broadbill are very sociable birds—they like a lot of company. A very good setup is shaped like a fishhook. You follow the shank of the hook, come around to the barb and extenuate the barb.

"One of the great sights is the broadbill coming in. They'll come in quite high, and they'll see the rig. They'll spill the wind right out of their wings. They come down incredibly fast, and the next thing you know they're boring right in at you and landing right there in the hollow of the hook. All you see is black. The black head and the black chest. We let them come until they're not going to want to come anymore. Then we sit up and these birds go into a flare, and they really are moving. All of a sudden they turn from black into a tremendous pattern of black and white, and if the sun's out, they're really beautiful."

When the broadbill season ends on January 31, O'Brien is depressed, though his wife Katie, he admits, "really has had her fill of it." But February and March are not lost time. In those months O'Brien does most of his serious contest carving for the U.S. National, which is held in mid-March. He spends hours studying his heads, going so far as to put them on the dashboard of his car so that he can study details on the drive to and from his office. "Another reason I drive to New York is so I can look out the window and watch the ducks," he says. "Even along the Harlem River by the Columbia boathouse, I see canvasback, broadbill and black duck."

In April, O'Brien forgets about ducks momentarily when he starts trout fishing. He has his own trout stream on his property and for a number of years he was entranced with the idea of breaking the world record for brook trout. But come summer, when O'Brien and his family vacation on Nantucket, he gets back to his carving, making decoy heads on the beach when the stripers and blues aren't hitting.

In September, O'Brien is busy getting ready for duck hunting. As befits a hunter of his ardor, he usually has several retrievers about the house. He trains them himself, but during the summer he may ship a dog off to a professional trainer for polishing. In the 1960s O'Brien competed in retriever field trials, and although he did well, it simply took too much time from real shooting.

O'Brien's passion for ducks has not gone unnoticed at his law firm. In a skit at the last Christmas office party, a young associate played the part of O'Brien dressed up in hunting clothes. O'Brien didn't complain. In fact, he wasn't around at the time—he was off on a duck hunt in Texas.

—SEPTEMBER 27, 1971

The Obsessions of a Late-Bloomer

Dick Wolters

A merican males, slumped in front of the tube, putting on a pot and approaching forty, arise! Take as your example in life Richard A. Wolters, the illustrations editor at *Business Week*. To middle-aged millions reared on the unrequited dreams of Walter Mitty or diverted by the brilliant ineptitudes of George Plimpton, the positive achievements of Dick Wolters offer direction, inspiration and thrust.

Thirteen years ago Wolters was just another weary commuter, slogging home to a loving family, a relaxing drink and an hour in an easy chair. Then he discovered sports, and now, at the age of forty-nine, he is a distinguished (and sometimes controversial) fly-fisherman, skeet shooter, retriever trainer, sailplane enthusiast and author of five books. *Beau,* a sporting memoir, *Gun Dog, Water Dog, Family Dog* and *Instant Dog.* The owner of multitudes of equipment, some of it ingeniously self-devised, he has a customized camper that draws wows on the back roads of Maine and Montana. In Manhattan he is a pillar of the Midtown Turf, Yachting and Polo Association, where he lunches with the likes of Lee Wulff, Ed Zern, Ernie Schwiebert and other big shots of the outdoors. Wolters is generous with advice, even among his peers, and comparative strangers often phone him to inquire about hatches on the Battenkill, the proper discipline for a listless Labrador or the name of a good little parachute rigger. Wolters is pleased to serve as a guru; as a matter of fact, he resembles one. He has a bushy mustache and an extraordinarily thick head of hair that grows almost to his shoulders, with the result that he looks rather like Mark Twain. Dressed in a vintage Abercrombie suit, his hatband studded with field trial pins, he is a sight to remember.

Wolters did not become interested in sports until he was thirty-six. Like many other American males approaching middle age, he was too busy with a career and building a home to get involved. He played tennis as a youngster in Philadelphia, but he gave it up when he entered Penn State to study chemistry. Upon graduation in 1942 he went into rocket and then atomic research for the government. He took part in A-bomb tests in Nevada and in the Pacific, but bored with research, he gambled on turning his hobby of photography into a living. He succeeded and became a magazine photographer.

In 1954 he became the first picture editor of *Sports Illustrated* and soon thereafter, more or less in the line of duty, was persuaded to go fishing. He returned to the office proudly bearing a four-and-one-half-inch trout—a catch that should have got him arrested but instead set him on fire. "Given the way I've always embarked on projects, I'm sure that had I been on a construction magazine I would have learned to operate a crane," he says. "But suppose I'd been on a woman's magazine?"

Fly-fishing helped establish two basic rules that Wolters has since followed in choosing a sport.

1. The sport must be readily available. Fly-fishing was only minutes away on the Amawalk, an excellent stream in northern Westchester.
2. The sport must be within reach financially so that he can afford the best in equipment and accommodations. "I must go first-cabin," he says.

Wolters is very methodical, and when he began fishing the Amawalk he kept a log noting stream conditions, water temperatures, fly hatches and the number of trout caught. In 1956 he fished a total of forty-five times and caught eleven trout, much to the merriment of his friends. After the season ended he practiced casting on his lawn and started tying flies.

He built a rotary tying vise from sundry spare parts, including a shaft stripped from a motor his son Roger found on the street, and he constructed his own tying table. He also designed a fishing jacket with all sorts of special pockets. "Anything I go into I go completely whole hog," he says. "I go *all the way out.* I don't fiddle around watching television."

In his second year on the Amawalk, Wolters improved. He fished fifty times and caught 166 fish. Having learned his basics, he began fishing elsewhere in the East, and he even made a special trip to England to fish the Test. He set new goals for himself, to fish with the tiniest of flies and to catch and release the limit of trout every time he fished the Amawalk. He was very fond of fishing and the men he met in the sport. One of his best friends was the late Jack Randolph, the outdoor columnist for *The New York Times,* who, on occasion, made Wolters the subject of jokes or misadventures. Wolters did not mind, because, as he says, "I enjoy humor, especially the give-and-take between friends." Randolph sometimes got as good as he gave. Once he spent a baffling afternoon on a stream casting some flies Wolters had tied, and every time a fly hit the water, the feathers would disappear. Wolters, who was hiding nearby and chuckling to himself, had used sugared water instead of head cement on the tying thread.

It was Randolph who, perhaps in an attempt to get even, suggested that Wolters go bird shooting. Wolters accepted the challenge, figuring he might be able to get some feathers for fly tying. On the trip Wolters fired three shots and hit three grouse, the only one in the party of six to get a bird. Randolph was stunned. Wolters was elated, and to improve his shooting he took up skeet, setting the private goal of winning the Outdoor Editors Shoot the next spring, a competition that he figured was within his class. He won it, all right, and gave a little bow toward Randolph.

Wolters enjoyed bird shooting, but what really intrigued him was watching a dog work in the field. He just had to have a dog, and he bought an English setter pup. It died of distemper, and he bought another, which he named Beau. He began training Beau when the dog was only seven weeks old. Gun dogs, so tradition has it, are not to be trained until they are at least six months to a year old, and they are then supposed to be approached with a spiked collar and a whip. Old-time handlers also have maintained that training a dog when he's a pup is supposed to take something out of the dog. But, as Wolters later wrote in *Beau,* he was able to take a fresh tack, because "I came to dog training late in life. I didn't have the advantage, or what I might now call the disadvantage, of having a father or grandfather to teach me how to raise a hunting dog. Traditional dog training is an art that's based on too many old wives' tales. Like the one about never keeping a hunting dog in the house, it will ruin his nose for game. That was written by an old woman who hated dogs and her husband."

By the age of three months Beau sat, stayed and came on command. Wolters took daily walks with the setter, and whenever the pup would start to walk behind, Wolters would turn around so that the dog was in front. Beau quickly learned his place was out front, but when he got too far out, beyond what would be shotgun range, Wolters whistled to bring him in closer. At five months Beau could quarter a field following hand signals. The dog learned to hold point on a bird in the front yard through an unusual trick. Wolters rigged a grouse wing on the end of a line on a fly rod. As he swung the rod, Beau would get excited seeing the "bird" in flight. Suddenly Wolters would lower the rod and drop the wing on the ground. Beau instantly would freeze on point. In the field Beau proved to have a good nose to go with his eyes.

When Beau was eight months old Wolters received an invitation to lecture at North Carolina State College, where Dr. Frederick Barkalow, Jr. of the zoology department was teaching an adult education course in hunting. Dr. Barkalow had read Randolph's columns in the *Times* about Wolters's training of Beau, and he offered Wolters some fine quail shooting if he would come down with Beau and lecture. Wolters went, and Beau did very well indeed, earning glory in the field on the final day when, as a substitute for older dogs that failed, he stood on point twenty-eight times for the excited class.

Wolters had no idea that he had been doing anything revolutionary in dog training, but after returning from North Carolina he happened to hear about a study on dogs being done at the Animal Behavior Laboratory at Hamilton Station, a division of the Roscoe B. Jackson Memorial Laboratory in Maine. Wolters, his wife and Beau drove to Bar Harbor, where they met Dr. J. Paul Scott, a former Rhodes scholar, who was heading a scientific investigation of the behavior of dogs in the hope that it might shed light on the behavior of humans. Olive Wolters, then doing graduate work in psychology, was able to put the research findings into layman's terms for her husband. It was immediately apparent to Wolters that he not only had been right in starting Beau so young, but that Dr. Scott and his colleagues had made some truly important findings for dog owners everywhere.

These discoveries were fodder for Wolters, and he immediately began work on a training book, *Gun Dog,* which was published in 1961. "I had never written, I was a poor speller, but I told myself I was going to do the book," Wolters says. "There is no use making excuses for yourself." The book got rave reviews and it is now in its twelfth printing.

By now Wolters was hooked on dogs. Unfortunately, the training fields he had used for Beau were giving way to shopping centers and housing developments, and there was a dearth of grouse and pheasant next to the Wolters' home. He decided to switch to Labrador retrievers, a breed he very much admired and which did not necessarily need a ready supply of live birds. Using Labs and what Dutton, his publisher, calls the Revolutionary Rapid Training Method, Wolters wrote two books, *Family Dog,* which deals with the dog as a house pet, and *Water Dog,* for the amateur retriever owner-handler. Both books have done well. His latest book, *Instant Dog,* is a humorous work done in collaboration with Cartoonist Roy Doty. There is some sound advice in the book, but most of it is broad satire, such as how to teach a dog to sit by stepping on his tail or how to feed a dog from the dinner table. There is even an elaborately long recipe, "Instant Supper," for dogs that calls for a dressed three-pound pheasant, green pepper, fresh asparagus, heavy cream and rice. To Wolters's delight, some reviewers have taken *Instant Dog* as a serious work.

By the early 1960s Wolters was moving in pretty doggy circles, and doggy people can be bitchy. "He had the gall to own one setter and to write a book about training gun dogs," says one doggy critic. "Just who the hell is he?" Another doggy acquaintance says, "When Dick moved into Labs he irritated some people, especially in the rich Long Island crowd. Dick is not the most self-effacing guy in the world, and a lot of people resented him." Wolters says, "Part of the resentment may have been caused by my books. New ideas go down hard, and there are people who just didn't agree with my theories, so they didn't like me. I wasn't in Labs for more than a few months when I saw they didn't have adequate training equipment. I went to a field trial when I first had my young Tar, and a woman said her dog couldn't compete because he didn't know how to work far enough. She said, 'I can't throw the dummy that far in training.' She was like most of us. She couldn't afford bird boys or raise live birds or hire a trainer. So that night I got to thinking, and some people couldn't take the results of my thinking."

What Wolters thought up was a sort of Rube Goldberg rocket device that could propel a dummy farther than any human being could fling it. He worked out a rough idea and then got in touch with Arthur Johnson, a ballistics expert in Washington. Together they codesigned the finished product, the Retriev-R-Trainer, a hand-held device that can shoot a dummy one hundred yards. Twenty-two blank cartridges serve as the propellant, and the charges can be changed to vary the distance. For some time Wolters took delight in visiting field trials to hear gasps of amazement from some of his critics. The Retriev-R-Trainer is sold nationally, and Wolters collects a small, but ego-pleasing, annual royalty. The Retriev-R-Trainer has since proved to have a number of other uses. It can be adapted to hurl a fishing lure 250 yards, throw a line one hundred yards and fire a flare, among other things. Once Wolters loaded up with a magnum charge and shot a golf ball out of sight. "This business of trying to come up with new things, with new ideas, innovations, this is really a lot of sport to me," he says. "To me, the sport of a sport is going in and giving it everything you can and coming up with something new."

In 1962 Wolters became president of the Westchester Retriever Club, and he approached the job with characteristic zest. Until then the club had been somewhat loosely organized, holding only "fun" or "picnic" trials. Wolters set out to make the club more attractive and more effective by getting American Kennel Club recognition and permission to hold sanctioned trials.

Meanwhile, Wolters was active on other fronts. Fishing and dogs were his passion, and if some Eastern field-trialers were snippy, Midwesterners and Westerners were friendly and open. Wolters bought a camper truck, and he and Olive, the two children, Roger and Gretchen, and a pair of Labs would drive west on vacation, stopping to fish, visit kennels or attend field trials. Wolters spent hundreds of hours remodeling the camper. For instance, he built a special kennel compartment for the Labs above the right rear wall, installed extra lights, put in a shower, made fitted dish racks, rigged up a canopy for an outside patio and built an observation deck on the roof. He bought a climbing bike, which fitted on the back, and when the family stopped to camp he would tootle off on the bike to fish. Should Olive need him, she only had to call on a walkie-talkie. The camper, named Lablubber's Landlubber II, is so self-sufficient that when they visit friends the Wolterses stay in the camper instead of the home. When the Wolterses visit a camper rally people line up at the door for a tour. To many persons, unfamiliar with Wolters's other sporting activities, he is reverentially referred to as "the guy with that camper." Wolters says, "The camper falls in with my idea of having things that are compact. I enjoy small things that are well designed."

Wolters stayed active in Labs until 1965. But by then he felt there was little more he could do with dogs, and some of the people were unpleasant. One day while walking down the street with a royalty check in his pocket, he saw a car he liked. It was an MGB GT, and he bought it at once. Why not race cars? He took driving lessons. But he was not long in finding that sports-car racing was not for him. He didn't care for too many of the people ("somewhat flashy," he says), and then he really did not understand engines. He would have to rely on someone else to do the tinkering. Moreover, racing looked as if it might be expensive. One day while racing at Lime Rock in Connecticut, Wolters saw a youngster cartwheel a car. "It didn't bother me to see the accident," Wolters says. "The boy walked away without a scratch. But he totally wrecked his car. I realized one thing then. He had a wealthy father, I didn't, and next week he'd be back in a new car. I wouldn't. I saw myself getting into something that was going to be over my head financially."

A year and a half ago a friend, Phil Gilbert, president of Rolls-Royce Inc. in America, suggested that Wolters try soaring. Wolters went aloft with another friend, Arthur Hurst, and he was enthralled.

Soaring was convenient at the Wurtsboro, New York airport, only an hour's drive from home. "It cost me $450 for lessons to get my license," he says. "And after you get your license you can rent, and the cost will come to about what it costs you to ski." In his first year of soaring Wolters set a personal goal of one hundred hours in the air. "I made it," he says. "I held my wheel off from landing until the sweephand came around to the minute, and then I touched down. That's a lot of flying for a sailplane, especially since my early flights were only twenty minutes long. But I find this to be one of the most challenging sports I ever set my mind to."

After getting his license Wolters bought a German-made sailplane, a Ka-8B, and then a Libelle, a compact fiberglass ship also made in Germany. He recently sold it and got back what he had invested, because the demand for sailplanes exceeds the supply. He now owns a new model Standard Libelle. "The people in soaring are tremendous," Wolters says. "They're hot competitors, but they help one another, and they are out to help you. Some dog people wouldn't talk to you if your life depended on it. They keep their little tricks to themselves. But the people in soaring, the top people I've met, George Moffat [the 1969 national soaring champion], Gordie Lamb, Gleb Derujinsky, are out to help others. George will come up to me and say, 'That landing wasn't quite right,' and then he'll tell me what to do. When I bought my first Libelle I got a phone call from Ben Greene down in North Carolina, the 1968 champion. I had met him briefly at the Nationals and had flown with him in Pennsylvania. And he warned me I was getting into a slippery little ship and told me what to watch for. This is the camaraderie in this field and I really enjoy it."

Last year Wolters qualified for the silver badge, becoming only the 1,494th American to meet the standards set by the *Fédération Aéronautique Internationale.* To do this, he had to climb 3,280 feet above release by the tow plane, make a flight of five hours' duration and make a thirty-two-mile cross-country flight. Olive crewed for him on the last, keeping in touch by radio (Wolters's call sign is "Old Dog") as she sped along roads in the camper truck with the twenty-eight-foot-long trailer for the glider hooked up behind. Wolters completed the flight by landing in the field of a startled farmer. Having gotten his silver badge, he qualified for the Eastern regional cross-country competition and won the standard class. During the flight he got extremely low and feared that he would have to land in an apple orchard. Inasmuch as the trees were only twenty-five feet apart and the wingspan of the Ka-8B is fifty feet, he thought he might have what he called "a real problem of geometry." Fortunately, he hit a good lift and shot up to 6,000 feet. Upon landing, he asked about the apple orchard and was told, "That's no apple orchard—them's cherries."

"I think I can get pretty good at soaring," Wolters says, "but I'm not too sure I want to become a really hotshot competitor. My ambition is to qualify for the gold badge in 1969 and then go for diamond. There are only 109 diamonds in the history of American soaring. In diamond you have to make a 300-mile flight and climb 16,000 feet above your low point. I'll probably go out to California to do that. I hear that the lee wave off the Sierra Nevada is sensational."

With fishing still available in season on the Amawalk, the Labs at home ready to retrieve and a book on soaring in the works, it would seem that Wolters's time is filled. Yet he has noticed a small chink in the calendar in January and February when the Wurtsboro airport is closed by snow. That happens to be the time of the year when the nearby Hudson is frozen over and iceboaters from a hundred miles around take to the river. "Iceboating sounds very attractive," Wolters says. "I am sure I will want to delve into it. Some of the principles I've learned in soaring apply. Iceboating might be just the sport to fill in the entire year very nicely."

—AUGUST 18, 1969

"Hey, You Wanna Deer?"

Joe DeFalco

It's hardly a night to entice a man out. The World Series is on TV, and it's raining heavily on Long Island. But by 7:30, half an hour before the 15th Annual Joe DeFalco Hunting Expo is to start at the Adelphi-Calderone theater in Hempstead, a crowd of 600 or 700 is already on hand waiting to watch Joe DeFalco, 53, an ex-butcher who had cut up more than 10,000 deer before he turned author and folk hero, show them onstage how to field-dress and carve up deer. In the lobby, beneath a banner proclaiming THE COMPLETE DEER HUNT BY JOE DEFALCO, pitchmen in blaze orange jackets are hawking copies of *The Complete Deer Hunt* by Joe DeFalco, a $5.95 paperback that has, according to Joe DeFalco, who first published it himself in 1969, sold over 700,000 copies. Inside, near the stage, a Joe Pastor band is playing and a vocalist is singing while Joe DeFalco checks the props onstage. Next, Joe DeFalco goes out to the lobby to see how the sale of $1 raffle tickets is doing. The prizes include "3 days & 2 nights, 2 adults & 2 children free, Plus 8 delicious meals at Fernwood in the Poconos." Fernwood is one of Joe DeFalco's clients.

Additional prizes are a quartz clock radio, a shooting-range pass, a free head mount, a Colt revolver kit and a grand prize of "$1,000 Value 3 Day All Expense Paid Hunting Trip with Joe, Private land,

Guides, Celebrities, Donated by the Paramount Hotel [another Joe DeFalco client], Plus a Remington 3006 Model 4 Semi-automatic, Donated by Remington Arms Company." All proceeds from the raffle are to go to two sick brothers in the Catskills who have let hunters shoot on their farm for 40 years. "Everything we do is four-star legitimate," says Joe DeFalco, who will use the first person plural when he isn't alluding to himself in the third person singular or, more commonly, as "Joe DeFalco" instead of "I."

In his life, Joe DeFalco has shot at least 100 white-tailed deer, hunting in New York, New Jersey and Pennsylvania. The biggest buck he ever took was an 11-pointer that weighed 198 pounds, field-dressed. The biggest deer he ever saw weighed 202 pounds field-dressed.

"Bein' a former butcher, I know what a deer weighs," Joe DeFalco says. "You hear all this talk about how this guy got a 280-pound deer, a 300-pound deer. No way. The average field-dressed deer, a buck comin' out of New York, don't weigh 110 pounds."

According to Joe DeFalco, "The smart hunter who is lookin' for food won't take a buck. If he has a doe permit, he will take a young doe. A young doe is gold on the table. The bucks have to age for a week. You handle a deer right, you get the blood out, you cut it up right, and you can serve veal Parmesan to people who say they don't like venison.

"But the average hunter don't know what he's doin'," Joe DeFalco continues. "You talk to a guy from the city and you ask, 'Where you gonna hunt tomorrow?' And he says, 'I don't know,' or 'I'm gonna go up the hill across the road.' He hasn't even sighted in his rifle. What you should do is take advantage of the small-game season, which opens a month before deer. You're out lookin' for rabbits or pheasants. It's the same fields or woods where you're gonna hunt deer, and so you see a buck, or you see four deer near a certain tree. Three days later you see the four deer again at the same spot. You put an X on that tree. On openin' day, you sneak up to that tree, and you get your deer."

During deer season, Joe DeFalco leads parties of hunters on drives over 3,000 acres of land in the Catskills. Hunters from as far away as Maine pack into the Paramount Hotel in Parksville, N.Y. to hunt with Joe DeFalco. They pay $30 a night to sleep four or five in a room, plus another $30 a season to cover the cost of four guides, the lease on the land and insurance. "When you hunt with a guy like Joe DeFalco, you're gonna have excitement," says Joe DeFalco. "We're gonna push deer. You're gonna see deer. You're gonna have a chance at a shot, but you gotta be ready for a movin' target. The worst hunters in the world are target shooters. They're shootin' at targets 6 feet high, and the biggest deer is 36 inches at the shoulder. The chest is best, but sometimes you gotta shoot at the rump on a movin' target. Last year we never had a day when we didn't see deer. Last year, on average, 20 out of 25 guys on our drives got deer. The average in New York State was one out of six."

A Joe DeFalco hunt is organized like a campaign out of Caesar's *Gallic Wars*. Joe DeFalco will have reconnoitered the land beforehand and marked off various sectors. As many as 35 hunters may be in a day's party. Half of them will be posted at key spots that Joe DeFalco has marked, and the other half will drive the deer. "We've divided them up into four different teams," says Joe DeFalco, "and we know exactly where we're gonna go. The guides have white arm bands. They have sideband radios, like the police, that have a range of eight miles. We're in constant communication, and we know where everybody is. It's like a football game, and I'm sendin' in the plays from the sidelines. This guy has gotta block at the line and the quarterback has gotta throw the ball, but he's gotta know where his receivers are."

After Joe Mallia, Joe DeFalco's assistant, fires a shot in the air to signal the start of a hunt, the drivers begin shouting to move the deer. A drive lasts half an hour to an hour, and there may be as many as 12 in a day. At the end of each drive, a truck air horn blasts so that people and deceased deer can be picked up and regrouped or field-dressed.

Joe DeFalco's hunting companions have included Willie Mays, Catfish Hunter, Joe Namath, Rich Caster, Spider Lockhart, Dave Kingman and any number of other past, present or ex-New York Jets, Giants, Mets and Yankees. "The athletes are so coordinated they can go all day," says Joe DeFalco. Joe DeFalco is big on celebrities. "I never hunted with Richard Todd, but I gave him his first bow," Joe DeFalco says of the Jet quarterback. "He's had dinner at my house three times. I gave guns, black powder from Classic Arms—I get a lot of stuff to field test—to Tom Seaver, Mickey Lolich, Jon Matlack, Telly Savalas, George Savalas." Indeed, Joe DeFalco was the chairman of the first Telly Savalas Charity Ball.

Joe DeFalco was nine when he shot his first deer. His father, Al, a butcher in New York City's borough of Queens, drove Joe and an older brother, Phil, up to the Adirondacks the night before opening day. "By 10 in the morning my father couldn't keep his eyes open," says Joe DeFalco. "He says, 'If you see any deer, boys, wake me up,' and he falls asleep under a tree. An eight-point buck is runnin' toward me. I pick the gun up, brace it on a rock and hit the deer a half inch above in between the eyes.

"My father jumps up, grabs me by the arm and asks, 'Are you O.K.?' Phil points to the deer and my father smacks me in the face. 'You're not old enough to shoot this deer,' he says. 'You tell anyone, and we'll all go to jail.' When we got home, my mother kissed my father. He took bows all over the place and gave us a wink."

At a little after eight in the Adelphi-Calderone theater, with 1,200 people on hand, the band strikes up the national anthem, and Joe DeFalco's niece, Donna DeFalco Lipari, sings "The Star-Spangled Banner." As she begins, the curtains part. There, at the center of the stage behind a lectern, is Joe DeFalco in a checkered shirt. In front of him are a stuffed deer and a stuffed bear. On a wall behind him are the heads of four bucks shot by Joe DeFalco, the mounted rear end of a deer that DeFalco shot precisely there, a couple of tanned deer hides, a bullseye and two targets featuring a deer. At stage left are celebrities Joe DeFalco will soon introduce. At stage right, Joe DeFalco's brother Tommy, who runs the Veteran's Supermarket in Saint Albans, L.I., stands at attention in a butcher's white apron, butcher knife upraised by his side, next to an eight-point buck hanging from a rope by its antlers.

The master of ceremonies, Vince Lipari, Joe DeFalco's "nephew-in-law," welcomes everyone to the 15th Annual Joe DeFalco Hunting Expo: "I married into a legend," Lipari exults. "Joe DeFalco is a legend in the hunting world. Joe DeFalco will field-dress a deer right here on this very stage tonight! . . . I'd like to present the legend, Joe DeFalco!"

"Everybody comes to this affair 'cause they love the sport of huntin'," Joe DeFalco says. He then begins introducing the celebrities. "Chuck Wepner! Sylvester Stallone came to New York with $109 in his pocket and saw Chuck Wepner fight Muhammad Ali on closed-circuit TV from Cleveland, and Chuck nearly kicked Muhammad Ali's ass! So he made *Rocky*. The *real* Rocky, Chuck Wepner! Number Seven of the New York Mets, Ed Kranepool, Number Seven! Vito Antuofermo! He's Italian. Give him a big round of applause!" Ten of the New York Jets, at the time on strike, are introduced. Father David, of St. Rita's Church in Queens, takes a bow and says that Joe DeFalco has done a great deal for children.

Joe DeFalco starts talking about hunting rifles. "People ask me what kind of a gun do I buy," he says to the hushed house. "Buyin' a gun is like marryin' a girl. You don't know what she's like until you squeeze her. I'd like you to meet my wife, Eleanor." Mrs. DeFalco stands up. Applause. Joe DeFalco picks up a rifle with lever action and then puts it down. "I don't want to knock any gun companies, but I'd flush that one down the toilet," he says. He recommends a 220-grain bullet, saying, "When I go into the woods I don't go to play around. See it, knock it down, one, two, three."

Joe DeFalco quit high school in his first year to join the Merchant Marine. Only 13, he was 6 feet tall and weighed 200 pounds, and "People used to say, 'Why aren't you in the service?' " He spent 16 months in the Pacific and then came back home to become a butcher. He was in the Army for two years during the Korean War and served as a sergeant in meat-cutting school at what was then Camp Gordon in Georgia. In his spare time he hunted, and once served as a guide for General Eisenhower, who was in Augusta to play golf. Later on, Joe DeFalco spent an afternoon hunting mule deer with Lyndon Johnson in Texas, but, he says, "Drivin' up and seein' a deer sittin' there and shootin' it is not a sport to me." In 1965, hunting rabbits on Long Island, Joe DeFalco met another hunter, who happened to be Kranepool, and the ballplayer and the butcher became close friends. They have hunted together every year since. After the Mets won the '69 World Series, Kranepool, Jerry Koosman and Joe DeFalco were invited to hunt on an Indian reservation in South Dakota, "The only white men ever allowed in," says Joe DeFalco. "The Indians wanted to meet Joe DeFalco."

Joe DeFalco brings Walter Seville of Bear Archery and Howie Noll, the New Jersey state bow champ, out on the stage. Howie shoots out all the balloons on a target with his arrows. "Now some Life Savers!" exclaims Seville. Howie shatters the first Life Saver, but misses the second. Boos. He misses several more. Joe DeFalco intervenes. Peering up at the balcony, he says, "This man cannot see on accounta the goddam lights in his eyes." Applause for Howie.

Joe DeFalco moves on to apparel. "A lot of hunters don't know what the hell to wear," he says. Suddenly there is a blare of loud music as a black man comes out on stage with ghetto blaster and belts of machine-gun ammunition strung all over him. Joe DeFalco looks dumbfounded. Joe DeFalco reaches into an ammo box hanging on the guy and keeps pulling on a belt of ammunition. The audience cheers. Lipari introduces the man as Willie Womper—actually Willie Hollingsworth, who "is in the *Guinness Book of World Records* for walking more than 18 miles with a bottle on his head." Joe DeFalco says a hunter should be quiet in the woods: "You stand still and that goddam deer will walk up to you." Joe DeFalco talks about the new Joe DeFalco Game Winner huntin' jacket that he has endorsed. "Give myself a plug," he says. "Same material as the astronauts used on the moon, O.K.?" He talks about where to hunt. "My favorite spot is the Paramount Hotel in Parksville, New York. Anyone who wants to hunt with us, come on up. Paramount Hotel, O.K.?" Joe DeFalco tells of the time his son Al, then 16, got lost hunting and walked for 22 miles until the state police found him. Joe DeFalco says, "I wanted to kill him but he said, 'Don't worry, Dad, I told them my name was Greenberg.' " Joe DeFalco introduces Joan Murray, owner of a modeling school. The crowd whistles as she walks onstage. Ms. Murray says that because this is an audience of hunters, they might like to see something primitive. The New York Jet players carry scantily clad models onstage over their heads. The crowd cheers.

Joe DeFalco's rise to fame began in 1968, when he got a phone call at the Starlight Meat Center in Franklin Square, Long Island, where he was working, from a hunting club asking if he would show 25 of its members how to field-dress a deer. He agreed, and so many people showed up that traffic was snarled. Joe DeFalco had to cover the last six blocks to the store on foot. Frank Keating of the *Long Island Press* reported, "The police estimated the overall crowd at between 2,000 and 3,000. A bewildered woman member of an adjacent Republican club called the turnout 'the biggest thing that ever happened in this neighborhood.' She added that presidential candidate Richard Nixon drew only 500 people at a recent appearance."

A local weekly, the Franklin Square *Bulletin,* took on Joe De-Falco as its hunting and fishing columnist, and he began calling himself "Franklin Square's Own Famed Hunter-Guide-Rifle-Long-Bow Expert." (He later became, briefly, "Long Island's Famed Hunter," but he now simply refers to himself as "Joe DeFalco, Famous Hunter," on the grounds that "if I was under oath and was asked who the most well-known hunter in the country is, I would have to say, from the bottom of my heart, Joe DeFalco.") In response to the 5,600 letters he received after the demonstration at the Starlight Meat Center, Joe DeFalco announced that he would put on another demonstration three weeks later at the Plattdeutsche Park Restaurant, which could hold more people than his butcher store. Three thousand jammed into the restaurant, and a neighbor suggested that if Joe DeFalco could draw crowds like that, he ought to write a book. He immediately started on *The Complete Deer Hunt.* To help pay for 25,000 hard-cover copies he had printed for 88¢ apiece, he sold a brand-new Cadillac. "Only 1,800 miles, and my ex-wife said, 'You're crazy.' "

To promote the book, Joe DeFalco quit butchering. "I wrote to every sporting-goods store I could to tell them the book was coming out," he says. "I had friends who would call a store and say, 'Have you got *The Complete Deer Hunt* by Joe DeFalco?' In them days, you had to push Joe DeFalco down people's throats. But the week before we came out, every store must have had 10 calls, and when we would walk in they would say, 'Wow, have we been waitin' for you!' "

Joe DeFalco rented space at the sportsman's show in New York City. Through happenstance, the promoters of the show had hired Namath, who knew Joe DeFalco, to make an appearance. "When he saw me there, he came over to the booth," says Joe DeFalco. "He started autographin' books with me, and I got an award for drawin' the biggest crowd of the show. We ran out of books." He had more printed. "We probably blew out legitimately more than a couple hundred thousand copies," Joe DeFalco says. Playworld stores bought 2,500 copies when Joe DeFalco made an appearance, and drew "one of the biggest crowds they ever had. They had a parade for me." A representative of Times Square Stores was there at the time, and as a result, the firm bought 10,000 copies and hired Joe DeFalco to promote guns at its 12 stores. Grosset & Dunlap, the publishers, asked to publish the book, but just before Joe DeFalco sold them the rights, he printed up another 100,000 copies for himself. By this time he had started referring to himself in the third person. "I made Joe DeFalco another person so I could talk about him," Joe DeFalco explains.

He also began promoting himself as the best-known hunter in the country. For several years, in the mid-1970s, Joe DeFalco had his own program, *The Outdoorsman,* on Long Island cable TV: He would feature athletes and celebrities as guests.

Back at the Adelphi-Calderone, Joe DeFalco is saying, "Outdoor Life Book Club called me 'one of the leadin' authorities in the country on the white-tailed deer,' O.K.?" The book club printed an excerpt from *The Complete Deer Hunt* in 1969 and says it was "so good that we've brought it out again."

Lipari introduces a magic act—Steve Rodman and Linda. Steve pulls doves out of handkerchiefs and Linda twirls offstage with them. Jack Fontana, a comedian, comes on next. "I hunt," says Fontana. "I got an Italian dog. Ever hear an Italian dog bark? *Woofa, woofa.*"

Joe DeFalco comes back onstage, and with brother Tommy wielding the knife, demonstrates how a deer should be dressed in the field. Joe DeFalco is adamant that a deer be dressed out on the exact spot it was downed. He says the hunter should cut a half-inch hole in the upper belly and then step back to let gas escape. He tells how to remove the intestines, the liver, the heart and the kidneys, and how to cut the windpipe and the esophagus. He says make a cut around the anus and pull firmly on the rectal tube to facilitate drainage of the blood when the deer is hung high.

Joe DeFalco makes a lot of appearances for nothing. "Nobody has ever paid Joe DeFalco a fee for a charity," he says. "If it's for kids, it's for nothin'. I love kids. Kids are not black, Hispanic, Italian. Kids are kids." But if any kid gives Joe DeFalco some lip, he lifts them up against the wall and says, "Shut up, ya little bastid." Joe DeFalco and a couple of Jets helped put a stop to most of the kid pilfering in the Times Square Store in Hempstead several years ago by talking to youngsters in the neighborhood, but he got in trouble when he gave a speech to the Chamber of Commerce and was quoted in *Newsday* as saying that the store had no problem with kids because it was policy to kick their butts. "Their families don't give 'em discipline," says Joe DeFalco. "I do. I tell 'em to stay straight with sports. I tell 'em about huntin' and fishin' and I take them outdoors. I put on shows. I bring athletes. We go to grammar schools, churches, Little Leagues, you name it."

Onstage, there is much sawing and chopping. Joe DeFalco holds up the liver, the heart and lungs. "Anybody hungry?" he asks. "O.K., Tommy," he says, "take the legs off. O.K., let's talk about glands for a minute, O.K.?" Then it's "Cut the shoulder off. O.K., the youngest kid in the house, bring him up." A man climbs onstage with a year-old boy in his arms. Joe DeFalco gives them some venison. He asks for the oldest man in the house. An 82-year-old with a cane limps onstage. "Let's give him a big round of applause," Joe DeFalco says. "Is everybody having a good time?" It is 10:40 when the show ends, and Joe DeFalco thanks everyone for coming.

In 1979, just after Joe DeFalco had finished making a TV pilot with Catfish Hunter for a hunting series that was to be nationally syndicated, he was riding his motorcycle when a truck hit him and sent him flying 60 feet. "I had $9,000 worth of medical bills," Joe DeFalco says. "I sued, but I lost 'cause a jury thinks that if you're 50 and ridin' a motorcycle you're retarded."

After the accident Joe DeFalco stopped working full time for Times Square Stores and joined his wife, Eleanor, in a business she had started called VIP Promotions. For a fee, VIP will supply celebrities for commercials and store openings, among other things, while a branch of the business, VIP Vacations, books rooms in resorts in the off-season and sells them at a discount to stores that offer two free nights' vacation to people who buy so much in merchandise.

All in all, Joe DeFalco is doing very well. He has a 14-room house in Baldwin Harbor, L.I., with his own trophy room, which contains, among other things, a pistol case labeled JOE DEFALCO, FAMOUS HUNTER, mounted deer heads, bulging scrapbooks with stories about Joe DeFalco and a wall full of awards. "I got 135 awards," he says. "Nassau County had a Joe DeFalco Day." He also owns a 38-foot motor home and four cars, including a new custom-made Lincoln, complete with fuzz buster. He has many, many friends, and his kids are healthy.

Next fall, Joe DeFalco plans to move the 16th Annual Joe DeFalco Hunting Expo from the Adelphi-Calderone theater to the New York Coliseum. "With all the publicity Joe DeFalco is gettin', and with one hundred celebrities onstage, Joe DeFalco will draw 20,000," says Joe DeFalco. "They'll be standin' in the streets outside. It costs $20,000 to rent the Coliseum for one night, and it will be a free show as always. It's just about locked up with Herman's Sportin' World and the NRA [National Rifle Association] sponsorin' the show.

"It's been so excitin' and adventurous," says Joe DeFalco. "To think that it all started with huntin'!"

—JANUARY 10, 1983

Step in and Enjoy the Turmoil

Chanler Chapman

It was a splendid day in Paris in the 1920s when William Astor Chanler, former African explorer, big-game hunter, Turkish cavalry colonel and patron of the turf, limped into Maxim's for lunch with a friend. The colonel had lost a leg, not on the field of battle but as the result, it was whispered, of a brawl in a bordello with Jack Johnson, the prizefighter. A familiar figure in Maxim's, Colonel Chanler informed the headwaiter that he wished to be served promptly because one of his horses was running at Longchamps that afternoon. The colonel and his friend sat down, and when, after taking their order, the waiter did not reappear swiftly, the colonel began tussling with something beneath the table. With both hands he yanked off his artificial leg, bearing sock, shoe and garter, and hurled it across the restaurant, striking the waiter in the back. Colonel Chanler shouted, in French, "Now, may I have your attention?"

Back home in the United States, the colonel's oldest brother, John Armstrong Chanler, known as Uncle Archie to members of the family, had a simpler way of obtaining service: when dining out, Uncle Archie would carry a pair of binoculars around his neck to keep close watch on his waiter's comings and goings. His manners at table were memorable. He would consume a fish as though he were playing a harmonica, and a fellow member of one of his clubs was intrigued to watch Uncle Archie douse a dozen batter cakes with melted butter and maple syrup and then roll them up and tuck them behind his ears like a Polynesian adorned with hibiscus blossoms. Wherever he went, Uncle Archie was likely to get attention. He sported a silver-headed cane engraved with the words LEAVE ME ALONE. He had spent three and a half years involuntarily confined in the Bloomingdale lunatic asylum in White Plains, New York, because, among other peculiarities, he liked to dress as Napoleon and often went to bed wearing a saber. In a farewell note he left the night he escaped from the Bloomingdale asylum in 1900, Uncle Archie wrote to the medical superintendent, "You have always said that I believe that I am the reincarnation of Napoleon Bonaparte. As a learned and sincere man, you therefore will not be surprised that I take French leave."

Given the drabness of the present age, it is heartening to note that the spirit of the eccentric sporting Chanlers lives on in Barrytown, New York, one hundred miles up the Hudson River from New York City. Here, in the decaying but still gracious estate country on the east bank of the river, a handful of Chanler descendants carry on in their own fashion. There is Richard (Ricky) Aldrich, grandnephew of Uncle Archie and grandson of Margaret Livingston Chanler Aldrich, who fought for the establishment of the United States Army Nursing Corps. Ricky, thirty-six, manages Rokeby, the family seat and farm, where he collects and rebuilds antique iceboats (such as the *Jack Frost,* a huge craft that won championships in the late nineteenth century), and ponders the intricacies of Serbian, Croatian and Polish grammar. Ricky studied in Poland for a spell, but left in 1966 after he was caught selling plastic Italian raincoats on the black market. The most noticeable fact about Ricky is that he seldom bathes. As one boating friend says, "Ricky would give you the shirt off his back, but who'd want it?"

Then there is Chanler A. Chapman, regarded by his kin as the legitimate inheritor of the family title of "most eccentric man in America." As Ricky's brother, J. Winthrop (Winty) Aldrich, says, "Only members of the Chanler family are fit to sit in judgment on that title." Winty, who is Chanler Chapman's first cousin once removed, says, "Television has done *Upstairs, Downstairs, The Forsyte Saga* and *The Adams Chronicles,* but they should do the Chanlers. The whole story is so improbable. And true."

Everyone who has met Chanler Chapman regards him as brilliantly daft. While teaching at Bard College, Saul Bellow, the Nobel laureate, rented a house on Chapman's estate, Sylvania ("the home of happy pigs"), and found in him the inspiration for his novel *Henderson the Rain King.* In the novel, written as an autobiography, Henderson shoots bottles with a slingshot, raises pigs and carries on extravagantly in general. "It's Bellow's best book," Chapman says, "but he is the dullest writer I have ever read."

At seventy-six and possessed of piecing brown eyes, a bristling mustache and wiry hair, Chapman nearly always wears blue bib overalls and carries a slingshot. He is fond of slingshots, because "they don't make any noise," and he shoots at what tickles his fancy. Not long ago he fired a ball bearing at a Jeep owned by his cousin, Bronson W. (Bim) Chanler, former captain of the Harvard crew, inflicting what Chapman calls "a nice dimple" in the left front fender. Ball bearings are expensive ammunition, however, so, for four dollars, Chapman recently bought 600 pounds of gravel. He calculates this supply of ammo should last at least five years.

Before his infatuation with slingshots, Chapman was big on guns. He hunted deer, small game and upland birds and ducks, mostly on his estate. Indeed, at one time he had 115 guns, and his shooting habits were such that friends who came to hunt once never cared, or dared, to return. Chapman had only to hear the quack of a duck and he would let loose with a blast in the general direction of the sound. On a couple of occasions it turned out that he had fired toward hunters crouched in reeds, using a duck call. "Almost got a few people," he says matter-of-factly.

Chapman is the publisher of the *Barrytown Explorer,* a monthly newspaper that sells at the uncustomary rate of twenty-five cents a copy at the newsstand and four dollars a year by subscription. The paper's slogan, emblazoned above the logo, is WHEN YOU CAN'T SMILE, QUIT. "You can abolish rectitude," Chapman once expatiated opaquely, "you can abolish the laws of gravity, but don't do away with good old American bullshit."

The *Explorer* prints whatever happens to cross Chapman's lively mind. "Opinions come out of me like Brussels sprouts," he says. There are poems by Chapman (who always gives the place and date of writing, for example, Kitchen, September 13, 7:15 A.M.), and a regular spiel column, also by Chapman, in which he offers his unique observations of the world ("A sunset may be seen at any time if you drink two quarts of ale slowly on an empty stomach" or "What's good for the goose is a lively gander" or "Helen Hokinson has turned atomic" or "Close the blinds at night and lower the chances of being shot to death in bed. That goes for the district attorney who wants to be a judge"). Chapman always signs the spiel column, "Yrs. to serve, C.A.C., pub."

The *Explorer* publishes pieces about nature, written by Mrs. Stuyvesant Chanler under the nom de plume of "Country Cousin," and about horse racing. "Racing entertains me," says Chapman. "It's an absolute fool's game. It is the incense of the ethos. It's glorious!" For years, Chapman has been a close friend of Abram S. Hewitt, who recently completed an eighty-seven-part series on sire lines in *The Blood Horse.* Any contributions by Hewitt, even personal letters, are welcomed by Chapman. Last year Hewitt sent a letter from Lexington, Kentucky, and Chapman printed it in part in his paper: "Your kind note finally caught up with me here, where I am enthroned for the moment, having taken charge of N. Bunker Hunt's matings (not personal!) for 1976. He is a Texan who does things in true Texas style—the sky's the limit. His training bills in France alone amount to about three-thousand five-hundred dollars a day!

"The horse copers in this area have kept the W. C. Fields tradition alive, of swindling one and all—especially 'outsiders'—with an air of fraudulent dignity. Once you know what is going on, the spectacle has its entertaining aspects—like sending a crew of men out in the night to move the three-eighths pole one hundred and fifty feet, so that the New York millionaire . . . would be sure to see a high-priced two-year-old work three-eighths of a mile in world-record time! . . ."

Chapman likes the W. C. Fields touch, and on occasion he will print Fields' picture in the *Explorer* for no reason other than this fondness. People in the news sometimes get worked over by Chapman in Fieldsian fashion. Of Leon Botstein, the new president of Bard College, Chapman wrote, "His diction seems to be improving. Obviously he has never been trained to speak, so that every word can be understood when it is uttered. There is no elocution." The Reverend Sun Myung Moon, the Korean messiah who bought the old Kip estate across the road from Chapman, gets evenhanded headlines: DARK SIDE OF THE MOON and THE MOON RISE OBSERVED. Chapman is not prejudiced against any race, creed or color, but he does harbor a grudge against the state of Ohio. "It is occupied by blind, moneyed baboons," he says.

Chapman has been married three times. His first wife, from whom he was divorced, was Olivia James, a grandniece of Henry and William James. Robert, a son by that marriage, lives in a house in Florence, Italy, which his father thinks is called "the place of the devil." (Robert reportedly used to live in a cave, where he made kites.) Another son by this marriage, John Jay Chapman II, lives in Barrytown. After attending Harvard, he went to Puerto Rico, where he became a mailman. He married a black woman, and they have several children. When Chanler Chapman's old school, St. Paul's, went coed, he was enthusiastic about his grandaughter's chances of getting a scholarship. "She's a she," he said, ticking off the reasons. "She's a Chapman. She's a Chanler. And she's black."

Five years ago, John Jay Chapman II persuaded post office authorities to transfer him from Puerto Rico back to Barrytown, where he now delivers the mail. Asked if his son truly likes delivering mail, Chapman exclaimed, "He can hardly wait for Christmas!" Not long ago, Chapman and Winty Aldrich, who lives with Ricky at Rokeby, the ancient family seat next door to Sylvania, were musing about the twists and turns in the family fortunes. Winty observed, "Isn't it remarkable, Chanler, that Edmund Wilson called your father the greatest letter writer in America, and now your son may be the greatest letter carrier!" Chapman, who is, upon occasion, put off by his cousin, let the remark pass without comment. ("Winty is the essense of nothing," says Chapman. "He has the personality of an unsuccessful undertaker and he uses semicolons when he writes. He knits with his toes.")

Chapman's father was John Jay Chapman, essayist, literary critic and translator. A man of strong convictions, John Jay Chapman atoned for having wrongly thrashed a fellow student at Harvard—it happened to be Percival Lowell, the then future astronomer—by burning off his left hand. At the same time, Chapman used to go to bed at night wondering, according to Van Wyck Brooks, "What was wrong with Boston?"

Chanler Chapman's mother, Elizabeth Chapman, was one of the orphaned great-grandchildren of John Jacob Astor, each of whom came into an inheritance of some one million dollars. They were called the "Astor Orphans" by Lately Thomas in *A Pride of Lions,* a biography of the nineteenth-century Chanlers. Winty Aldrich says, "There was never anything wrong with the Chanler blood until crossed with the yellow of the Astor gold."

By blood, the Chanler descendants are mostly Astor, with an admixture of Livingston and Stuyvesant. Knickerbocker patricians, they are related, by blood or marriage, to Hamilton Fish Sr., Franklin

Delano Roosevelt, Jimmy Van Alen, Francis Marion the Swamp Fox, Julia Ward Howe and General John Armstrong. It was the last who built Rokeby in 1815 after he blotted his copybook as Secretary of War by letting the British burn the Capitol and the White House.

It has been said of Chanler Chapman that the genes of the Chapman side of the family provided the polish, while the Chanler genes imparted the raw psychic energy. Chapman's middle name is Armstrong; he was named in honor of Uncle Archie, his mother's oldest brother. "Archie was a pure bedbug," Chapman says. That may be understating the case. After escaping from the Bloomingdale asylum, where he had been committed by his brothers (with the help of Stanford White, the architect and a close family friend), Uncle Archie fled first to Philadelphia, where he was examined by William James, and thence to Virginia. He changed his last name to Chaloner and started a long legal battle to have himself declared sane in New York.

At his Virginia estate, Merry Mills, Archie indulged his love of horsemanship and hatred of automobiles. He discovered an obscure state law requiring the driver of a motor vehicle to "keep a careful look ahead for the approach of horseback riders, [and] if requested to do so by said rider, [such driver] shall lead the horse past his machine." Mounted on horseback, clad in an inverness cape and armed with a revolver, Uncle Archie would patrol the road in front of Merry Mills demanding that motorists comply with the law. "A green umbrella was riveted to the cantle of his saddle, a klaxon to the pommel," J. Bryan III, one of his admirers, wrote in *The Virginia Magazine of History and Biography*. "After nightfall, he hung port and starboard lights from the stirrups and what was literally a riding light from the girth. The klaxon was his warning, the revolver his ultimatum."

In the midst of the legal battle for his sanity, Uncle Archie shot and killed a wife beater who had invaded his house. To commemorate the encounter, he sank a silver plate in the floor with the cryptic inscription HE BEAT THE DEVIL. He was absolved of the killing, which occurred in 1909, shortly after Harry L. Thaw shot Stanford White, but the *New York Post* noted, "The latest prominent assassin has taken the precaution to have himself judged insane beforehand." Archie sued for libel, and the case dragged on to 1919, when he won both the suit and his fight for sanity in New York.

By now Uncle Archie had come to love automobiles and made peace with his brothers and sisters. He came visiting in a Pierce-Arrow he had had custom-made. Parts of the rear and front seats were removed to make room for a bed and a field kitchen, and the car was painted with blue and white stripes copied from a favorite shirt. Chanler Chapman would meet Uncle Archie in Manhattan, and they would drive back and forth between the Hotel Lafayette and Grant's Tomb. "He told me he was the reincarnation of Pompey," Chapman says, "but that he was going to have more luck than Pompey and take over the world. His eyes would gleam and glitter. He would also rub an emerald ring and say to the chauffeur when we came to a light, 'Watch, it's going to turn red! See!' " In Barrytown, Uncle Archie dined, as family members pretended not to notice, on ice cream and grass clippings.

At St. Paul's, Chanler Chapman was nicknamed Charlie Chaplin, after his own exploits. From the start Chapman had what the masters at St. Paul's called "the wrong attitude." Some years afterward he wrote a book with that title about his days at St. Paul's. (In *Teacher in America*, Jacques Barzun praises *The Wrong Attitude* for Chapman's "penetrating remarks.") Once young Chapman jumped into an icy pond to win a fifty-dollar bet, and he collected a purse of one hundred dollars for promoting a clandestine prizefight in which he was knocked out. On another occasion, boys each paid fifty cents to watch Chapman fill his mouth with kerosene and strike a match close to it. Flames shot across the room. On the side, he dealt illegally in firearms, selling the same Smith & Wesson .32 over and over again. It jammed every third or fourth round and, invariably,

Chapman would buy it back from the disgruntled owner at a reduced price. A center in club football, he practiced swinging a knee smartly into the ribs of an opponent, but when he cracked the rib of a boy he liked, he felt such remorse that he gave the boy a silver stickpin shaped like a broken rib with a diamond mounted over the break.

Chapman was too young to serve in World War I. He desperately wanted to serve after his half-brother, Victor, was shot down and killed while flying for the Lafayette Escadrille. Fortunately, he was distracted by his Uncle Bob, Robert Winthrop Chapman, the youngest, biggest and, in many ways, the most raffish of the Chanlers. "Uncle Bob dreaded the thought that Chanler would be filled with the pieties," says Winty Aldrich.

After studying art in Paris for nine years, Uncle Bob settled on a farm near Sylvania and ran for sheriff of Dutchess County. He won the election after acquiring acclaim by hiring a baseball team, which included Eddie Collins of the Philadelphia Athletics and Heinie Zimmerman of the Cubs, to play against all comers. While sheriff, Uncle Bob wore a cowboy suit and retained Richard Harding Davis as his first deputy. Having divorced his first wife, Uncle Bob returned to Paris, where he vowed to marry the most beautiful woman in the world. He fell in love with Lina Cavalieri, an opera singer, who, if not the most beautiful woman in the world, was certainly one of the most calculating. After only a week of marriage to Uncle Bob, she left him to live with her lover. That was bad enough, but then it was learned that Uncle Bob had signed over his entire fortune to her. Uncle Archie, down in Virginia busily fighting for his sanity, remarked to reporters, in words that became famous, "Who's loony now?"

Uncle Bob divorced Lina, who settled for a lesser sum than his entire fortune, and back in New York he began living it up again, with his nephew, Chanler, sometimes in tow. During this period he was doing paintings of bizarre animals and plants, which became the vogue, and he bought three brownstones in Manhattan, made one establishment of them, and called it the "House of Fantasy." The place was filled with macaws and other tropical birds, and parties held there (orgies, some said) lasted for days. Ethel Barrymore is reputed to have remarked of the House of Fantasy, "I went in at seven o'clock one evening a young girl and emerged the next day as an old woman."

Chapman found two of his other Chanler uncles tedious. One, Winthrop Astor Chanler, was extremely fond of riding to hounds. Indeed, when Uncle Winthrop died, his last words were, "Let's have a little canter." Then there was Lewis Stuyvesant Chanler who, like all the Chanlers, was a staunch Democrat. In 1906 he ran for the lieutenant governorship of New York—at the time the candidate for that office ran separately—and in 1908 he was the Democrats' choice to run for governor against Charles Evans Hughes. Hughes won, but the memory of the campaign waged by Uncle Lewis, which began with an acceptance speech on the front steps of Rokeby, still stirs the family. Not long ago, Hamilton Fish Sr. visited Rokeby, where he strongly urged Winthrop Aldrich to run for office. When Winty demurred, Uncle Ham, sole survivor of Walter Camp's 1910 All-American football team, six-feet four-inches tall and ramrod straight at eighty-eight years of age, said, "Look at your Uncle Lewis!" Winty replied, "But Uncle Ham, Stanley Steingut [State Assembly speaker] and Meade Esposito [Brooklyn Democratic leader] wouldn't know anything about Uncle Lewis. Nobody remembers Uncle Lewis." Eyes blazing, Uncle Ham exclaimed, "Everyone remembers Uncle Lewis!"

Chanler Chapman went to Harvard in 1921. "He ran a gambling den there," recalls Peter White, a cousin, who is a grandson of Stanford White. "He had a bootlegger, and all the gilded aristocracy from St. Paul's, St. Mark's and Groton as his customers. Chanler and his partners took in $300 to $400 a week. They didn't drink until their customers left at three in the morning, but then they drank themselves blind."

While in Cambridge, Chapman joined the Tavern Club, founded by nineteenth-century Boston literati. "Two years ago Chanler celebrated his fiftieth anniversary as a member of the club," Winty Aldrich says. "It is a tradition to present a gold medal to a man who has been a member for fifty years. Being proper Bostonians, the members do not have a new medal struck, but give the honoree one that had been presented to some deceased member. Chanler was very excited—I had heard he was to get the gold medal that belonged to Oliver Wendell Holmes—but for one reason or another he couldn't attend the ceremony. The members were relieved. They thought Chanler might bite the medal in half, or hock it."

After Harvard, Chapman went to Paris where he acquired his lasting affection for horse racing. He went broke at the track, and his Uncle Willie, Colonel William Astor Chanler (also known as African Willie, because he had explored parts of the Dark Continent where Stanley said he would not venture with a thousand rifles), gave him a job at an ochre mine he owned in the south of France. Six weeks in the mine were enough. Seeking fresh adventure, Chapman joined an acquaintance who was sailing a forty-seven-foot ketch, the *Shanghai,* from Copenhagen to New York. But Chapman found the trip a bore—"The ocean is the dullest thing in the world. The waves just go chop, chop, chop"—except for the stop in Greenland, where he swindled the Eskimos by trading them worn-out blankets for furs. Off Nova Scotia he lost the furs and almost everything else when the *Shanghai* foundered on rocks, forcing all to swim to shore.

Back in the United States, Chapman undertook a career as a journalist. He worked for the *Union* in Springfield, Massachusetts for two years and then joined *The New York Times.* "Anyone who spends an extra week in Springfield has a weak mind," he says. The *Times* assigned Chapman to the police beat on the upper East Side but Chapman decided that crime, like the ocean, "bores the hell out of me." He spent a year playing cards with the other reporters and then quit to work for a book publisher.

In 1932 Chapman took over Sylvania and became a full-time farmer. He devoted a great deal of effort to organizing dairymen so they might obtain better milk prices, but division in the ranks made the task impossible. Then, during World War II, Chapman, with the seeming compliance of President Roosevelt, worked up a plan to seize from Vichy France the islands of St. Pierre and Miquelon located off Newfoundland. However, Roosevelt, who had apparently been having a lark at his neighbor's expense, called off the plan at the last moment. Chapman next volunteered as an ambulance driver for the American Field Service and served in Africa and Burma. Nautically, his luck seemed to pick up where it had left off with the sinking of the *Shanghai*—a freighter taking him to Egypt was torpedoed 600 miles southeast of Trinidad. "It was very entertaining," he recalls. "The vessel was carrying 1,900 tons of high explosives." Fortunately, the ship, which had been struck in its boilers, went down in seven minutes and did not explode. Chapman had the foresight to stick $200 in traveler's checks and a bottle of Abdol vitamin pills in his life jacket before scrambling into a lifeboat. After a week's sail, he and the other survivors made it to Georgetown, British Guiana.

After the war, Chapman and his wife were divorced and he married Helen Riesenfeld, who started the *Barrytown Explorer* with him. She died in 1970, and three years later Chapman married Dr. Ida Holzberg, a widow and psychiatrist. "It's convenient for Chanler to have his own psychiatrist in the house," says Winty Aldrich. Like the second Mrs. Chapman, Dr. Holzberg is Jewish. While chaffing her recently Chapman said, "Jesus Christ, maybe I should have gone Chinese the third time around." Mrs. Chapman, or Dr. Holzberg, as she prefers to be called, is listed on the masthead of the *Explorer,* but her duties are undefined. "She wants to get off the masthead because she gets angry at me every other day," Chapman says. Dr. Holzberg is petite, and Chapman affectionately refers to her as "Footnote" or "Kid," as in "O.K., Footnote" or, "Kid, I like you, but you've got a long way to go." As Chapman figures it, his wives are getting shorter all the time, but he likes that because they have a lot of bounce-back, Dr. Holzberg especially, "because she's got a lower center of gravity."

Over the years, Chapman has conducted his own radio interview show, but at present he is off the air. His last sponsor was a dairy, for whom he used to deliver remarkable commercials, such as, "Their man is on the job at five in the morning. You might even see him back at a house for the second time at nine, but let's skip over that." Some of Chapman's taped interviews are memorable, like the one in which he kept referring to the mayor of San Juan, Puerto Rico, where Chapman happened to be on vacation, as the mayor of Montreal. "San Juan, Señor," the mayor would say plaintively every time Chapman referred to Montreal.

Perhaps Chapman's greatest accomplishment with a tape recorder came at a great family gathering at Rokeby in 1965. About 150 Chanlers, Astors, Armstrongs and other kin assembled to celebrate the sesquicentennial of the house. Among those present at the main table were William Chamberlain Chanler, who is known as Brown Willie, and Ashley Chanler, the son of African Willie. Ashley is generally accounted a bounder by the rest of the family, and on this occasion he was wearing a Knickerbocker Club tie, which disturbed Brown Willie, a retired partner in the proper Wall Street firm of Winthrop, Stimson, Putnam, and Roberts. Believing that Ashley had been dropped from the Knickerbocker Club (as indeed he had been previously, for nonpayment of dues), Brown Willie voiced his annoyance and a loud debate ensued. "No one knew what was going on," says Winty Aldrich. "It wasn't until later that we found out it was all over a necktie. But Chanler was seated near them, and the moment the argument started he turned on his tape recorder, held up the microphone and began egging them on. When Ashley said that he had been reinstated in the Knickerbocker Club, Chanler shoved the microphone at Brown Willie and said, 'You lose that round, counselor.' "

Nowadays Chapman is primarily confining his attentions to the *Explorer* and his slingshot, with an occasional reversion to his guns. "Stop the presses!" he exclaimed the other day to a caller. "We're replating for wood alcohol! An unlimited supply of energy. No fermentation at the North and South Poles, so the penguins and Eskimos are out of luck. First flight to Venus by booze." He also was elated about reprinting a piece by Abram Hewitt on War Relic, "really a second-rate horse, still being promoted as quite a stud."

The shooting in early spring, Chapman said, had been superb. The frozen Hudson was breaking up, and he liked to go down to the river with a .22 to shoot at pieces of ice. The most challenging shot was at twigs floating by. "Crack a little twig when it's just barely moving!" he exclaimed. "It's better than any shooting gallery. You feel like a newborn baby." Friends who happen along at this time of the year may be greeted as was William Humphrey, the novelist. Chapman insisted he shoot his initials into the snow next to the front porch. "Chanler can be trying," Humphrey says. "A few years ago I broke my right foot playing baseball barefooted with a gang of ten-year-olds. It was not put in a cast. Chanler came to dinner. He had stowed away six or eight martinis when he got out of his chair, crawled across the drawing room floor, took my bare foot in his big hands and broke it all over again. I beat him in the face with my crutch until he let go." Despite this, Humphrey considers Chapman a great friend.

Chapman is hopeful that this year will be a good year for seventeen-year locusts. Good, that is, from his point of view, not theirs. "They don't come every seventeen years, you know," he says. "They come every five or six. I use twenty-two longs with birdshot in them and, boy, those locusts can absorb a lot of dust. They're only three-quarters of an inch long, but they're built out of armor plate. You have to hit them just right. I like to take a little stool that unfolds and pop them when they're swarming. Shooting on the wing. That's the only way. I wouldn't shoot them while they're sitting down."

Chapman says now he's just looking for things that give him pleasure. Has he a word of advice for others who would seek a happy life? Yes. "Things are going up and coming down," he says. "Earthquakes are expected. Step in and enjoy the turmoil."

—JUNE 13, 1977

An Absence of Wood Nymphs

Vladimir Nabokov

To an army of admirers, Vladimir Nabokov, a balding Russian émigré of sixty, is best known as the author of the spectacular bestseller *Lolita.* To a comparative handful, however, he is V. Nabokov, lepidopterist. Respectful colleagues have named four species of butterflies after him. He is the discoverer of at least two subspecies of butterflies, one of which, it should be noted, is called (accidentally, but prophetically) Nabokov's wood nymph.

Nabokov has described his findings, usually signed V. Nabokov, in a number of scientific periodicals ranging from *Psyche*—"A Third Species of *Echinargus* Nabokov (Lycaenidae, Lepidoptera)"—to the *Bulletin* of the Museum of Comparative Zoology at Harvard College—"The Nearctic Members of the Genus *Lycaeides* Hübner (Lycaenidae, Lepidoptera)." Rarely can the reader deduce that V. Nabokov, the lepidopterist, is Vladimir Nabokov, the novelist. Only when writing for the *Lepidopterists' News,* a rather chatty journal, is V. likely to peep through as Vladimir: "Every morning the sky would be an impeccable blue at 6 A.M. when I set out. The first innocent cloudlet would scud across at 7:30 A.M. Bigger fellows with darker bellies would start tampering with the sun around 9 A.M., just as I emerged from the shadow of the cliffs and onto good hunting grounds." Conversely, Vladimir sometimes artfully assumes V.'s vocabulary, as in describing Humbert Humbert's first wife in *Lolita:* "The bleached curl revealed its melanic root." Melanic is an entomological term meaning "with a blackish suffusion."

Nabokov has had a passionate interest in butterflies since he was a boy of six in Russia. By the time he was ten, he had made such a nuisance of himself with the net that solemn Muromtsev, the president of the first Russian Duma, intoned, "Come with us by all means, but do not chase butterflies, child. It mars the rhythm of the promenade." In 1919 in the Crimea, a bowlegged Bolshevik sentry, patrolling "among shrubs in waxy bloom," attempted to arrest him for allegedly signaling with the net to a British warship in the Black Sea. Later, in France, a fat policeman wriggled on his belly through parting grass to observe whether or not Nabokov was netting birds. Shortly after Nabokov arrived in the United States in 1940, he became a Research Fellow at the Museum of Comparative Zoology at Harvard, one place, presumably, where his passion was better appreciated. In 1948 he became a member of the Department of Literature at Cornell, but he has kept his summers free for his beloved butterflies. Net in hand, he roams the West, unmindful of hooting motorists, chiding cowpokes or snarling dogs that, he says, "ordinarily wouldn't bark at the worst bum."

In late May of 1959 Nabokov and his wife, Véra, were staying in a cabin at Forest Houses in Oak Creek Canyon, a sort of watchpocket Grand Canyon, eighteen serpentine miles south of Flagstaff, Arizona. There, tucked away in the woods, Nabokov devoted himself to literature (working on translations of the *Song of Igor's Campaign,* the twelfth-century Russian epic, and *Invitation to a Beheading,* a novel he wrote in Paris during the 1930s) and lepidoptera. For a couple of days, lepidoptera won out.

On a Monday morning, for instance, Nabokov, dressed in dungarees, sport shirt and sweater, emerged from his pine cabin to sniff the air and see the morning sun. "It is now nine o'clock," he said, lying. It was really only eight-thirty, but Nabokov keeps moving all of his clocks and watches ahead to make his wife move faster so he can get to his butterflies all the sooner. "The butterflies won't be up for another hour," he admitted, however. "This is a deep canyon, and the sun has to go some way up the rim of the mountain to cast its light. The grass is damp, and the butterflies come out when it's dry. They are late risers. Of course, in the plains they are up earlier at eight o'clock and flying merrily."

He moved inside, sat down on a sofa and picked up a thick brown volume entitled *Colorado Butterflies*. He opened to Nabokov's Wood Nymph on page eleven. "This butterfly which I discovered has nothing to do with nymphets," he said, smiling. "I discovered it in the Grand Canyon in 1941. I know it occurs here, but it is difficult to find. I hope to find it today. I'll be looking for it. It flies in the speckled shade early in June, though there's another brood at the end of the summer, so you came at the right time." He turned to page 161 showing Nabokov's Blue. "Another group of butterflies I'm interested in are called Blues. This I discovered in Telluride in southwest Colorado." He picked up another book, Alexander Klots's *A Field Guide to the Butterflies,* and opened to the page on the Orange-Margined Blues. Proudly, he pointed to a sentence which read, "The recent work of Nabokov has entirely rearranged the classification of this genus." A look of bliss spread across his face. "The thrill of gaining information about certain structural mysteries in these butterflies is perhaps more pleasurable than any literary achievement," he said. Two pages later he pointed to the entry on *Lycaeides melissa samuelis,* a subspecies known as the Karner Blue, and said, "I discovered it and named it *samuelis* after Samuel Scudder, probably one of the greatest lepidopterists who ever lived. Karner is a little railway station between Schenectady and Albany. People go there on Sundays to picnic, shedding papers and beer cans. Among this, the butterfly."

Mrs. Nabokov called him to breakfast—soft-boiled eggs, toast and coffee. "The Southwest is a wonderful place to collect," he said over his soft-boiled eggs. "There's a mixture of arctic and subtropical fauna. A wonderful place to collect."

At 9:35 (Nabokov standard time), he got up to get his net and a blue cloth cap. The thrill of the chase was upon him as he left the cabin and headed south down a foot trail paralleling Oak Creek. "Good luck, Professor!" the motel manager shouted. Nabokov chuckled. His eyes sweeping the brush on either side of the trail, Nabokov said, "This Nabokov's Wood Nymph is represented by several subspecies, and there's one here. It is in this kind of country that my nymph occurs."

He stopped and pointed with the handle of his net to a butterfly clinging to the underside of a leaf. "Disruptive coloration," he said, noting the white spots on the wings. "A bird comes and wonders for a second. Is it two bugs? Where is the head? Which side is which? In that split second the buttery is gone. That second saves that individual and that species. You may call it a large Skipper."

Nabokov walked on. At 9:45, he gave a quick flick with the net. "This is a checkered butterfly," he said, looking at his catch. "There are countless subspecies. The way I kill is the European, or Continental, way. I press the thorax at a certain point like this. If you press the abdomen, it just oozes out." He took the butterfly from the net and held it in the palm of his hand. "This," he exclaimed, "is a beauty! Such a beautiful fresh specimen. *Melitaea anicia.*" He took a Band-Aid box from his pocket, shook loose a Glassene envelope and slid *Melitaea anicia* home to rest. "It's safe in the envelope until I can get to a laboratory and spread it."

In good spirits, he pushed on. Something fluttered across the trail. "A common species," he said, walking on, maneuvering the net before him. "The thing is," he said, "when you hit the butterfly, turn the net at the same time to form a bag in which the butterfly is imprisoned." No sooner had he spoken than he darted forward. "A large male!" he cried as he deftly made a backhand volley. He held the net up for examination. "I'm not going to kill it," he said. "A common species." He released the butterfly which flew off.

Nearby, another butterfly was feeding on a flower, but Nabokov ignored it. "A dusky-wing Skipper. Common." At 10:03, he passed a *clarus* sitting on a bare twig. "I've seen that same individual on the same twig since I've been here," he said. "There are lots of butterflies around, but this individual will chase the others from its perch."

Further down the trail, Nabokov swung but missed a Blue. "Thirty-fifteen," he said. He walked off the trail into an apple orchard where he detected a Hairstreak feeding on a flower. He caught it, then released it. "Forty-fifteen," he said.

Nabokov started walking back toward the cabin. He noted a day-flying Peacock moth. "In quest of a female. It only quiets down at certain hours of the day. I have found them asleep on flowers. Oh, this is wretched work. Where is my Wood Nymph? It's heartbreaking work. Wretched work. I've traveled thousands of miles to get a species I never got. We went to Fort Davis, Texas, but there was no Wood Nymph. Toad-like sheep with their razor-sharp teeth had eaten everything. Horrible!"

At 10:45, Nabokov lunged wildly off the trail and raced up a rocky incline. Whatever it was had escaped in the underbrush. As he picked his way down, he sighed, "There I did something I shouldn't have done. I went up there without looking for rattlesnakes, but I suppose God looks after entomologists as He does after drunkards." At 11:00, he stopped short. "Ah," he said, a tremor of delight rocking him ever so slightly. "Ah. Oh, that's an interesting thing! Oh, gosh, there it goes. A white Skipper mimicking a Cabbage butterfly belonging to a different family. Things are picking up. Still, they're not quite right. Where is my Wood Nymph? It is heartbreaking work," he complained. "Wretched work."

Back at the cabin, Mrs. Nabokov, fresh from writing letters, greeted her husband in Russian. "Let us hurry, darling," he said.

Mrs. Nabokov smiled indulgently and followed him down the porch steps to their car, a black 1956 Buick, where she got behind the wheel. Nabokov, who does not drive, did not want to go fast, and to be sure that his wife did not exceed forty miles an hour a warning klaxon was attached to the speedometer. But just as he moves clocks forward a half-hour, his wife moves the klaxon up to sixty. "I always put it a little higher so he doesn't know," she said as he listened intently. "Now I'll put it at forty."

The car would not start. "The car is nervous," Nabokov said. "The car?" asked Véra. "The car," said Vladimir. At last it started. Mrs. Nabokov drove onto Highway 89A and headed to a butterfly hunting ground several miles north. The klaxon went off, and Mrs. Nabokov slowed down. A motorcyclist whizzed by in the opposite direction, and Nabokov shuddered discreetly. The Nabokovs wheeled past the Chipmunk Apartments. The name delighted him. "They have considerably improved all the motels across the country," he said. "No comparison with what they were in the early '40s. I shall never forget the motel-keeperess who said, when I complained that they didn't have hot water, 'Was there any hot water on your grandmother's farm?' " A gale of laughter swept over him.

At 11:26 (Nabokov standard time), Mrs. Nabokov swung over to the left side of the road and parked by Oak Creek. Nabokov leaped out. "Now we'll see something spectacular, I hope!" He hopped across the rocks in the creek, slipped and soaked his right leg. He ignored it. His eyes were on a swarm of butterflies flitting around a puddle. "These are all males and this is their pub," he said. "They suck moisture in the ground. In mountains, European mountains, where the mules have passed and pissed, it's like a flowery carpet. And it's always the males. Always the males."

He waved farewell to his wife who had stayed on the other side of the creek, and he jogged down a rough trail. He stopped. A butterfly was sipping nectar from yellow asters. "Here's a butterfly that's quite rare. You find it here and there in Arizona. *Lemonias zela.* I've collected quite a few. It will sit there all day. We could come back at four, and it would still be here. The form of its wings and its general manner are very mothlike. Quite interesting. But it is a real butterfly. It belongs to a tremendous family of South American butterflies, and they mimic all kinds of butterflies belonging to other families. Keeping up with the Smiths, you know."

He walked on, then stopped. He said softly, "Now here is something I really want." He swung his net. " 'One flick, one dart, and it was in his net.' I'm not suggesting anything." He pressed the thorax of the prey and displayed the butterfly in his hand. "A Checker," he said, "but it seems to be another form of the butterfly we took earlier. Quite interesting. I would like to take some more."

He pushed off the trail into a stand of bushes. From behind one, he exclaimed, *"Chort!"* Reappearing he explained, "I have been doing this since I was five or six, and I find myself using the same Russian swear words. *Chort* means the devil. It's a word I never use otherwise." Back on the trail he swung his net in forehead fashion and missed a butterfly. "Fifteen all," he said.

Nabokov clambered up a pile of rocks. "Haha! Haha!" he shouted, backhanding a butterfly. "A prize! One of the best things I've taken so far. That's a darling. Wonderful! Ha, so unexpectedly. Haha, look at it on this fern. What protective coloration. *Callophrys.* I'm not sure of the species." He turned it over in his hand. "Isn't it lovely? You could travel hundreds of miles and not see one. Ha, what luck! That was so unexpected, and just as I was about to say there was nothing interesting here today. A female that has hibernated. That was very nice, very nice indeed. Quite exciting. That was one of those things that make coming here worthwhile. This will go to Cornell, this little green thing. The best way to put it is, 'A green Hairstreak not readily identified in the field.' " Beaming, Nabokov boxed it.

Woosh! Nabokov had suddenly struck again. He grinned savagely. "I took two in one diabolical stroke of my net. A female

Blue. A Lygdamus female Blue, one of the many species of Blues in which I am especially interested. This other, by freakish chance, is a male Blue of another species that was flying with it. That's adultery. Or a step toward adultery." He let the offending male fly free unpunished.

Nabokov worked over a dry stream bed. "Quite a number of little things have appeared today which I haven't seen before. It's picking up. The next week will probably go much faster. I give the Wood Nymph a week to be out. I may go to Jerome for my Wood Nymph. It's a ghost town on the side of a mountain. I know of several collectors who were there and brought back my butterfly a few years ago."

He returned down the trail. Just before crossing Oak Creek to join his wife, he swung his net. "Three with one sweep of the net. This one is an Angle Wing. It has a curiously formed letter C. It mimics a chink of light through a dead leaf. Isn't that wonderful? Isn't that humorous?" He discarded the other two butterflies and danced across the creek to Véra where he carefully boxed the Angle Wing. "They won't lose any color," he said. "I saw an Indian moth, probably taken in the middle of the eighteenth century, that had been presented to Catharine the Great, and the color was still fresh. Some of the butterflies of Linnaeus, the first great naturalist, a Swede, are quite fresh. They are less fragile, I suppose, than pickled human beings."

Mrs. Nabokov headed the Buick south to Sedona for lunch. "I lost two butterfly collections," Nabokov recalled as the car sped along (someone had tampered with the klaxon). "One to the Bolsheviks, one to the Germans. I have another I gave to Cornell. I dream of stealing it back."

At 12:15, the Nabokovs drove into Sedona, which a sign proclaimed as the Flying Saucer Capital of the Universe. "It's a kind of quest, but they are going the wrong way," Nabokov said. After gathering their mail and lunching in a local restaurant, the Nabokovs drove south. "We would like to see if I can get a Blue butterfly." His eyes wallowed in the gorgeous wind-swept buttes. "It looks like a giant chess game is being played around us." At 2:20, Mrs. Nabokov parked the car by the side of the road. Net at the ready, Nabokov was off like an eager boy. "Mind the snakes," his wife called. "I'm going to inspect the grove," he said. "It interests me." Mrs. Nabokov took a net from the back seat and joined him. "You should see my wife catch butterflies," he said. "One little movement and they're in the net."

The grove was disappointing. "*Rien*," Nabokov muttered. He probed some bushes. "There is nothing," he said. "A hopeless place." He cautiously inspected a rocky area. " 'Suddenly we heard an ominous rattle, and Mr. Nabokov fell like a log.' " He went back to the car. "I'm sorry this was not a very great show," he said. "Sad." Still, he couldn't leave quite yet. He moved down the edge of the highway peering into bushes. "In Alberta you have to watch for bear." At 2:35, he got in the car, and Mrs. Nabokov drove back to Sedona to shop. There he followed her into the supermarket. "When I was younger I ate some butterflies in Vermont to see if they were poisonous," he said as his wife hovered over the cold-cuts counter. "I didn't see any difference between a Monarch butterfly and a Viceroy. The taste of both was vile, but I had no ill effects. They tasted like almonds and perhaps a green cheese combination. I ate them raw. I held one in one hot little hand and one in the other. Will you eat some with me tomorrow for breakfast?"

Back in their cabin, the Nabokovs set up drinks and hors d'oeuvres for the owners of Forest Houses, Robert Kittredge and his wife. The Kittredges arrived promptly at four (4:30 NST) and Nabokov excused them for being late. He and Kittredge, a fledgling novelist, have the same publisher in England. The conversation hopped from subject to subject. Nabokov expressed an enthusiasm for Dinah Shore and Jayne Meadows ("I like her big teeth"), his fascination for Lawrence Welk ("the most antiartistic man"), and an interest in birthdays ("William Shakespeare, Shirley Temple, and I have the same birthday, April 23."). Occasionally the talk would alight upon butterflies. In delight, Nabokov recalled a pregnant White butterfly that came all the way from Ireland by ship ("She laid her eggs immediately in a kitchen garden in Quebec in 1860"), a marvelous day in Alberta when he found a "treasure, a Nitra Swallowtail, sitting there on bear dung."

When the Kittredges left at 6:30, Nabokov burrowed into a pile of scientific papers and pulled out the thickest one, his article on the Nearctic members of the Genus *Lycaeides* Hübner. "The most interesting part here," he said, settling himself on the sofa, "was to find the structural differences between them in terms of the male organ. These are magnified thirty-four times. These are hooks which the male has to attach to the female. Because of the differences in the size of the hooks, all males cannot copulate with all females. Suddenly in Jackson Hole, I found a hook intermediate between the two. It has the form of the short-hooked species, but the length of the long-hooked species. It is almost impossible to classify. I named it *longinus*. This work took me several years and undermined my health for quite a while. Before, I never wore glasses. This is my favorite work. I think I really did well there." Yes, the Soviets were aware of his work on butterflies. Only in November of last year, one Lubimov had attacked him in the *Literary Gazette.* "He said that I was starving in America, compelled to earn a precarious existence selling butterflies." Nabokov laughed merrily and picked up another paper, this one dealing with an elaborate count of wing scales. "It's impossible to understand," he said, beaming. "But I proved my point, and it will stand forever."

The next morning, Nabokov was as chipper and as restless as ever. "Come on, darling," he called to his wife during breakfast. "The sun is wasting away! It's a quarter to ten." Mrs. Nabokov took her time. "He doesn't know that everyone is wise to him," she said. At 10:10, Nabokov at last succeeded in luring her behind the wheel. "We are going to Jerome, a ghost town," he said happily as the car moved south on 89A. "We are looking for my butterfly, the Wood Nymph, which should be out, I hope, on Mount Mingus." While the car sped through a veritable Lolitaland ("See Tuzigoot Ruins," "See Historic Fort Verde"), Nabokov said, "Butterflies help me in my writing. I wrote most of *Lolita* this way. I wrote it in motels or parked cars. The funny thing is in Russian the word 'motil' means moth. The English word motel spelled backwards is 'letom.' That means 'in summer' in Russian. T. S. Eliot spelled backwards is toilets. You have to transpose the t and the s. Powder backwards is red wop! Red wop! Isn't that wonderful?"

Nabokov reached Jerome ("Welcome to Ghost City. 3 Places to Eat") at 11:10. "Shall we catch my butterfly today?" Nabokov asked. While Mrs. Nabokov stopped to let the car radiator cool, Vladimir nipped into a store to ask directions. "Are you from merry old England?" the proprietor asked him. Nabokov came back to the car, and his wife drove up Mount Mingus. "We're getting into oaks and pines," he said, joyfully. "The greatest enemy of the lepidopterist is the juniper tree. Charming! Charming! Charming butterfly road!" Mrs. Nabokov swung off the road and parked by a marker announcing the elevation to be 7,023 feet. Both took nets from the back seat and walked up a dirt road bordered by pines. A yellow butterfly danced crazily by. Nabokov swung and missed. "Common," he said. "I'm just getting warmed up." A fifteen-minute search of the terrain revealed nothing. At 12:20, Mrs. Nabokov drove to the Potato Patch Picnic Ground, a quarter of a mile back down the mountain. Nabokov headed toward an iris-covered meadow. "I can't believe there won't be butterflies here," he said. He was mistaken. "I'm very much disappointed," Nabokov said after searching the meadow. "*Rien. Rien.* Iris is not very attractive to butterflies anyway. It's rather ornamental, and that's it." On the way back to the car, Mrs. Nabokov called excitedly. "Here's a yellow! Here's a yellow!" "I saw it, darling," Nabokov replied calmly. "It is very common. Just an orange Sulphur."

Nabokov got in the car. "It was very sad. 'And then I saw that strong man put his head on his forearms and sob like a woman.' " At 12:40, Mrs. Nabokov stopped again. "This will be our last stop today," Nabokov said. Véra took a net, and they walked up a dirt road. "It is this kind of place that my nymph should be flying, but with the exception of three cows and a calf, there is nothing." "Do we have to mix with cows?" asked Mrs. Nabokov.

They got back in the car and drove back to Jerome. "Sad," said Nabokov. " 'His face was now a tear-stained mask.' " Five minutes later, he had Véra stop at Mescal Canyon. "We may be in for a surprise here," he said. Nabokov walked up a dirt road alone. Mrs. Nabokov lent her net to their visitor. With a whoop of joy, the visitor snared a white-winged beauty. Cupping it in his hands, he showed it to Nabokov who dismissed it. "A winged cliché," he said. It had been a poor day for hunting. There would be other days to come, but the visitor wouldn't be there. As the car swung out for the journey home, Nabokov spread his arms and said sadly, "What can I say? What is there to say? I am ashamed for the butterflies. I apologize for the butterflies."

—SEPTEMBER 14, 1959

Trick or Truite

Joe Hyde

E legance and simplicity are the why and the wherefore of Chef
Joe Hyde, sportsman, savant of fish and game and author of the
new cookbook *Love, Time & Butter.* At Gay Head on Martha's Vineyard, where fishing for striped bass can be a pretentious production
calling for belted waders, plug bags and floating flashlights, Hyde
once appeared on the beach carrying a rod and wearing a dark blue
suit, brightly polished black shoes and a derby hat. As the other anglers watched in silence, Hyde waded into the surf up to his armpits,
caught two twenty-pound stripers, tipped his bowler to onlookers
and departed, dripping wet.

On the Vineyard, in New York City, Kansas City, Jupiter Island
and Santa Barbara, all locales where he has cooked or taught cooking, Chef Joe Hyde is, in the words of novelist Robert Crichton,
"sort of semilegendary." Should a client's dinner party flag, Hyde,
looking like a white-hatted Brendan Behan, has been known to
bound from the kitchen to supply the missing ingredient, his own
good cheer. At one dull gathering in New Jersey, he enlivened the
proceedings by Indian wrestling with the guests. Some years ago at
a garden party for Patrice Lumumba's delegation to the United Nations, he showed the befuddled Congolese how to eat corn on the

cob. Having done so, he threw the finished ear behind him with a flourish. A week later, at least so the story goes, the Congolese attended a formal dinner in the state dining room at the United Nations. Corn on the cob was served and the Congolese startled everyone by tossing the cobs over their shoulders. But Hyde has his shy moments, too. When Elizabeth Taylor sought him out to congratulate him on a dinner, he hid under the kitchen table, where he pretended to fuss with pots and pans. "I didn't want to get involved," he says.

Gastronomically, Joe Hyde belongs to the classic French school, with the emphasis, as an admiring food critic of *The New Yorker* once put it, on "preserving the essential greatness of the ingredients, rather than exalting them to complicated and unrecognizable heights." Hyde preaches the gospel of simplicity in food with such fervor that he sometimes refers to himself as "the backlash to the Galloping Gourmet and other TV chefs. While the bird is drying out more and more, they just confuse and snow the audience. Teaching cooking should be about detailed simple processes."

Hyde does about sixty dinner parties a year, and one of his simple spreads—enhanced with a touch of game fish here, a game bird or so there—can cost the host up to twenty dollars a guest. Hyde and his family live in Snedens Landing, New York, but they also have a house on the beach at the Vineyard, which Hyde visits often for seafood. "I love nothing better," he says, "than to have a client ask, 'Is this fish fresh?' And I say, 'Yes sir, I caught it myself last night on Martha's Vineyard. Would you like some more?'" Among Hyde's favorite seafoods are minnows, known as spearing, dipped in beer and then in a mixture of bread crumbs and flour and fried in deep fat; bay scallops, either smoked or sautéed meunière (the floured scallops are in the hot pan only one minute; if they stay longer they toughen); boiled periwinkles served cold with a vinaigrette dip of chopped onions, salt, pepper, oil and vinegar; fresh mussels and poached fish, preferably a striped bass or salmon of from five to twelve pounds. "The way to cook fish is to poach it whole," Hyde says, explaining that this is the best method to keep it juicy. "People have simply gotten used to fish being dry, because it is so often served that way."

Dryness is only one of the horrors that Hyde sees in American cooking of fish and game. He is aghast at the idea of storing venison or rabbit in a freezer. Instead he marinates them in crocks filled with red wine. Similarly, he feels game birds should be hung for a sufficient period of time. Adhering to French custom, he hangs a woodcock until it has one or two maggots in it. "Not fifty or one hundred," he says. "Just one or two." He also contends that all birds, except turkeys with exceptionally large breasts, should be roasted breast down and not up. "The hottest part of the oven is the top," Hyde explains, "and the back should stick up in the hot air because it has little meat on it." As fond as he is of game, Hyde regrets that he cannot get it often enough. Recently he roasted some starlings for a friend. "They weren't bad," he says, "but I suspect blue jays are better."

Hyde, who is now forty-three, was born surrounded by the "Beautiful People." His maternal grandmother, Mary Tonetti, a sculptress, started the artistic colony at Sneden's Landing on the Hudson River. Hyde's neighbors have included Orson Welles, John Steinbeck, Katharine Cornell, Jerome Robbins, Mike Wallace, Aaron Copland, Noel Coward, Vivien Leigh, Laurence Olivier and Burgess Meredith. As a youngster, Hyde taught Olivier how to sail; his boat was named *Fiddle-dee-dee,* a favorite expression of Scarlett O'Hara in *Gone with the Wind.*

Hyde's father, Robert McKee Hyde, was a well-to-do eccentric. He occupied his time writing ("His *Winds of Gobi* is a perfectly beautiful book about China," says Hyde. "He had never been there."), practicing nudism, collecting spiders and hunting mushrooms, an avocation inherited by his son. Joe went to prep school at Millbrook and then to college at Trinity in Hartford. Upon graduating from Trinity in 1950, Hyde decided on a conventional enough career, the hotel business, because he enjoyed meeting people. He went to work at the Hotel Raleigh in Washington, D.C., and there he started in the kitchen. He perceived immediately, he says, that cooking was his destiny. He spent three weeks with the roast cook, two weeks in the pastry shop, three weeks in cold meat and a week in the storeroom, where his first task was to clean all the cans on the shelves. He had no sooner absorbed the location of the canned goods than he was drafted into the Army. There, amazingly, he wound up serving as a cook for a heavy-mortar company in Korea. Hyde took along a Betty Crocker cookbook. "When the menu said steak, I always made stew," he recalls. "I made a casserole with the hamburger meat. I browned the meat, poured off the fat, added garlic, bay leaf, onion and tomato puree and simmered the sauce for two hours. Then I put layers of cooked elbow macaroni, sauce and sliced American cheese into the deep pans until they were full. The whole affair was baked for an hour; one pan went to each platoon. The boys liked it. They called it 'Holy Mattress.'"

On return to civilian life, Hyde worked as a room clerk at the Statler Hilton in New York for six months before going to France. There, through UNESCO, he got a job as an apprentice in Chez Nandron, a two-star restaurant in Lyons, a city considered by some to be the culinary capital of France. His first day was almost a disaster. The usual apprentice is a 13-year-old, and here was Hyde, the only American apprentice in the country, twenty-five years old, burly—almost six feet tall with a beard that needed shaving every twelve hours. When he appeared in the kitchen dressed in white, the dozen cooks stopped working to stare in amazement. With an atrocious accent, Hyde introduced himself. *"Bond jour!"* he exclaimed. *"Je m'appelle Joe!"* Several of the cooks almost swooned. "I was the grossest thing that had ever happened to French cooking," Hyde says. "They'd never seen anyone like me before. And the name Joe. They flipped out over it. It sounds like a peasant's name. Even today French chefs who have known me for years recoil at the mention of it. They always call me Joe-ceph!"

Given his appalling debut, Hyde was assigned the lowest job in the scullery, plucking larks beneath a splashing drainboard. Eventually, because of his age, the first cooks allowed Hyde to eat with them, and he acquired a taste for fried tripe, pig heads and coq au vin made with just the peeled chicken gizzards.

Hyde next became an assistant *poissonier,* or fish cook, at the Pyramide in Vienne. At the time it was regarded by many as the best restaurant in the world. While there, Hyde, a follower of the turf, won $1,000 in the *tiercé,* a form of French off-track betting. According to local custom, a winner is supposed to spend it all on one spree. Hyde invited nearly two dozen friends including the man who had sold him the ticket, to dine at the famed Pont de Collonges. "It was a fantastic, endless meal," he recalls. "I ate two pheasants. We had a meringue and ice cream dessert that was four feet tall. Each tier was covered with spun sugar and illuminated with a little light inside. We drank the finest of champagne—it didn't have anything written on it except dust."

After two years in France, Hyde returned to the United States to become chef at the Jupiter Island Club in Hobe Sound, Florida. One of his triumphs there was a chicken poached inside a pig's bladder, which he prepared for Sir Osbert Sitwell and Marshall Field. Hyde had brought back with him a supply of pig bladders from France, but when he later tried to import more, United States Customs seized them, and ever since he has had to make do with ones obtained from local slaughterhouses. Once, while he was cooking at Chalet Frascati in Santa Monica, California, he procured some bladders, washed them, blew them up through a stick of macaroni and set them out to dry on a clothesline. One of them got away and sailed over the fence like an expiring balloon. Hyde's wife, Gail, ran next door, shouting to the neighbors, "Excuse me, but one of my husband's bladders just landed in your yard."

Hyde spent a summer as head chef at the Misquamicut Club in Watch Hill, Rhode Island, but then quit to work, once again, as an assistant because "I felt I had to learn a great deal more." Cole Porter wrote a letter of introduction to Le Pavillon—how chic—but Hyde says, "It was the wrong way to come in. I should have entered through the cellar." He was shunted off to the Waldorf in 1956 as assistant sauce cook and afterward spent a year at the Brussels. A little while later he decided to teach cooking at UCLA. When his mother's home in Snedens Landing fell vacant, he returned East to teach in the family mansion known as the Old Library because it had served as one in the nineteenth century. Built in 1685, the house was also celebrated as a meeting place of George Washington and Lafayette. Although Washington never slept there, he had eaten there, and Hyde's classes were held in the enormous kitchen with its original fireplace.

In a roundup of cooking schools, *The New York Times* went beyond the city line to include Hyde's school because his classes had "too much merit." Similarly another Manhattan food expert wrote, "It is not my custom to concern myself with matters beyond the limits of my own borough, but I have an excuse in this case—that I would go a lot farther afield than Rockland County to find a teacher with Mr. Hyde's combined gifts for cooking and teaching."

In 1966 Hyde gave up teaching to devote himself full-time to catering. He shifted his kitchen from the Old Library to a sort of miniature palace nearby that had been built by his uncle, Eric Gugler, an architect and designer of the executive offices in the West Wing of the White House. There, amid historic frescoes, triumphant arches and heroic busts, Hyde turns out smoked bluefish, stuffed eggs, poached salmon, orange mousse and other dishes that can be prepared in advance for a dinner party. Hyde is thus well prepared when he arrives at a client's house with his staff of six, headed by Selma Andersen, a brisk Swedish woman who superintends the table setting while Hyde himself prepares the canapés, heats the oven for the saddles of lamb, sautés endives air-expressed from Belgium and chops shallots. Hyde never goes anywhere without shallots. Just in case he might find them unavailable, he keeps a supply in the glove compartment of his truck. "And I always have kosher salt with me," he says. "I just love the feel of it."

Hyde has cooked and catered in all sorts of places. At a party at a manufacturing plant, he used a forklift truck to serve the appetizers. When the Broadway musical *Camelot* opened, he catered the party for lyricist Alan Jay Lerner. He has also catered parties for the Josh-Logans, including one party in honor of Princess Margaret and Anthony Armstrong-Jones. Armstrong-Jones was so pleased that he shook the hand of one of Hyde's assistants under the mistaken impression that he was Hyde. "Another first for Chef Joe Hyde," says Hyde, who sometimes refers to himself in the third person when things go awry.

Occasionally Hyde falls out with a client. Robert Montgomery objected to the bill, and Carter Burden, the social New York City councilman, wrote Hyde several letters complaining he could not find the persimmon ice cream that was left behind.

Every so often Hyde caters a dinner for the New York Mycological Society. The mushroom enthusiasts often show up with unusual fungi, and they joyously sing their anthem:

"Deep, deep in the murky shadows,
There where the slime mold creeps,
With joy the stout mycologist
His pallid harvest reaps."

A year and a half ago Hyde and Everett Poole, who runs a fish market in Menemsha, on Martha's Vineyard, began turning out a line of frozen fish and shellfish dishes, prepared by "Famous Chef Joe Hyde." They sell soups, chowders, bouillabaisse, Menemsha thermidor (lobster and fish) and stuffed clams direct to customers or through fancy food stores in cities all across the country. (While Hyde objects to many frozen foods, he believes these dishes, prepared his way—with juices to conserve fresh taste—are worthy of a first-class chef.) One Vineyard resident went to three dinner parties in a week, and all the hostesses passed off Hyde's dishes as their own. They should know better, the Vineyard being true Hyde territory. It is there that Hyde does some truly debatable things. For example, he will take one of his antique bass boats and head south five miles for the deserted island called No Man's Land. When Hyde gets to No Man's, he either trolls off the beach or goes ashore for a stroll. There is only one difficulty. No Man's Land is used as a bombing and target range by the armed forces. Hyde rather likes trolling offshore, especially when the planes are strafing. With the fastidious taste of a haiku poet, he is fond of describing the puffs of smoke that are emitted from the wings of an attacking plane.

But for all this *joie de vivre,* he has moments of depression. On occasion he wonders if he does not repeat himself too much with menus. A couple of years ago he got so depressed by this thought that he consulted a psychiatrist. The doctor was elated because Hyde had such an unusual cause for depression. "People are eating your art!" the psychiatrist exclaimed. To which Hyde adds, "That was still another first for Chef Joe Hyde."

WILD DUCK À LA CHEF JOE HYDE

3 or 4 wild ducks for 6 persons (four ducks offer a second helping)
2 medium-size onions cut into eighths
1 onion chopped fine
1 stalk celery roughly cut
1 carrot roughly cut
2 cloves garlic halved but unpeeled
1 tbs. peppercorns
8 juniper berries
1 cup white wine
1 quart water salted to taste
1 stick butter
1 bunch watercress

Pluck ducks. Cut necks flush with bodies of birds. Split and clean gizzards. Fry gizzards and necks with liver in one-half stick of butter over medium-high heat in a large cast-iron skillet. When brown, add cut-up onions, celery and carrot, garlic, peppercorns and juniper berries. When all are tinged with brown, remove to saucepan, add white wine and let simmer for two hours. Strain off resulting juice and boil down to one-half cup liquid. Refrigerate. (You can do all this the day before the dinner.)

On day of dinner preheat oven to 500°. Salt and pepper ducks; smear with one-half stick of soft butter. Place in oven breast down on top shelf and roast for 25 minutes. This will cause some smoke. Don't worry. Remove ducks, sprinkle with chopped onion, and perhaps a handful of pine needles or several branches of rosemary. Return to 350° oven for 10 minutes.

Remove ducks. Make an incision between second joint and breast and rip off the legs. Make another cut at top of wishbone and on both sides of the backbones and strip breasts from carcasses. Place breasts skin down on platter and put to one side.

Place legs in a duck press or orange juice squeezer. If neither is available, simply squeeze the blood from meat with hand, and set aside.

Place the carcasses in a roasting pan. Pour one-half cup of the cooled juices over them. Put in oven and let simmer. Remove from heat and pass the juice through a sieve. Simmer again.

Place dinner plates and platter of breasts in the oven at 100°for three minutes. (Plates should be warm when served, not hot.) Garnish breasts with watercress. Just before serving, remove juices from heat, whisk in blood and pour over duck breasts.

VENISON STEAK AU POIVRE

6 1½-inch-thick venison steaks cut from haunch	⅔ stick butter
	1½ tbs. finely chopped shallots
3 tbs. peppercorns	

Put peppercorns on chopping block or cutting board. Using heel of heavy pot or round stone, crack corns. Do not grind. Distribute peppercorns on both sides of steaks and press in with palm of your hand. Heat 12-inch cast-iron skillet and put in 1 tbs. butter. Let butter brown and begin to smoke over high heat. Put in steaks. Brown three minutes to a side. Remove steaks, wipe out pan and put in remaining butter over medium high heat. When butter is brown, add shallots and remove from fire. Stir briskly and pour shallot-butter sauce over steaks. Serves six.

If steaks are frozen, do not thaw completely before cooking; too much juice will run. One of the important principles of game cooking is preservation of all juices. Do not presalt steaks. Salt draws juice from the meat. Let your guests salt their own venison at table.

—NOVEMBER 8, 1971

Yep, Another Nymphmaniac

Paul Schmookler, Ken Stewart & Company

It is a balmy May evening in Port Jervis, N.Y., and the folks stacked inside the Kentucky Fried Chicken restaurant off Main Street are crunching away and lickin' their fingers, and you expect to see the Colonel show up at any minute—white hair, goatee, white suit and all. But instead, here comes a short, blond man in a safari hat, approaching the huge plate-glass window with an ecstatic, dreamy look. He then begins to pluck insects delicately off the glass with a pair of tweezers. "*Epeorus pleuralis,*" he murmurs. His name is Paul Schmookler, and he is a trout fisherman hooked on trout-stream insects. *Epeorus pleuralis* is a mayfly, and there are thousands plastered against the window. Inside, some customers stop eating; others grind on abstractedly, oblivious of the sicko outside. Schmookler continues to collect, carefully placing each mayfly in a small vial which he tucks inside a pouch hanging from his shoulder. The manager appears behind the thick glass, looking for all the world like Franklin Pangborn suddenly confronted by W.C. Fields. Pangborn gestures. The gesture says, "Get the hell out of here!" Schmookler continues to pluck away until his pouch is full. "Best collecting place around," he says. He gets into his car to head home to the Bronx, 90 miles away. "Strange world," he says. "People get upset if someone is picking insects off a window."

Although an advanced case, Schmookler is typical of an increasing number of fishermen who are becoming more fascinated by the insects trout feed upon than the fish themselves. Among their quarry are the delicate mayflies that emerge from a stream to live only for a day or two. Because of this fleeting existence the order to which mayflies belong is called the Ephemeroptera. Then there are the wormlike caddis larvae of the order Trichoptera that weave nets like underwater spiders or build houses out of twigs, leaves and grains of sand. And there are the Plecoptera, stoneflies, ranging from the tiny dark *Allocapnia* that emerge in midwinter to the cholate-brown *Pteronarcys,* some fully two inches long and a succulent snack indeed for a trout.

All these bugs have their buffs. Schmookler, for instance, is particularly smitten with stoneflies, the Plecoptera. In Manhattan, Larry Solomon, a former president of the Theodore Gordon Flyfishers, raises mayflies and caddis in his apartment. In Branford, Conn., Dr. Wilbur G. Downs, professor of epidemiology at the Yale Medical School, has pretty much put aside his fly rod in favor of collecting caddis, mayflies and stoneflies from streams in the Northeast. "It's an epidemic!" exclaims the epidemiologist of the burgeoning interest in the life-styles of aquatic insects.

In Portland, Ore., Rick Hafele, an entomologist, teams up on winter weekends with Dave Hughes, a freelance writer, to conduct an eight-hour workshop, Entomology and the Artificial Fly, in which they discuss insect identification and behavior and collecting methods on the stream. Touring Oregon, Washington and California, they rent motel conference rooms and charge $30 a person for a session, lunch included.

In Denton, Texas, Kenneth W. Stewart gets himself up for the day by playing a tape recording of the drumming signals of courting stoneflies. Some male stoneflies signal for unmated females by drumming the ground with their abdomens, and the females respond in kind to a male with the right vibes. A trout fisherman, Stewart is head of the Department of Biological Sciences at North Texas State University, and he and a colleague, Bill Stark of Mississippi College, have a five-year grant from the National Science Foundation to study the stonefly nymphs of North America. Like other aquatic insects, stoneflies live underwater as nymphs before emerging from a stream to mate as adults.

Working out the life histories of the 500 or so stoneflies known in the U.S. and Canada is an intricate business. Most species can be identified with certainty only by means of an examination of the genitalia of the adult male. Indeed, this holds true for most insects, but stoneflies offer a further difficulty in that their lives sometimes develop erratically. The eggs and nymphs of some species can go into "diapause," a state of arrested development that may last as long as a year. This is one reason why the nymphs of more than half the stoneflies in the U.S. have yet to be identified by species. To identify them positively, in most cases, it is necessary that they be reared in cages set in a stream or in a laboratory aquarium. When they emerge, the adults can be correlated with the cast outer skins of the male or the female nymphs of a given species. Stewart's passion for categorizing stoneflies is such that he once rushed maturing nymphs of *Isoperla rainiera* from a small stream on Mount Hood in Oregon 1,740 miles to Denton by plane and pickup truck so he could observe them when they emerged as adults in his lab.

Both sporting and ecological considerations have triggered the explosion of interest in aquatic insects. They make up the bulk of the diet of trout and other fishes, and some species of mayflies and stoneflies in particular can serve as indices of water quality. Many aquatic insects are vital links in the energy flow of a stream because they eat dead leaves that fall from trees. Most of the carbon in the world is tied up in plants, and insects have a major role in freeing it. Moreover, a daily phenomenon known as "behavioral drift," which presumably has been going on as long as aquatic insects have been around but which was not discovered until 1960, has caused great excitement among scientists and the few anglers who know about it. Put simply, many mayflies, caddis, stoneflies, blackflies and Gammarids (crustaceans) release their hold on the bottom of a brook, stream or river in the first few hours after sunset to drift downstream, often in enormous numbers. During a 24-hour period, 170 million mayfly nymphs of the genus *Baetis* drifted past a sampling station on the Green River in Wyoming. According to Dr. Thomas F. Waters of the University of Minnesota, a leading authority on behavioral drift, trout especially select and defend territories in a stream best suited for intercepting the drifting nymphs. Put in fisherman's terms, this means that an angler would do well to fish a nymph imitation at the head of a pool after the sun goes down.

As a result of the booming interest, the Entomological Society of America now has an aquatic insects subsection, and the Midwest Benthological Society, which started in 1953 with 13 charter members devoted to the study of organisms that live on the bottoms of rivers and lakes, now has 1,100 members and has changed its name to the North American Benthological Society. Fittingly, NABS has a stonefly as its emblem. There is a new international journal, *Aquatic Insects,* catering to bug lovers of all sorts, and there are even three newsletters for, uh, nymphmaniacs: *Eatonia,* for mayfly mavens and named for the Rev. A.E. Eaton, an Anglican vicar who studied the Ephemeroptera as a hobby in the late 19th century; *The Trichoptera News-letter,* which is about caddis; and *Perla,* for stonefly enthusiasts.

However, the glut of information is such that even the newsletters are often a couple of years behind the breaking news on the entomological front. Then again, these publications do not feel as compelled to rush the latest news into print as, say, a football tip sheet. The editor of *Perla,* Dr. Richard Baumann, formerly of the Smithsonian and now at Brigham Young University, often appears to lapse into blissful torpor simply thinking about what he's going to print. The idea of *Perla* was first hatched in 1968 at the Fourth International Symposium on Plecoptera held in Abisko, Swedish Lapland, but Baumann didn't get out the first issue until 1974. He explained to eager readers of the premier issue, "It might appear to be late to outsiders, but anyone familiar with the habits of many stoneflies should not be surprised. Only the first drumming signals were heard at Abisko, but even after oviposition [egg-laying], development is often not straightforward, and considerable spans of time may be spent in the dormant stages."

On the popular side, books for fishermen, such as Ernest Schwiebert's *Nymphs,* Larry Solomon and Eric Leiser's *The Caddis and the Angler,* and Al Caucci and Bob Nastasi's *Hatches,* have fueled interest. "A lot of interest has to do with all the books," says Downs, who started collecting systematically six years ago. Downs is assembling a reference collection of Northeastern aquatic insects for the Peabody Museum at Yale, and so far he has picked up about a dozen species that appear to be new to science. "This part of the country really hasn't been worked over thoroughly for a long time," he says. Downs spends the summer collecting and fly-fishing in Colorado and Wyoming, where he owns a couple of ranches, and all his Western caddis go to John Unzicker, who is working on the order at the Illinois Natural History Survey. Thrice a year the doctor also visits West Africa to look over tropical-medicine programs he has set up for Yale and the U.S. Agency for International Development, and he has collected mayflies in Tanzania, Senegal, Kenya and Nigeria. "Too much of mayfly collecting there has to be done on a one-night-stand basis," he says, "but I must say I've had some good collecting nights at airports, where the windows are brightly illuminated. If I could ever get into the upper Senegal River to work, I'd be in country with some interesting mayflies and caddis."

While collecting in the Northeast in June, Downs keeps an eye out for *Siphlonisca aerodromia,* a mayfly that has not been seen alive for more than 40 years. Apparently only two entomologists, C.P. Alexander, who discovered the species in 1907 along the Sacandaga River in northern New York, and G.C. Crampton, who collected a few specimens there in the 1930s, have ever seen *Siphlonisca* alive, but Downs hopes that this primitive species, a kind of dinosaur of mayflies, can be found in rivers in Vermont and New Hampshire that are similar to the Sacandaga, which has long been done in by a dam. "Everybody collecting in the East sort of has it in the back of their minds to get Siphlonisca," says Downs, who regularly drops in on the 90-year-old C.P. Alexander, the discoverer of the species, in Amherst, Mass. And what would happen to the person who found *Siphlonisca* again? "Among the small group of cognoscenti around the world, there would be those who know that Joe Blow found *Siphlonisca* in 1980," says Downs with a chuckle. "Everyone who reads *Eatonia*—and what a crowd that must be!—would surely know it. Joe Blow wouldn't be elected President of the United States, but he might get a free ticket to the next International Conference on Ephemeroptera, of which there already have been two."

Newsflash: In the slow-moving world of aquatic entomology, word has just filtered out that Dr. K.E. Gibbs informed the Third International Conference on Ephemeroptera in Winnipeg last year that she had found *Siphlonisca aerodromia* in abundance in central Maine. Says Downs, "My life is far from ruined. I would still like to find it myself. It's like climbing Mount Everest."

Driven as these insect trackers are, perhaps no angler is more bugs about aquatic insects than Schmookler. Now 34, he has been a collector since he was five. He also used to collect safes, but, as he says, "They got too heavy." For a long while Schmookler specialized and dealt in butterflies as a sideline, but eight years ago, when his growing lust for aquatic insects could no longer be controlled, he sold his cigarette and candy vending-machine route, which just happened to parallel several trout streams in New York and Connecticut, to turn over rocks full-time. Up to his knees in a stream, he will bend down and suddenly yank a 50-pound rock from the bottom to look at the startled creatures still clinging to the underside with their claws. "Love it, love it!" he exults. Although Schmookler has a license to collect aquatic insects in streams officially classified as trout water in New York (a number of states require just such a license or a permit), he often collects in non-trout waters that have been junked up with debris because he can use the trash to advantage. Hellgrammite larvae dearly love to crawl under a tattered mattress on a stream bank to pupate, and several hundred nymphs of the stoneflies *Taeniopteryx nivalis* and *Brachyptera fasciata* can be found around the tubes in an old TV set where leaves have gathered.

Under the corporate names of Visual Life Sciences, Inc. and 20th Century Angler, Ltd., Schmookler has found a way to make his avocation pay off. He embeds and sells individually identified specimens of stoneflies, mayflies, caddis and other aquatic denizens in clear polyacrylic blocks for $6.75 each. Entombed in these transparent mausoleums, with their natural colors still vivid and their legs extended, the insects provide flytiers with a far more accurate model to imitate than any two-dimensional photograph or even a soggy specimen adrift in a vial of alcohol." A stack of them makes an instant reference library for a fisherman," Schmookler says. "He doesn't have to worry about collecting, breaking his own leg or breaking off a leg of a specimen." The polyacrylic concoction is of Schmookler's own devising, and recently he embedded a parrot in it without loss of plumage color. "I could do a mouse," he confided to a friend. "I could do a human being."

A couple of years ago, Schmookler started his own mayfly experiment in a stream on a friend's property in the Catskills. He catches pregnant females of *Ephemera simulans* and *E. varia* and has them deposit their eggs in cages made from mosquito netting, which he then places in the stream next to a silty bank. "When the eggs hatch into nymphs, they immediately go through the netting into the silt, where they will be safe from predators," he says. "In nature, many of them would be eaten before they could get into the silt. When they emerge as adults to mate and lay eggs, the trout will have a chance at them." Inasmuch as *E. simulans* and *E. varia* use less oxygen than many other species because they are silt burrowers and because they are better able to withstand heat, Schmookler sees possibilities of stocking them in trout streams that have lost their mayfly hatches.

Schmookler's own fly tying and fishing have improved greatly as a result of collecting. "I don't claim to be a great fisherman," he says, "but I have all the confidence in the world. I know just how to tie my nymphs and just how and where to fish them in a stream. I know what's going on *down there*."

One evening a couple of months ago, Schmookler was at home happily looking over his collection of Plecoptera when the phone rang. The caller was a woman taking a political survey.

"Are you a Republican?" she asked.

"No," replied Schmookler just before the line went click, "I'm a Plecopteran."

Another newsflash: the manager of the Kentucky Fried Chicken restaurant in Port Jervis has put up curtains.

—AUGUST 18, 1980

Spitmouth Puffers in the Living Room

Bob Abplanalp

When Bob Abplanalp was a boy, he used to go black fishing in Long Island Sound. Other kids might wear themselves out chasing fiddler crabs for bait, but Abplanalp got a better idea from his father. At low tide he sank a row of tin cans in the mud and herded the crabs toward them. Crabs fell in by the dozens.

Ingenuity runs in the family, and Bob picked up a good share of it. Faced with a challenge nowadays, ideas light up in his head, not so much like the bulb in the funnies but more like an exploding theater marquee. He holds more than 100 patents, and 20 years ago he invented the first reliable aerosol valve, the gismo that goes "sssssst" on top of a pressurized can. The company that this single invention started, Precision Valve Corporation of Yonkers, N.Y., now manufactures more than half the aerosol valves used in the world. Not many inventors make money on their brainchildren, but Abplanalp has more than made up for the unfortunate saps who have failed. He is the sole owner of Precision Valve, and last year the company grossed more than $50 million.

With no stockholders due an accounting, Abplanalp has been able to do as he pleases with the profits, and as a result Precision Valve has flipped over fish. By way of example, subsidiaries of the company run a unique trout fishing preserve and hatchery in the Catskills, are planning to raise and market hitherto expensive tropical marine fish for home aquarists and own almost a dozen islands in the northern Bahamas, including Walker's Cay, one of the finest big game fishing camps in the world.

Now 47, Abplanalp is a burly 6-footer built along the lines of a beer hall bouncer. His manner is affable and down to earth, and his employees call him Bob. His idea of a good time is to spend the day fishing and the evening playing poker with friends, such as Joe Trombetta, an old schoolmate who is a vice-president of Precision Valve, and Bill Ruppel, a former mate on Abplanalp's sport-fisherman who now runs the trout operation. One of Abplanalp's closest friends is President Nixon, who sometimes vacations at Grand Cay, seven miles from Walker's. Abplanalp, who acquired Grand Cay on a long term lease, has enlarged a house there for the President's use, but he makes it a rule not to discuss his friendship with Nixon because, he says, the President has a right to personal privacy.

Of Swiss extraction, he was born and raised in the Bronx. His father Hans, known as Pop around Precision Valve, was a machinist. After settling in the U.S. he began fishing in Long Island Sound and often took his son along. At home Pop spent hour upon hour teaching Bob all there was to know about machine tools. "When I was 7, I knew how to run a lathe," Abplanalp says. "My father and I took care of all the household repairs." Pop earned a comfortable living, and Bob went to Fordham Prep, a Jesuit school, and then to Villanova to study engineering. He stayed only two years, returning to the Bronx, not unhappily, to open his own machine shop, R. H. Abplanalp & Co.

World War II had just started and, as Abplanalp jokes, "I thought I was going to be a war profiteer." Before the profits started rolling in, Pearl Harbor was bombed and he spent three years in the Army where he served with a railroad battalion in France.

After the war Abplanalp went back to his machine shop and all but starved for the next several years. "There were many weeks when I was lucky to take $10 out of the operation," he says. "There were times when I wished I could have gotten the hell out and found a job." He hung on by making all kinds of parts for a variety of machinery, ranging from lace knitting looms to electronic gear. Then one June afternoon in 1949 his luck took a turn.

A washing machine customer, John J. Baessler, stopped by with a problem. He had started distributing a line of aerosol products, which were new at the time, but buyers complained that the valves leaked. Baessler wondered if they could not be made reliable. "After we talked for several hours," Abplanalp recalls, "I said, 'Leave all the stuff here and I'll look at it.' I did and I got absorbed in the problem." For three months Abplanalp devoted himself to aerosol valves. He dissected them to find out why and how they leaked. Having his own machine shop gave him a great advantage. He was able to design a new part, cut it himself and test it immediately. If it did not work, he tried another approach. Baessler introduced Abplanalp to Fred Lodes, who was working for a chemical company, and Lodes gave him a crash course in the chemistry and physics of aerosol containers. By September 1949, Abplanalp had invented a new and dependable valve, made of seven simple metal, plastic and rubber parts, for which he was later granted U.S. patent #2,631,814. That same month, Abplanalp, Baessler and Lodes formed the Precision Valve Corporation as equal partners. Sales were meteoric, and Abplanalp was eventually able to buy out his partners by 1962. Precision Valve now has 2,000 employees, plants in Yonkers and Chicago, additional plants in Mexico, Canada, France, Argentina, Japan, West Germany, South Africa and Australia and a licensee in Great Britain.

Precision Valve's entry into the world of fish came more or less by accident four years ago when a company attorney urged

Abplanalp to buy an Adirondack estate on Tupper Lake that belonged to another client. Abplanalp bought the place with the idea of using it as a retreat for Precision Valve employees or customers. Then he wondered if trout could not be raised there. He formed a subsidiary, Adirondack Fisheries, but for various reasons no trout were ever raised there. Instead, two years ago Adirondack Fisheries acquired a privately owned trout hatchery at Eldred in the Catskill Mountains.

The hatchery was enlarged, and public fishing ponds, now stocked with brook, brown, golden, rainbow and tiger trout, were dug. Admission is 50¢, with an additional charge of $2 a pound for each trout caught. A fisherman may sell his catch back to the preserve for $1 a pound or trade his fish for smoked trout. No fishing license is required, and there is no closed season. A snack bar and a picnic grove are on the premises, and attendants are on hand to teach youngsters the art of fly casting.

Although the pond fishing at Eldred was an instant success, Abplanalp realized it was not the sort of angling to attract the dry fly purist. Last spring Adirondack Fisheries opened a half-mile stretch of Halfway Brook, which flows through the preserve, for fly fishing only. Trout average more than a pound, and no more than 10 licensed fishermen a day are allowed on the stream. The charge is a flat $30 a day per angler with a limit of 10 fish.

Inasmuch as the Eldred hatchery can easily raise a quarter of a million trout a year, Abplanalp has plans to establish similar preserves elsewhere. He also has toyed with the idea of shipping live fish to markets and restaurants. "We cannot market frozen fish in competition with trout hatcheries in Denmark or Colorado," he says, "but we can compete delivering live fish. Live fish command a premium because people know they're fresh." For the past couple of years a truck has made a number of trial runs transporting live fish from the Catskills to Yonkers.

When the experiment began, Abplanalp thought about the possibilities of a one-piece aquarium unit to carry the fish. His thinking did not stop there. It so happens that Precision Valve has two sub-sidiaries, U.S. Thermo-Plastics and Tiros, which manufacture plastics that the corporation uses to make valves. These subsidiaries are headed by Dr. Hans Hafner, a nephew of Baessler and a scientist Abplanalp calls "one of the world's great polymer chemists." Perhaps Hafner and the subsidiaries could make aquariums not just for trout but for tropical marine fish as well. Regular aquarium tanks made of metal corrode when filled with salt water. There was another problem. A saltwater aquarium, whether made of plastic or metal, is usually a chancy affair, primarily because the self-contained water can become polluted. The whole tankful then goes bad, and everything dies, from sea anemones to angelfish. As a result the market for tropical saltwater aquariums has never come near to realizing its potential.

Abplanalp thought the problems could be solved. While Hafner and the subsidiaries worked on the basic tank, Abplanalp hired a couple of marine biologists, Dr. Henry Feddern and John Sabol of the Institute of Marine Sciences (since renamed Rosenstiel School of Marine and Atmospheric Sciences) at the University of Miami, and put them to tinkering in a lab at the Precision Valve headquarters in Yonkers. They tested plastic filters and protein skimmers that would automatically remove the wastes. The experiments were a success, and Abplanalp plans to start manufacturing a complete saltwater aquarium unit next spring. All a hobbyist need do is plunk down his money for a unit (a 20-gallon aquarium should cost between $50 and $60), take it home, plug it in and stock it with fish to have instant Caribbean right in his living room.

When it became obvious that a foolproof saltwater unit could be built, Abplanalp still was not satisfied. "What good does it do to sell a unit like this if you don't have fish to put into it?" he asked. There, seemingly, was another problem: most saltwater tropicals have to be netted in the wild and shipped vast distances, with all sorts of attendant dangers, and they are usually expensive and beyond the purse of the average hobbyist, the very customer Abplanalp wants to reach. For instance, the blue angelfish, a common species in the Caribbean, sells for as much as $15 in the aquarium stores of New York City. Abplanalp told Feddern and Sabol to see if some species could be bred in captivity. After scoring a breakthrough in Yonkers with the neon goby, they have since moved down to Miami where Precision Valve is setting up a pilot hatchery.

Two years ago, when Abplanalp first thought of breeding tropical fish, he looked for a native setting where they could be raised in great numbers. He began buying islands in the northern Bahamas. Then he discovered that the islands he was acquiring were zoned against commercial use, and, moreover, the Bahamian government was skeptical of the whole venture, especially since Abplanalp had unknowingly hired a consultant who was wanted for taking protected fish from Bahama waters. To allay fears, Abplanalp discontinued the consultant's services and turned to scientists at the Institute of Marine Sciences for advice. As a result, Abplanalp was able to overcome the skepticism of the Bahamian government, and a new Precision Valve subsidiary bought nearby Walker's Cay, which was zoned for commercial use since it had been a game fishing resort for more than 30 years. "Walker's Cay will serve as the basic site of this whole concept of saltwater fish raising and breeding," Abplanalp says. "We'll be using our own breed stock. We're not going to rape the reefs or exploit the islands. I think this breeding will become a new industry for the Bahamas, and I like the idea of developing something new and different."

Werner Geiser, a former curator of fish at the Zurich Zoo, is in charge of the Bahamian breeding operations. It is coincidence that Geiser happens to be Swiss. Abplanalp simply hired the best man available and, in landlocked Zurich, Geiser demonstrated that he had a truly wet thumb by successfully breeding and raising two dozen different species of marine tropical fish for the first time anywhere. "Ya, I bred, yiick, two dozen, ya, about two dozen," says Geiser, who is just learning English. "Puffer fish I breed first in der world. Den der spitmouth puffer from Zambézia." If Abplanalp has any fears, it is that Geiser will not live to complete his work. An enthusiast of nature in the raw, Geiser is fond of chumming for sharks at night in the harbor at Walker's and then diving in to watch them feed.

When Abplanalp bought Walker's Cay, he was uncertain about what to do with the fishing camp. It had been run as a sort of "mom and pop" operation and was in need of repair. After thinking things over and doing a lot of fishing himself, he decided to enlarge the accommodations and make them plush. The camp will reopen on March 1, 1970, and the daily rates are $35 single and $45 double, European plan. A one-day sport-fisherman charter is $130, 22-foot inboards and outboards are $70 and Boston Whalers are $35 a day. Cost of all boats includes guide, tackle and bait.

Without question Walker's is a spectacular island. One hundred acres in size, it is 50 miles to the east of the Gulf Stream, and the weather is delightfully cool. Twelve world records have been set at Walker's, and some of the best fishing is to be had only five minutes away from the old hotel. An angler can wade nearby flats for bonefish, cast off the reefs for snappers, jig in the deeper holes for groupers or troll at sea for blue marlin, white marlin, sailfish, dolphin, wahoo, bonito and bluefin tuna.

A year ago last summer, while trying to figure out what to do with the fishing camp, Abplanalp landed a 535-pound blue marlin. As pleasant as this was, his favorite fishing at Walker's is to troll live bait for wahoo or king mackerel. Just before the fish strikes, Abplanalp can see the bait squirm, moving the outrigger; when the fish does strike, it often leaps 25 feet into the air. "Getting the slack out of the line and setting the hook then takes some doing," says Abplanalp. "I don't know of any fishing to beat it."

This past summer Abplanalp spent more than two months on Walker's, supervising enlargement of the camp, the building of breeding pens and improving the airstrip. One major problem was finding a new source of fresh water, and Abplanalp set himself to the task of seeing what he could devise. To be brief, he has invented what he believes to be a revolutionary way of desalting seawater, and the gismo he thought up can convert salt water into fresh water at a very low cost. Abplanalp's invention, for which he is now seeking patents, obviously has great potential, not just for Walker's but in providing fresh water for arid parts of the world, such as Southern California and the warring Middle East. If it works out as Abplanalp hopes it will, the invention will be one of the greatest boons to mankind since the wheel.

Is Bob Abplanalp, boy crab catcher turned aerosol tycoon, happy about all this? Yes, and maybe no. "You know," he says with a sigh, "I've been so damn busy working on this freshwater thing that I just haven't had time to do any serious fishing."

—DECEMBER 8, 1969

"You Spigotty Anglease?"

James Joyce's
Finnegans Wake

Poaching is illegal, but I am going to trespass upon the "stream of consciousness," the private preserve of the world-wide army of academics who have made an industry out of attempting to explain the most inexplicable work of fiction ever written in any language, James Joyce's *Finnegans Wake,* the so-called *Work in Progress* on which he labored for 17 years. What I have to say amounts to a revolutionary declaration about the *Wake,* as Joyceans simply call it, and my declaration is this: Fish and fishing, fly fishing in particular, constitute a major theme, indeed *the major theme,* in the novel. The evidence that I have discovered is so overwhelming that the *Wake* must be considered as belonging in great part, albeit a bizarre part, to angling literature.

I am amazed that this fish theme has escaped the army of Joyceans, particularly those who are both Irish and anglers, to say nothing of members of the hundreds of James Joyce and *Finnegans Wake* societies throughout the world. For instance, under the leadership of Murray Gross, the members of The *Finnegans Wake* Society of New York, gather above the Gotham Book Mart at six in the evening on the fourth Wednesday of every month, and there they take five years to go through the book, reading every word aloud and commenting upon the meaning.

I got started on the *Wake* accidentally in 1996 while engaged on my own work in progress, *Flagrante Delicto Fly Fishing.* I was doing research on Preston Jennings, the first American author to codify scientifically the aquatic insects that trout eat so that anglers could imitate them with artificial flies. Jennings wrote *A Book of Trout Flies,* published in 1935, four years before the *Wake,* and in the course of my research, I chanced to run across the photograph of Jennings shown here. It seemed similar to another photograph I had seen before. I searched my mind, and then I remembered that it was this one of Joyce shown next to it.

Preston Jennings   *James Joyce*

The resemblance between the two men is extraordinary. They have identical hair lines, hair cuts, facial configurations, eyeglasses, noses, mustaches, and mouth shapes, and both hold an optical object in the right hand. Recalling that Vladimir Nabokov, whom I once accompanied on a butterfly chase in Arizona, maintained that Salvador Dali was Norman Rockwell's twin brother who had been kidnapped by Gypsys, I thought that I would write a facetious article, based on these photographs, stating that the Joyce and Jennings had been separated at birth, even though Joyce was born in Ireland in 1882, 11 years before Jennings was born in Virginia.

I felt that I was in a unique position to make this jocular judgement by right of apostolic succession, a literal laying on of hands. I shook the hand of Art Flick who shook the hand of Jennings, and I shook the hand of my dear friend, the late Dr. Hans Kraus, the celebrated alpinist and father of sports medicine, who shook the hand of Joyce. In fact, I once exclaimed to Hans, "Just think, James Joyce, your English teacher! He taught your family English in Trieste and then after Italy entered the first World War, he was your English teacher in Zurich! He used to read to you from *Ulysses* while he was writing it! Hans, James Joyce, your English teacher!" To which Hans replied, "Ja, he dint doo a goot chob, dit he?"

In college 50 years ago, I found the *Wake* impossible to read, but I knew now that I would have to read it through, no matter the effort, in the hope I could find one or two references to fish—just a couple would suffice, dear God—to justify my jocular judgement that Joyce and Jennings were identical twins. But before I waded into the *Wake,* I knew from my stock of general knowledge that Joyce and Jennings, in addition to their remarkable facial resemblance, had a number of quirks in common.

Both were vexed by former acolytes who wrote a book. For Jennings, the acolyte was Flick, who wrote *The Streamside Guide,* a popular work that Jennings thought stole the thunder from *A Book of Trout Flies.* For Joyce the disdained acolyte was Robert McAlmon, who wrote *Being Geniuses Together,* an account of expatriate life in Paris, that Joyce said should have been called *The Office Boy's Revenge.* Moreover, Joyce and Jennings each had three mental hangups. For Joyce, they were a fear of dogs, a fear of thunderstorms and a loathing for red wine. For Jennings, the three hangups were the unorthodox beliefs that the Royal Coachman, a preposterously gaudy artificial fly actually imitated the mayfly *Isonychia bi-*

color; that returning Atlantic salmon feed in freshwater; and that trout could not see a 2x leader turned purple with Tintex dye.

Finally, Jennings and Joyce both had water on the brain. In addition to fishing all the rivers that he could for trout and Atlantic salmon, Jennings was actually in the water business: he was a sales engineer for the Filtrine Manufacturing Company that dealt in bottled water.

Although Joyce never fished so far as I can determine, two friends recalled that he was absolutely bonkers about rivers. Dr. Carola Gieddion-Welcker of Zurich wrote that Joyce "observed the life of waters. River-nature, river-myth merged with that 'river-civilization' which seemed to him fundamental. Repeatedly he sought out regions with rivers, the lovely idylls of Luxembourg, the harsh beauty of the Dauphin near Grenoble with its rivers, woods, and mountains, or the broad epic flow of the rivers in France. Even the rushing of little Wolf Creek behind our garden could charm him. Referring to this little creek he implored us never to give up a house that was suffused with such a sound of nature. 'Here I experienced an illusion of old age,' he added ironically. To him the confluence of the Limmat and Sihl was an elemental and dramatic meeting, and when I once wanted to take a picture of him in Zurich, it had to be exactly at this spot and with this river background."

Similarly, Paul Leon, who assisted with the proofs of the *Wake,* wrote that whenever Joyce "went on holiday, he immediately looked for a river, a stream, or even a brook, and his first walks led him along its banks. How many hours we passed together, watching the calm flow of the Seine from the Pont de l'Alma or the Pont Royal!"

For the *Wake* Joyce coined words, took words from 62 languages and dialects, and inserted words within words, with every word "bound over to carry three score and ten toptypiscal readings." He advised the reader to "Wipe your glosses with what you know."

Wits its potpourri of words and phrases, the *Wake* has been subjected to a medley of interpretations as to what it's really about. Indeed, as Louis O. Mink wrote in *Critical Essays on James Joyce's Finnegans Wake,* "Reading *Finnegans Wake* is somewhat like playing charades, with the mounting excitement that goes with the recognition that one is getting warm and the certainty and triumph when the answer is finally guessed. Every paragraph, almost every sentence, and most phrases and even single words rise from the page, signalling and gesturing, acting out a hidden meaning with body English, appealing to every resource to hint at some arcane allusion. From this standpoint, *Finnegans Wake* is a virtually inexhaustible game of solitaire charades, ready to play whenever you are."

Based on the number of references to Shakespeare and his words in the *Wake,* influential Joyceans claim that the Bard is the major theme, "the rock mass in which metal, fossils, gems are enclosed or embedded," to quote from Adaline Glasheen's *Third Census of Finnegans Wake.* They base this on the number of allusions to Shakespeare and his works, 300 all told in 625 pages of text, an average of 0.48 for every page. Indeed, in *The Western Canon,* Harold Bloom proclaims that Shakespeare "has always guided my reading of the *Wake.*"

Really? By my count, the number of allusions to fish and their watery world (200 to water alone) comes to at least 2,200, an average of 3.52 per page. From the very first word, "riverrun," the *Wake* is awash in fishy phrases, such as "Songster, angler, choreographer!", "compleat anglers," "And if you're not your bloater's kipper . . . you're rod, hook and sinker," "Holy eel and Sainted Salmon, chucking chub and ducking dace," "one man's fish and a dozen men's poissons," "catching trophies of the king's royal college of sturgeone by the armful to bake pike," "Flies do your float," "mother-in-waders," "Were these anglers or angelers?", "his own length of rainbow trout and taerts [young salmon] . . . devour his threescoreten of roach per lifeday, ay, and as many minnow a minute (the big mix, may Gibbet choke him!) was, like the salmon of his ladderleap," "What wouldn't I poach—the rent in my river-

side, my otther shoes, my beavery, honest!—ay, and melt my belt
for a dace feast of grannom with the finny ones, those happy grep-
pies in their minnowahaw, flashing down the swansway, leaps
ahead of the swift MacEels, the big Gilaroo redfellows and the
pursewinded carpers, rearin antis rood perches astench of me,"
"And whenever you're tingling in your trout," "crying stinking
fish," "The trout will be so fine at brookfisht," "It's only another
queer fish or other in Brinbrou's damned old trouchorous river
again," "Be trouz and wholetrouz!", "some blowfish out of school-
ing," "he would not hear a flip flap in all Finnyland," "he gaining
fish considerable," "By the unsleeping Solman Annadromus, ye
god of little pescies, nothing would stop me for mony makes multi-
mony like the brogues and the kishes," "bellyhooting fishdrunks,"
"my magic fluke," "leaving tealeaves for the trout," "fishngaman
fetched the mongafesh," "the way of all fish," "Splesh of hiss spalsh
springs your salmon," "Hake's haulin! Hook's fisk! Can you beat
it? Whawe! I say, can you bait it?" and "My herrings!"

The word play on the initials of the major male character, H. C.
Earwicker, sometimes have a fishy connotation, as in "Human Con-
ger Eel," "erst crafy hakemouth" and "Ear canny hare" (the hare's ear
is a trout fly). His wife, Anna Livia Plurabelle, personifies the River
Liffey that flows from the Wicklow Mountains to the Irish Sea and
whose delta smells of fish, while son Shem has a "trio of barbels" on
his chin, "a salmonkelt's thinskin," and "eelsblood in his cold toes."

Here and there, Joyce checks to see if the reader has caught on to
his angling game. Page 16: "You spigotty anglease?" In other
words, "You speak angling?" Page 485, "Are we speachin d'anglas
landadge . . . ?" Page 532: "Angleslachsen is spoken by Sall,"
which means, to me, "Angling language is spoken by us all." Added
touch: lachsen also stands for salmon because *lachs* is the German
for that fish.

All told in the *Wake,* the word fish itself occurs 85 times alone or
in combination, as in "fishy fable," which could be another title for

the book. Some of the combined words: "fishandblood," "fishmummer," "fishnetzeveil," "soulfisher," "wifish," "turfish," "Fisht," "Sickfish," "wangfish," "merfish," "streamfish," "fishabed," and "supperfishies," The *Wake* also has variations on the Latin for fish: "piscines," "pisciolinnies," "Piscisvendolor," "piscivore," "piscman," and "Pisk," while a fishy footnote reads: "Gee each owe tea eye smells fish. That's U." Deciphered, that means a letter from each word spells "ghoti," which in turn spells fish. Joyce got this from George Bernard Shaw who declared that ghoti spells fish when you pronounce the gh from enough, the o from women and the ti from nation. As for "That's U," "yu" is the Chinese for fish according to Roland McHugh's *Annotations to Finnegans Wake* (Johns Hopkins University Press, 2nd edition, 1978).

There are 100 references to salmonid fish and aspects of their life history, e.g., Atlantic, coho and chinook salmon, rainbow, brown, Dolly Varden ("dolly farting"), lake and sea trout, grayling (in English, French and German), spawn, ova, milt, redd, alevin, fry, parr, smolt, "troterella" (the Italian for little trout), grilse, kelt, gillaroo (an Irish trout with stomach muscles that can crush the shells of mollusks), and sockdologer (angling slang for a huge trout).

References to other species of fish, often multiple in number and in different languages, include ide, orf and oarfish (both in "orfishfellows"), argentine, scup, sennett, sergeant major, shiner, skate, skelly, rudd, cod, catfish, snook, mackerel, bullhead, spearing, lampern, sprat, taimen, scup, stickleback, stargazer, bass, turbot, tuna, jack, halibut, grenadier, squawfish, tang, tarpon, ling, crappie, drum, flounder, fusilier, lampern, gag, roach, haddock, gar, gudgeon, gunnell, shad, smelt, croaker, dab, darter, goby, ray, tope, shark, slippery dick, and fugu, embedded in "fuguall," or what a Japanese chef might say to diners dying after eating this potentially poisonous fish.

"Sour deans," "sourdine," and "sardinish" mean sardines. "Omulette" means omelet to Joyceans who contributed to McHugh's

Annotations. To me, "omulette" is an omelet that has two species of fish in it: *omul,* the Russian for the prized whitefish from Lake Baikal, and mullet. Joyceans gloss "Untie the gemman's fistiknots" as meaning untie the entanglements in a bride's nightdress made by bridesmaids. To me it means untie the gentleman's fishing knots. Joyceans read "greased lining" as greased lightning, but greased line fishing is a way of angling for salmon. Joyceans say that "Reefer was a wenchman" refers to the Taffy was a Welshman nursery rhyme, but wenchman is the common name of a reef fish, a snapper scientifically known as *Pristipomoides aquilonaris.*

"Swimmyease bladdhers" is a fish's swim bladder, while adipose, pectoral, pelvic and caudal are fins on salmonids. The word fin, alone or in combination, occurs at least 25 times, not counting the times Joyce embedded it in Finnegan. The *Wake* names angling methods: casting, skittering, dapping, legering, trolling, spinning, and paternostering, as well as natural and artificial flies: e.g., cinnamon quill, silver doctor, cowdung, hawthorn, palmer, variant, buzzer and creeper.

The *Wake* dwells most on a favorite food of trout, mayflies, the ephemerids. Joyce uses that word, plus nymph, dun, imago and spinner, all angling terms for mayflies in different life stages, as well as "Mayjaunties," in reference to the species with the common name of the Yellow May (*jaune* is the French for yellow). The scientific name of the Yellow May is *Heptagenia sulphurea,* and the *Wake* notes that "*maikar, has been sulphuring.*"

Angling authors abound, e.g., Izaak Walton is obvious in "any Wilt or Walt who would ongle her as Izaak did to the tickle of his rod"; "davors" is the angling poet Jo. Davors, a favorite of Walton; "Lang . . . Wurm" is a punning allusion to Andrew Lang, author of *Angling Sketches* and an editor of Walton; "rheadoromanscing" and "speckled trousers," could refer to Louis Rhead, editor of *The Speckled Brook Trout;* "Humphrey's unsolicited visitor, Davy" certainly refers to Sir Humphry Davy, who wrote *Salmonia, or Days of*

Fly Fishing; and "scrope" (stroke to Joyceans) is William Scrope, author of *Days and Nights of Salmon Fishing in the Tweed,* published in 1843. The book has a famous color plate, "Burning the Water," a night scene depicting three fishermen spearing salmon attracted by torchlight. The *Wake:* "burning water in the spearlight."

The phrase "scotcher grey, this is a davy" refers to George Scotcher, author of *The Fly Fisher's Legacy,* Sir Edward Grey, author of *Fly Fishing,* and Davy. Similarities in language indicate that Joyce took words and phrases from Grey's book published in 1899. The *Wake:* "Chuck a chum a chance." Grey: "a 'chuck and chance it' style." The "Itcher" and "test" in the *Wake* are the Itchen and Test rivers that Grey described fishing on holidays from the House of Commons. The "Coquette" in the *Wake* is the Coquet, the river that Grey fished in Northumberland where he lived. The *Wake:* "Northumberland Anglesey." To me that is Northumberland angler Grey. The *Wake:* "Up wi'yer whippy!" Grey: "no greater misery than to be using a whippy rod." The *Wake:* "Olive quill does it." Grey: "favourite dry flies . . . 1. Olive quill." A final point: Grey gives only two dates in his book, and one of them is June 16, 1894, precisely 10 years from "Bloomsday," the day in which the action in *Ulysses* takes place, a fact that would intrigue Joyce.

Also in the *Wake:* "Ausonius . . . gillie" is the Latin poet Decimus Magnus Ausonius, circa 310–393 A.D. A gillie is a fishing guide, and Ausonius's tenth Idyll, *Ad Mosselam,* a great favorite with Walton, is about fishing in the Moselle River. The poem is the first to use the words *Salar, Fario,* and *Esox lucius* later adopted in the scientific names for salmon, trout and pike. The *Wake:* "Was it *esox lucius* or *salmo ferax?"*

Anglican vicar Alfred Eaton was the 19th century author of two major treatises on mayflies, the ephemerids, and a sentence in the *Wake* reads in part, "He had eaten all the . . . ephemerids . . ." Eaten? Eaton? Ephemerids? A reach? Possibly, but Joyce made a practice of separating words or themes and then repeating them, much as a composer repeats chords or motifs in a composition. When young Hans Kraus asked Joyce how he could do this in writing, Joyce answered, "A man might eat kidneys in one chapter, suffer from a kidney disease in another, and one of his friends could be kicked in the kidneys in another chapter." Another possible reach, perhaps a far one: "hal" ends a word on page 582, and "ford" ends a word on the opposite page, thus making halford, as in Frederic Halford, the lord on high of the dry fly.

Here is another reach: "proving aye the death of ronaldses." Joyceans say this refers to the death of Roland in the *Chanson de Roland.* I suggest that it refers to Alfred Ronalds, the author of *The Fly Fisher's Entomology* who died of unknown causes. This landmark work in angling literature went through numerous editions after publication in 1936, but despite its success Ronalds emigrated to Australia in the 1850s where his fate and death remain a mystery. Coincidentally, Jennings became known as "the American Ronalds" with the publication of *A Book of Trout Flies.*

Surprise, the very name of Jennings is in the *Wake*! Its inclusion may be what Jung called "synchronicity," a meaningful coincidence. Even so, I must note that in *A Book of Trout Flies* Jennings mentions streamers, polar bear hair (used in tying streamers) as well as the Esopus, his favorite trout stream, and the Ausable, both in New York. In the *Wake,* Joyce mentions "streamers," "polarbeeber hair" (note well, hair, not fur), as well as "esophagous" and "auspicable." Was Joyce aware of Jennings' book, and if so, did he use it as a source?

Joyceans say "Lochlunn" is from Lochlann, a Scandinavian landlubber. To my mind it could also stand for a loch, a lake, and William James Lunn, river keeper for the Houghton Club on the Test and the subject of J.W. Hills 1936 biography, *River Keeper.* Hewitt, a name used by Robert Emmet according to Joyceans, could also refer to Edward Ringwood Hewitt, the great American trout and salmon fisherman and author of a half dozen books on the subject.

The most widely known fact about the *Wake* is that it contains the names of at least a thousand rivers and other bodies of water, e.g., "Dove," "hudson," "missus, seepy, and sewery," "muddy terranean," "Sassqueehenna," "O'Delawarr," "hat . . . peak" (Hot Creek), "canoedler" (Canoe), "damazon" "der went" (Derwent), "kennet," "Animas," "sacco," "wabbash," "Amoor" (Amur), "usking" (Usk), "Shoebenacaddie," "Tombigby," "Saint Lawrence," "trinity," "moos" (Moose), "Snakeshead," "dneepers," "platteau," "wyerye" (Wye), "gangres" (Ganges), "Suchcaughtwan" (Saskatchewan), "Yokan" (Yukon), "coneywink" (Conewango), "absantee" (Santee), "dee," "bow," "Wendawanda" (Wende and Wandle), "Zambosy," to name only a pittance. In addition, I have found other rivers that Joyceans have not identified, most notably the Frying Pan, "praying fan" and "freiung pfann."

Yet all this absolutely baffles Joyceans. As James Atherton declared, "nobody has ever been able to suggest what purpose is served by this inclusion of names."

Hey, *Wake* watchers, wake up! Fish live in water. Have an ephiphany on me.

—JULY 23, 2000

Nomen Piscis est Morone Saxatilis— And It Is Best Not to Argue About It

When I was a boy, it was my luck to hang out with kids who devoured *The Sporting News* and could reel off batting averages of players from the majors to the Three-I League. As an adult, it has been my lot to find myself surrounded by botanists, zoologists and knowledgeable fishermen who derive considerable delight from reciting the scientific names of plants and animals. A largemouth bass is *Micropterus salmoides,* and when a mayfly hatch is on, knowing trout anglers speak of *Ephemera guttulata* as readily as my childhood friends talked of Joe DiMaggio.

I guess because I have spent so much time with people who rattle off these exotic terms, many of them stick in my mind like the names of certain TV newscasters. For years I have been trying to shake my memory free of Sander Vanocur. I haven't seen him on television for quite a long time, but his name just won't go away. It seems I am equally taken with the bilateral symmetry of Sander Vanocur and the binomial nomenclature established by an 18th century Swede, Carl von Linné, who in the spirit of things Latinized his name to Carolus Linnaeus.

The idea of using scientific names instead of common names, such as bass or mayfly, is to allow scientists anywhere in the world to identify species exactly and to place them in relationship to other forms of life. The right to name a species belongs to the person who first describes it in print. That sounds simple, but it is complicated by the fact that botany, bacteriology and zoology have separate codes for nomenclature. And in zoology there are disputes over who named what first. There is actually a periodical entitled *Opinions and Declarations Rendered by the International Commission on Zoological Nomenclature.* As a kid I had no way of guessing that someday I would be more interested in it than in *The Sporting News.*

Scientific names ideally are supposed to be reasonably simple and descriptive. The striped skunk is *Mephitis mephitis,* which means "stink stink." Some scientific names even have come to be used as common names, among them hippopotamus and chrysanthemum. But despite the strictures, there are plenty of tongue twisters, including my favorite, *Leucophthalmoechinogammarus crassus,* a crustacean from Lake Baikal.

I have a friend, Dr. Dominick J. Pirone, who is the director of the environmental studies program at Manhattan College. Without using any reference books, he can identify and give the scientific names of 5,000 insects. And his expertise hardly stops there. When I first met Dom, we collected fish together. "*Menidia menidia!*" he would exclaim at the sight of a silversides. He was especially enamored of collecting near sewer outlets, and while I would gag, he would paw his way through strands of algae, giving them their Latin names as he went. Crowds would occasionally gather while Pirone was so joyously occupied, and inevitably an onlooker would step forward to ask Dom who he was and what he was doing. Dom would whip out his card, and there printed beneath his name was COLLECTOR OF WORLDWIDE ORTHOPTERA, ESPECIALLY THE PHASMATIDAE. Orthoptera is the order that includes roaches, grasshoppers, crickets and Phasmatidae, or walkingsticks, bizarre creatures that look like twigs with legs.

Dom, who is now 39, began soaking up scientific names at the age of three, under the tutelage of his Uncle Pat—Dr. P.P. Pirone, a recently retired plant pathologist at the New York Botanical Garden. Uncle Pat has a species of fungus named in his honor, and a horticulturist called a variety of cultivated tree "Pirone's ash," sudden mention of which always provokes gasps at ladies' garden clubs. There also is a worm, *Lumbricus pironei,* named in honor of the family. "Some years ago, my cousin Joe, who is now a psychology professor, and I were camping in a tent for a week near Kingston, N.Y.," says Don. "I was collecting a subspecies of butterfly called *Lycaena phlaeas americana,* the American copper. Joe was there chasing some girl. He was very sloppy—he's half Irish—and he would throw his underwear on the ground every night. When we got home, his mother dumped out his drawers to do the laundry, and there was a red, white and blue worm. His mother got scared, and his father thought Joe had become infected with some internal parasite and shipped the worm off to Cornell in alcohol. It turned out to be a new species of earthworm, and it was named for Joe."

I am an avid striped bass fisherman, and back in the 1960s, when I was doing research for a book on the Hudson River, I was shocked to learn from Dr. C. Lavett Smith of The American Museum of Natural History that the scientific name for the striper, *Roccus saxatillis,* had just been changed to *Morone saxatilis.* I was more than shocked; I was outraged. *Roccus,* dog Latin for rocks, was an appropriate name for striped bass, which like to hang around rocks. It was one scientific name that every surf caster knew by heart. The *Salt Water Sportsman* once ran an article with the headline WHAT MAKES ROCCUS RUN, and readers instantly knew what the article was about. *Roccus* was close to becoming like hippopotamus.

Dr. Smith told me that after exhaustive research some scientists had taken striped bass out of the genus *Roccus* and put it, along with kindred fish such as the white perch, in the genus *Morone,* because that was the name originally used for those fish ages ago. Therefore,

Morone had priority under the rules of zoological nomenclature. And, Smith went on, the change to *Morone* had already been approved by the Committee on Names of Fishes, composed of members of the American Fisheries Society and the American Society of Ichthyologists and Herpetologists. He told me that if I wanted to protest this change I would have to write an elaborate brief for presentation to the International Commission on Zoological Nomenclature, which meets only once every five years. To put it bluntly, I didn't have a prayer. At least, I was not alone in my outrage. Susan Smith, a biologist and artist with the National Marine Fisheries Service, wrote a poem entitled *Taxonomic Tragedy,* which reads in part:

> *Oh,* Roccus saxatilis *is a name we'll surely miss.*
> *The culprit is, I'm sad to say, a taxonomic twist.*
> *Yes,* Morone's *now the genus name I never figured why,*
> *But when that old name* Roccus *goes*
> *I'm sure I'm going to cry.*
> *Why,* Roccus *cracks right off the tongue!*
> *Like speed and strength and size!*
> *While* Morone *kind of rolls around*
> *Then gives a sigh and dies.*

In my book on the Hudson, I noted that *Morone* was now the generic name, although no one knew what *Morone* meant. I received a letter from a reader, Bert Kruse of Clear Lake, Iowa, who wrote, "You stated that no one knows what *Morone* means. Webster notes it's New Latin, meaning 'type genus.'"

I seized on this and wrote to Dr. Smith: "Does this mean we still have a chance of going back to *Roccus* since *Morone* is obviously a scientific term in itself and not really a generic? After all, *Type Genus saxatilis* is a bit stupid for the striper (or any fish)."

Dr. Smith replied: "In regard to this business of the derivation of *Morone,* I'm quite sure what your correspondent is referring to is the fact that *Morone* has been used as a type genus of a family of fishes, which, of course, is the Moronidae and which we are temporarily considering Percichthyidae.

"Jordan and Evermann, who looked into such matters, said the name is unexplained, and a casual perusal through some lexicons suggests it may have come from the same Greek word as our word moron, meaning stupid or foolish. There is also a possibility it is involved in the stem of the word mulberry, which is the genus *Morus.*

"All this is academic, however, because under the International Code of Zoological Nomenclature it makes no difference what it means, and even if it meant type genus it would still be usable. Article 18 of the International Code states that 'a genus—or species-group name—once established cannot afterwards be rejected, even by its own author, because of inappropriateness.' As a matter of fact, they give the generic name of paddlefish as a horrible example— *Polyodon* means 'many teeth' and, of course, the paddlefish is toothless. So for the time being I think we're safe to stay with *Morone.*"

I passed Smith's letter on to Kruse, and he replied: "I don't know about the paddlefish being a bad example because the young of *Polyodon spathula* have a great many teeth indeed and sharp ones."

Not toothless! I was speechless and let the matter rest.

—OCTOBER 27, 1975

"I Am a Bit of a Fanatic"

Cus D'Amato

When Floyd Patterson was heavyweight champion, his eccentric manager, Cus D'Amato, often disappeared mysteriously. For weeks on end no one knew where to look. Rumors flew that D'Amato was in Detroit or Spokane or Indianapolis lining up some palooka for Floyd to flatten in two.

Now that Patterson is no longer champion, the truth may be told about those mysterious trips: D'Amato had gone f-i-s-h-i-n-g. Cus has been fishing for the past few years, and he has entered into it with all the zest, verve and passion that he used to bring to boxing. "I am," he whispers in conspiratorial fashion, "a bit of a fanatic."

Cus is putting it mildly. Never has there been such an angler as he. He plots against the bass in much the same way he used to hatch schemes to foil Jim Norris. He talks to the fish. He shouts at the fish. He buys lures by the ton. He dreams about fish. He lives to fish. Fishing is all he cares for. "It's a good thing I didn't fish when I was a kid," he says. "I never would have done anything else."

Cus began fishing in 1960, when he went to upstate New York to get away from the aftermath of the Rosensohn investigation. But in the country, he became bored. A kindly friend suggested that he pass the time fishing. Cus went, and he liked it. He did not catch

anything the first day (neither did his friend), but he was just fascinated casting a lure with a spinning rod. "I didn't even know what a
lure was!" he exclaims. On the second day out, he caught a smallmouth bass. That did it. "Catching a bass," Cus says, "is like getting
bit by a mosquito with malaria. You get a disease."

The friend could not fish the next day, but he arose at sunrise to
drive Cus to a nearby creek. "I was all alone," Cus recalls, "and then
in a while it began to get dark. I thought I was gonna get caught in a
thunderstorm. I began to get the gear together, and then, suddenly, it
dawned on me. It was gettin' darker and darker! It wasn't a thunderstorm. It was nighttime! The whole day gone! I lost a whole day in
my life without realizin' it. I wondered what happened. I thought I
was ill. A day went by, it seemed like an hour!

"When I saw my friend, he laughed and said, 'This is normal.
This is what happens to people who like fishin'.' Holy smokes, I
said to myself, I better be careful. If I do this every day, one day I'll
look in the mirror and see an old man. You don't know how many
times I've been in bed and wondered whether this is an illness. A
particular type of illness, where you get pleasure, not pain, where
you get reinfected each time. Where you want to get reinfected!"

When D'Amato goes fishing now, he wears everything: jacket,
creel, hat, the whole bit. "If I look like a nonfisherman," he says, "the
fish won't want to be caught. They have pride. So I remove this possible area of resistance. The fish look up, and they say, 'Ah, there's a
real fisherman.' " Should the fish balk, Cus pleads with them. "I sort
of talk it up," he says. "I invent stories for them. I think all the fish, all
the adult fish, are tellin' all the others not to bite. Somebody must be
instructin' them! If you go out there with confidence and proceed
with enthusiasm, you'll get better results. When I'm there, it seems
normal." When Cus lands a fish, he will call out to the bass below,
"Hey! He needs some company! C'mon up here with him." Asked
why he does this, he explains, "The fish don't care about me. They

care about one another. I try to appeal to their emotional side. Hey, people are gonna think I'm crazy altogether."

D'Amato loves tackle almost as much as he loves fishing. At last count, he had 34 rods, 20 reels and countless boxes of lures, in which were entangled 1,500 Mepps spinners. He's just crazy about Mepps spinners. When the world is troubling him and a trip upstate is impossible, he will quietly close his office door, haul forth the loot from a closet and gloat over it. "My vice," he confides.

D'Amato does not dare to walk past a tackle shop with money in his pocket. Yet he cannot keep away. When he walks into a shop, the salesmen shout, "He's here!" Who he is they do not know. All they know is that he reappears periodically to buy out the stock. "They act like I'm a character," Cus says, a trifle irked. He is such an easy mark that the salesmen now try to talk him out of buying things. They have to keep in practice some way. "How much is that?" Cus asked the other day at Herman's, a Manhattan sporting goods store, his hands greedily grabbing and encircling an imported Swedish reel.

"You don't want that," the clerk said, reaching for it hastily.

"Why not?" Cus demanded, affronted.

"Because it's for trolling, and you said you didn't troll."

"How do you know I won't?" Cus asked.

"I don't," the clerk said, "but why don't you wait until you do?" By now, the clerk's fingers had worked their way around the reel, and with a triumphant cry he snatched it away from a defeated D'Amato.

"I guess you're right," Cus said sadly.

D'Amato's fascination with fishing has led him into the larger world of nature. Not long ago, he told a friend, "I've been hearing about a guy I want to learn about. I've heard a lot of quotes, and after I heard his name with the fourth or fifth one, I said to myself that I gotta know this guy better."

"Who's the guy?" the friend asked.

"Thoreau," Cus said.

"Thoreau!" the friend exclaimed.

"You know him?" Cus asked excitedly.

The friend explained that Thoreau had died 100 years ago. Then he went on somewhat to talk about Thoreau's philosophy. D'Amato was entranced. It was, Cus said, too bad that Thoreau was dead. He would have liked to have known him personally. "You probably would have become friends, Cus," the friend said. "Ah," Cus said, "you're just makin' fun of me."

But the chances are that if Thoreau were alive today, he and Cus would be friends indeed. Both would have at least one thing in common—an unusual approach to life. Cus bore this out recently while getting dressed for a fishing trip. As he sat on the edge of his bed, he carefully spread his trousers out on the floor. Then, with a joyous whoop, he quickly pulled both trousers legs toward him and in an instant was on his feet with his pants on. "I've always had a reason for doing that," Cus said. "You know when guys in boxin' come to me and try to put the bull on me, they say, 'Listen, D'Amato, you're no different from me. When you get dressed, you put your pants on one leg at a time.' And you know what I do when they say that? I laugh, I just have to laugh."

—OCTOBER 21, 1963

The Man's Hooked on Plugs

Seth Rosenbaum

S eth Rosenbaum lives in an apartment in Queens, N.Y. with 5,000 fishing lures. Some 3,000 of these lures are plugs, and there is little doubt that his plug collection ranks among the world's largest.

Originally carved from wood, plugs have been made of metal, cork and rubber, and in recent years, plastic. Designed to float, dive, sink, bob, pop or wobble and shaped to resemble baitfish, frogs, crayfish, mice or absolutely nothing at all found in nature, plugs have accounted for more than their share of world-record fish. Among them are a 69-pound 15-ounce muskie that glommed on to a Creek Chub Jointed Pikie, a 22-pound 4-ounce largemouth bass that fell for a Creek Chub Jointed Wag-Tail and an 11-pound 15-ounce smallmouth bass that tried to eat a Pearl White Bomber.

By profession Rosenbaum is a computer consultant, absolutely on top of digital science. Therefore, in an effort to keep up with his acquisitions, he is in the midst of a project to computerize his holdings on three different master lists: by name of lure, date made and manufacturer. For all this technological organization, complete with printouts, the truth is, Rosenbaum spends his idle hours mentally dwelling in the years 1910 and 1911, which he fondly refers to as "the golden age of plugs, when everybody was getting into the act."

On occasion, Rosenbaum lives out those golden days. He has been known to show up at seaside to pursue bluefish with a greenheart rod and Cuttyhunk line. And a few weeks ago he arrived at a friend's house to fish for largemouth bass—"the plug fish"—toting an ancient leather tackle box containing everything but a sled named *Rosebud*. There were bait-casting reels with braided silk lines, quill minnows from Victorian England, a selection of snelled-catgut hooks and, of course, plugs, among them an aluminum Shakespeare Revolution.

Once out on the friend's pond in a canoe, Rosenbaum tied on a 50-year-old Rush Tango plug five inches long. "One of the greats," he enthused. "The Tango floats when at rest, but almost half the plug is lip, and on a normal retrieve it dives to 25 feet, which is very deep indeed. That means my line takes a really sharp angle in the water, and even as this floating plug goes down it has very nice action. If I stop reeling, buoyancy brings it up again, so that I have a kind of three-dimensional action working for me." On his third cast, a 12-inch bass struck. Rosenbaum landed it with glee. "Camera! Camera!" he cried. "One doesn't see this every day!" He released the bass and confided, "What I've always wanted to have happen is to be fishing and have some stranger ask me, 'Hey, bud, what works on this lake?' and I'll casually answer, 'Oh, a 1902 Shakespeare Revolution and the 1921 Rush Tango are favorites here.'"

Now in his 40s, Rosenbaum has been fishing since he was seven. "I just bought lures for fishing back then," he recalls. "But by the 1950s I began buying some for esthetic reasons and I have simply kept on buying, plugs mainly. Because of my business, I always traveled a great deal, and whenever I hit a town I'd head for the local tackle stores. Tackle hadn't become as commercial as it is now. If a store didn't sell a plug in 1938, it was there in '39, and if it didn't sell in '39, it was there in '40. And it might still be there in

'52 or '53. Dealers didn't clean out their shelves then—the stuff just stayed on forever. I found I could buy very old material that might have been around 15, 20 or 30 years. After the '50s, with new merchandising methods and everything in little plastic envelopes or blister packs, and with the price getting knocked down in 30, 60, 90 days, it became harder and harder to find old tackle. I began to swap and advertise.

"Generally I'll run an ad in a publication with a circulation of 40,000 or under. I don't want to get inundated. I've had trouble keeping up with the moderate amount of mail I receive. In Glens Falls, N.Y., I advertised in the daily paper once or twice. I did O.K., maybe four or five responses. I got a Feather Gettum, which doesn't mean much to most people, but it's a rare lure. I also got a couple of old reels that I immediately passed on to Richard Miller in Hudson, Mass., who collects reels, along with rods and some plugs. I'm waiting to see what I get back from him. I'll take anything, but I can always pass the garbage on to another collector who thinks it's exotic stuff. I'm one of the few I know of who collect saltwater plugs; another is Dick Streater in Mercer Island, Wash. He and I trade Pacific Northwest salmon plugs. But I also have a nice collection of Atoms, particularly Reverse Atoms, and striped bass fishermen will pay $30 or $40 for a Reverse Atom because that type is not made anymore. Nowadays Bob Pond makes the Atom plugs, but they were originally made by Captain Bill on Cape Cod, out of wood. Then Pond came along with a plastic Atom. Actually, the rarest saltwater plug was made by Fuller Brothers, a popper that has beautifully tapered lines to it."

Like the bait-casting reel and the split-bamboo fly rod, the plug is an American invention. Despite the success of the balsa Rapala from Finland, plugs made in the U.S. have dominated the world angling market. As an authoritative English book, *The Penguin Guide to Fishing,* concedes: ". . . no British manufacturer has anything to offer as good as the plug baits imported from the United States."

According to a hallowed story about the invention of the plug, one day in 1888 James Heddon, a Michigan bass fisherman, was whittling a piece of wood on Dowagiac Creek while waiting for a pal to come by. Idly, Heddon tossed the piece of wood into the creek and was astounded to see a largemouth belt it into the air. Idea! Whittling while he worked, Heddon started turning out "Dowjack" plugs for friends, and by 1902 business had grown to such proportions that he built the first factory to turn out plugs in volume.

The early Heddon plugs were of cedar and invariably featured a propeller, as on the Artistic Minnow and the Double Dummy. Later plugs, such as the Deep O Diver, which is supposed to look like a crayfish, used a lip plate for diving. "Heddon specialized in hook gimmicks," Rosenbaum says. "His was the first company to come out with a hook hanger screwed into a plug. In 1911 Heddon introduced the Double Dummy, so called because of its unusual hooks. Let me read from an old ad. 'Jim Heddon's last invention, the Double Dummy design of hook, shows how triumphantly he satisfied his final ambition to produce a hook more certain of impaling the fish than any treble gang, yet free from its inhumanity and inconveniences. . . . The black bass, of all varieties and in all climates, always attacks the minnow at the side. . . . The single hook is placed to engage the upper jaw and the dummy portion comes into contact with the lower jaw, forcing the hook point into the upper jaw, without danger of disengagement.' "

To Rosenbaum, Heddon's finest achievement was the Luny Frog, which was manufactured in 1926. "Fishing with a Luny Frog is like playing with a deck of marked cards," he says of the plug he considers the greatest bass lure ever made. Unlike most frog imitations, which float on the retrieve, the Luny Frog's enticing action is displayed four or five feet underwater. It was made of Pyralin, similar to Bakelite, which was both its strength and weakness. "If you cast a Luny Frog and hit a rock," Rosenbaum says, "you have an 18-piece Luny Frog." On exceptional occasions Rosenbaum will fish a

Luny Frog in carefully scouted rockless areas using 40-pound-test line to make certain that a bass can't break off with it. "I couldn't bear to lose a Luny Frog," he says. "They are very rare. They are very precious to me." Not long ago when a friend suggested, with much throat clearing, that he would, ahem, like to borrow a Luny Frog, Rosenbaum raised a hand and cautioned, "My dear fellow, you can move into my apartment for a week, eat all the food in my well-stocked larder, wear my clothes, run up a huge phone bill, give wild parties and carry on in general, but I shall be in a motel, along with every Luny Frog I own."

Well before the Luny Frog or the Double Dummy, other companies had sprung up to compete with Heddon: Creek Club, South Bend, Pfueger and Shakespeare (started by a man named William Shakespeare, Jr.). "The finishes on Shakespeare plugs were probably better than anyone else's," Rosenbaum says. "Note the detail, right down to the painted fins." By 1910 a small company, K & K, had made the first jointed minnow. Rosenbaum is intrigued by its incorporation of metal fins, almost as much as its articulated movement.

Around World War I, an *Art Nouveau* artist named Louis Rhead began marketing imitations of frogs, crayfish and minnows under the name of "Nature Lures." Perhaps in an effort to knock down competition, Rhead decried "the faults of commercial baits made by machinery" in a book, *Fisherman's Lures and Game-fish Food*, published by Scribner's in 1920. Rhead is a controversial figure in American angling. Earlier, he had published a book on flies with most imaginative ties, but inasmuch as he gave his imitations of aquatic insects fanciful names, which beclouded entomological identification by anyone else, Rhead has been relegated to angling purgatory by fly-fishermen. In truth, Rhead belongs in angling heaven. He was far ahead of his time, and flytiers and plug makers have been taking ideas and inspiration from him for years. Rosenbaum has the finest collection of Rhead plugs in existence, as evidenced by the Shiner and very rare Crayfish, which he scooped up with joy and in numbers from the cellar of William Mills when that venerable Manhattan firm closed shop four years ago.

One of the truly exquisite plugs in the Rosenbaum collection is Schoenfeld's Sea Gull, made in 1923. "It's a relatively rare item," he says. "It's pretty, simply pretty. I've never fished with it." With its bulbous shape it might be considered a forerunner of the now popular Big O.

The Arbogast Sunfish Tin Liz was the first lure manufactured by Fred Arbogast. "He was a world champion plug caster, both for distance and accuracy," Rosenbaum says, "and he later made the Hawaiian Wiggler and the Jitterbug. His biggie was the Jitterbug, still as good as any surface plug made."

For all the plugs among his treasures, Rosenbaum lusts after a variant of the Rush Tango, called the Tigertango. "It has a blockier head than the regular Tango," he says. What would he swap for that, Rosenbaum was asked the other day by phone. "Anything except my life," he replied. A Heddon Luny Frog? "I wouldn't mention *that*," he said, abruptly hanging up. After the line went dead, one imagined Rosenbaum packing immediately to move to a motel.

—JULY 14, 1975

Salmon & Stoneflies from a Darwin Who Does Math

William Ricker

After years of following baseball and occasionally dipping into the sciences, I have arrived at these conclusions: Great mathematicians are like fastball pitchers. They're at their peak in their 20s, and after that they're finished. Great chemists are like curveball or screwball pitchers. They make their contributions in their 30s. But great biologists are like knuckleball pitchers. They can go on for years because they don't burn out. In fact, biologists get better with age.

I don't know why this is, but the truth of it came home to me forcefully not long ago when I had the good fortune to meet one of my longtime heroes, Dr. William E. Ricker, who at 76 is the Phil Niekro of fisheries biology. Ricker is the author of nearly 200 papers, articles and books about fish, aquatic insects and kindred subjects, and for a dozen years, from 1950 to '62, he served as the editor of the *Journal of the Fisheries Research Board of Canada* (now the *Canadian Journal of Fisheries and Aquatic Science*), which he made into the best publication of its kind in the world.

A tall, bespectacled man who sports a 1957 Johnny Unitas crew cut, Ricker is gracious and polite in that old-fashioned way that characterizes many Canadians, except when they're playing hockey. His office at the Pacific Biological Station in Nanaimo on Vancouver Island, B.C., where he served as chief scientist until his "retirement" in 1973, is awash with books and papers. No clean-desk man, Ricker works on two or three problems simultaneously until the answer to one, or all of them, suddenly pops into his head.

"Everybody doesn't work the same way I do," he says. "I've never consciously divided the day into sections. When there's a deadline I concentrate on the subject, whatever it is. I often wake up in the middle of the night and I stay awake for an hour or so, and some good ideas come to me at that time. When they do, I hop out of bed and write them down for fear they won't last. New or unusual ideas or relationships come spontaneously when you're not actively thinking about them."

The late Dr. George W. Bennett, who was the head of the aquatic biology section at the Illinois Natural History Survey and the leading authority on largemouth bass, once remarked, "Bill Ricker looks like a big country boy, but he's a genius." Dr. James Atz, a former curator of ichthyology at the American Museum of Natural History, says, "If Ricker worked in molecular biology or some other field in which Nobel prizes are given, he would have won at least one."

Ricker is the godfather of modern fisheries science, a different kettle of fish from fisheries biology, also a Ricker specialty. Fisheries science deals with the dynamics of fish populations, and Ricker figured out much of the mathematical methodology now used in this arcane field. The celebrated Ricker curve isn't a pitch but a graph representing the number of progeny added to a fish population by any given number of parent spawners. (The graph is based on the equation $R = \alpha P e^{-\beta P}$; where R = number of progeny, α = ratio of R to P when the stock is almost zero, P = size of parental stock, e = 2.718 . . . , and β = a parameter with dimensions of 1/P.) Ricker's 382-page *Computation and Interpretation of Biological Statistics of Fish Populations,* which is crammed with far more complex equations than that for the Ricker curve, is commonly known as "the Green Book" because of the color of the binding. It's *The Baseball Encyclopedia* of its field.

Also long intrigued by the fecundity of the Pacific salmons, Ricker proposed, in a paper published back in the 1950s, that they be stocked in waters to the east, such as the Great Lakes. A decade later, after sea lampreys had wiped out the lake trout in the Great Lakes and alewives had taken over, other scientists picked up on his suggestion, and chinook and coho salmon now flourish in the lakes, providing the basis of a multimillion-dollar sports fishery.

The Green Book is very heavy stuff, but Ricker's involvement with mathematics is only the means to any number of ends. Ricker's use of mathematics to check his insights helps make him unique. As another admirer, Dr. R. Ian Fletcher, former professor of fisheries and biomathematics at the University of Washington, puts it, "Darwin never wrote an equation in his life, but Ricker is like a Darwin who did."

Except for 11 years he served as a professor at Indiana University—he took over Alfred Kinsey's course in ornithology when Kinsey, who started out as an entomologist specializing in gall wasps, decided to devote himself to the study of human sexuality—Ricker has lived and worked in Canada. Yet in 1969, when the American Fisheries Society, a U.S. organization with international members, bestowed its first Award of Excellence medal, it bypassed several outstanding biologists in this country to give the award to Ricker for his "superb and original contributions" to the methodology of statistically sound sampling and interpretation of fish populations; the relationship between parent fish stocks and the numbers of surviving progeny; his new concepts about growth, mortality and predator influence on salmon; and his theory of lake circulation.

For all the accolades, Ricker's views don't always prevail. As he told the society a year later (he was unable to attend the award ceremony in '69 because he was in the U.S.S.R.), "Practically everyone who has ever gone fishing considers himself an expert in fish management and doesn't hesitate to say so. Also, the man who uses any particular type of fishing gear invariably regards all other types as pernicious and destructive; but he can insist, with a straight face, that *his* kind of fishing couldn't possibly do the stock any harm.

"And such illogical opinions can on occasion build up a head of pressure that cannot be resisted. Thus, there are many medium-sized streams, lakes and reservoirs on this continent that would benefit from a small net fishery but are wholly reserved for angling. As a result, fine stocks of whitefish and ciscoes go unused, suckers and buffaloes flourish, and even species like crappies may be greatly underutilized."

In bestowing its medal, the society noted, as an afterthought, that Ricker had a "sideline interest" in aquatic insects. This was like saying that Leonardo dabbled in painting. Ricker was then the world's leading authority on the insect order Plecoptera (stoneflies), an important food for trout. In the 1940s he completely rearranged some parts of the classification of this order, mainly on the basis of the evolutionary development of the genitalia. "Ricker smashed the old chaotic order of stoneflies," says Dr. Sandy B. Fiance, a stonefly specialist, "and what he built from the wreckage was a thing of beauty and simplicity that made evolutionary sense."

Ricker's stature in stonefly and fisheries research has been so outstanding that some scientists automatically assume that two experts working in two different fields happen to have the same name and middle initial. They are surprised to learn, as I have found, that there is only one William E. Ricker and that he is the expert in both fields.

Amazingly enough, Ricker first took up the study of stoneflies as a hobby. As far as he is concerned, anyone could become interested in them, and he cites the example of Raymond A. Hays, who began sending Ricker stoneflies for identification some years ago. Hays was a custodian in Bozeman, Mont., but he had a good reference library at hand because he happened to mop the floors in the zoology building at Montana State. He read voraciously, collected stoneflies from Hyalite Creek near the campus and corresponded with Ricker. "Hays was as good or better than I was," Ricker says.

Hays made Hyalite Creek perhaps the most studied stonefly stream in North America, if not the world. He collected a record 55 different species from it, including one previously unknown, which Ricker named *Isocapnia hyalita.* In honor of the energetic custodian, Ricker named a new stonefly species found in Yellowstone National Park *Nemoura haysi,* and when he collaborated with several other entomologists on a study, *The Stoneflies (Plecoptera) of Montana,* published by The American Entomological Society in 1972, Ricker saw to it that Hays was listed as one of the authors.

Although Ricker sometimes writes letters to friends in Latin, he doesn't necessarily use the customary Latin or Greek to name new species of stoneflies. "The classical languages have been rather thoroughly ransacked," he says. "Scientific names proposed for organisms should preferably be distinctive, euphonious and descriptive, in that order of importance," he says. Ricker prefers to use Spanish, native American Indian or Russian words for scientific names; he's familiar with, if not fluent in, these languages. But he says, "My only claim to linguistic virtuosity is that I can sing at least one song in English, French, German, Russian, Spanish, Italian, Latin and Japanese." He is the author of the *Russian-English Dictionary for Students of Fisheries and Aquatic Biology* and has translated about 100 Russian scientific papers into English. The species name *usa,* as in *Alloperia usa,* a stonefly that Ricker named, comes from the Russian word *usy* (mustache). He chose it because of the patch of hairs on the stonefly's behind. *Zapada chila,* another stonefly named by Ricker, is both Russian and Spanish. The generic name *Zapada* comes from the Russian *zapad* (west)—because the genus occurs mainly in western North America—while *chila* comes from the Spanish for red pepper. Ricker thought this particular insect was "a red-hot discovery" because it was the first one found in the East. He gave a specimen of Allocapnia the species name of *au-*

rora "because it suddenly dawned on me that this must be a new species."

In his spare time—what there is of it—Ricker golfs, trolls for salmon and does a bit of fly-fishing. "I was probably at my peak when I was in my 40s," he says. "Still, I suppose a biologist goes downhill more slowly than a mathematician or chemist because the accumulated background tends to make up for declining analytical powers. I'm not as strong as the young fellows, but I know the tricks a lot better."

—NOVEMBER 12, 1984

Friends of a Living Fossil

Bill Casper

all it Jurassic Lake. It is Wisconsin's Lake Winnebago, home of *Acipenser fulvescens,* the lake sturgeon, a member of a family of fish that evolved with the dinosaurs 200 million years ago. Like all sturgeons, the lake sturgeon is a "living fossil," a bizarre-looking creature whose retractable mouth can hang like a hose from the underside of its head and whose body is armored with rows of thick plates instead of scales.

Probably because they live underwater, sturgeons survived by adapting to the climatic changes at the end of the Cretaceous Period that led to the disappearance of dinosaurs 65 million years ago. But in the last 50 years most of the earth's 25 sturgeon species—which are found only in the Northern Hemisphere—have been threatened with extinction by pollution, habitat alteration and overfishing.

Happily, the lake sturgeon population at Lake Winnebago is not in immediate jeopardy. Thanks in large part to the efforts of Bill Casper, an affable but persistent retired machinist from Fond du Lac, Wis., and of Sturgeon for Tomorrow, the citizens' organization Casper founded 19 years ago, the 215-square-mile body of water has the largest self-sustaining population of lake sturgeon anywhere.

Casper, now 65, got the idea for the organization one winter day in 1977 while poised to spear a sturgeon through a hole cut in the ice of Winnebago. "I was concerned about what would happen if the stock were depleted, if the resource ever needed help," Casper says. Although lake sturgeon can live a long time (the record for longevity is 154 years) and grow to enormous size for a freshwater fish (the biggest was a 7'11", 310-pound female from Lake Superior), they are late to mature sexually. Females in Winnebago do not spawn until they are 20 to 25 years old, and then they do not spawn every year. In fact, only 10% to 20% of adult lake sturgeon spawn in a given year. Therefore, when an adult population decreases drastically, its group may not be able to rebuild for decades, if ever.

Lake sturgeon were abundant in the Great Lakes and the Midwest when Native Americans were the only human inhabitants. In Longfellow's *Song of Hiawatha* the biggest challenge facing Hiawatha is to catch a lake sturgeon, "the monster Mishe-Nahma . . . King of Fishes." Lake sturgeon began to decline in North America as the Great Lakes area became more heavily populated in the 19th century. Fishermen slaughtered sturgeon because they tore holes in nets set for whitefish and lake trout. As tastes changed in the late 19th century, the sturgeon became popular for its flesh, especially when smoked, and its eggs, which, when rinsed in cold water and lightly salted, became caviar, or "black gold." The sturgeon in the Midwest were further imperiled by pollution from industrial development and by dams that blocked the way to spawning rivers. (Despite their name, lake sturgeon need running water to procreate.)

To attract people to the first meeting of Sturgeon for Tomorrow, Casper posted notices in bars, restaurants and tackle shops all around Lake Winnebago. Almost 150 people, mostly local dairy farmers, showed up for the get-together in the Taycheedah (Wis.) Town Hall. Today the organization has 3,000 members spread among four chapters, and the adult sturgeon population in Lake Winnebago has risen to nearly 45,000 from about 11,500 in 1977.

Each chapter of Sturgeon for Tomorrow holds an annual fund-raising banquet, and members also sell T-shirts, caps and other items, such as Jim Beam bourbon in bottles shaped like sturgeon. Most of the nearly $200,000 raised to date has gone to the Wisconsin Department of Natural Resources (DNR) to fund sturgeon research.

Every spring, Sturgeon for Tomorrow underwrites the cost of lodging and food for 400 volunteers who, wearing caps emblazoned STURGEON PATROL, watch out for poachers along 125 miles of the Wolf and Fox rivers, which are tributaries of Lake Winnebago. There the fish are so absorbed in their spawning that they can be patted on the head. A 100-pound female, with about a quarter of her weight in eggs, might sell for $1,500 to a wholesale dealer out of state. "We always heard stories about eggs being sold illegally in the Chicago area," Casper says. "Not many dairy farmers around here eat caviar."

Initially, Casper wanted money raised by Sturgeon for Tomorrow to help build a sturgeon hatchery for the DNR near Lake Winnebago. "We didn't know very much about spawning back then," Casper says, "and I just wanted to learn how to raise these fish." Work on the hatchery began, but when it turned out that hatchery fish were not needed for Lake Winnebago—"We've learned that the system will take care of itself with careful management," Casper says—the DNR changed the focus and began stocking eggs, fry and fingerlings in Wisconsin waters that had lost their sturgeon. The DNR also has given eggs and fry to biologists in Missouri, Michigan, Minnesota and Ohio who are trying to restore those states' fisheries.

Sturgeon fishing on Winnebago is now strictly regulated. The season opens on the second Saturday in February and ends March 1; spearing is the only method allowed. Last winter 8,000 people bought $10 sturgeon permits. The lake was dotted with fishing shanties—complete with stoves, TV and other amenities—on the 20-inch-thick ice. Casper, a Green Bay Packers fan, built his shanty to look like a Packers helmet.

The spearers took a total of 3,175 sturgeon from the lake last winter. The season limit per spearer is one fish, which must be 45 inches or longer; possession of a sturgeon shorter than that can bring a fine as high as $3,000. The fish must be measured, weighed, sexed and tagged by DNR biologists waiting at registration stations onshore. (The resulting information is passed on to radio station WMBE in Chilton, which broadcasts four sturgeon reports each day.) The record Winnebago sturgeon, speared in 1953, was 6'6" long and weighed 180 pounds.

Some spearers use 45-inch weighted sturgeon decoys to lure live fish of legal length to their holes. Others use whatever they think will prove attractive to a sturgeon, be it an old white chamber pot, ears of corn attached to the ends of an iron pipe, or the twirling agitator from a washing machine. Why would a sturgeon be attracted to such stuff? "They're nosy fish," says Casper's wife, Kathy.

Still, not everything is O.K. with the sturgeon of Lake Winnebago. The Fox River has a history of fish kills going back to the 1960s. In 1988 some 37,000 fish, including 19 lake sturgeon, died in the Fox from a combination of environmental conditions. One contributing factor was carbon monoxide from motor testing on the river by Mercury Marine. The state of Wisconsin sued the company, and before the case went to trial, Mercury Marine agreed to pay $60,000 as a settlement. Since then the company and the DNR have been working together to maintain healthy environmental conditions on the river.

Of special concern to Sturgeon for Tomorrow is whether mining will be allowed at the zinc-copper sulfide deposit near Crandon, Wis. The deposit, one of the largest in the world, sits at the headwaters of the Wolf River, Lake Winnebago's main sturgeon spawning ground. The deposit was discovered by Exxon Coal and Minerals in 1975. The company backed off its plans for development in 1986, only to return in 1994 with a Canadian partner, Rio Algom, in a partnership called the Crandon Mining Co. Whether Crandon Mining gets to start digging depends on the disposition of its state and federal permit applications.

One Native American tribe fighting against the mining is the Menominee, but to Casper's dismay, part of the tribe's suit in federal court argues that the Menominees never gave up their fishing rights in Lake Winnebago. The tribe contends that it retains all fishing and hunting rights to those waters, including, presumably, setting its own limits on lake sturgeon.

"After Sturgeon for Tomorrow started, we got a lock closed in the Fox River to stop sea lampreys [which could parasitize and kill sturgeon] coming up from Lake Michigan," Casper says. "Then we dealt with outboard testing. Now we have Crandon Mining and the Menominee situation. We plan on continuing no matter what happens. Sturgeon for Tomorrow must carry on."

—November 12, 1984

Afterword

Of the men profiled in this book, most are still alive and pursuing their obsessions.

Harry and his wife Elsie are gone, and so are Charlie Brooks, Chanler Chapman (cousin Ricky Aldrich is the heir to the family-held title of "the most eccentric man in America"), and Dick Wolters (after a heart attack at age 55, he had given up parachuting but resumed hang gliding). Although long gone, Joyce and Zane Grey, like Nabokov, live on in their books.

From 1960 to 1977, my family and I lived in Croton-on-Hudson, and I began to take fishing very seriously. On my days off I fished local ponds, city reservoirs, streams and the Hudson River itself, often with Jack Olsen, another senior writer on the magazine. Olsen got me into fly fishing, and I went up to the Catskills to do a story on Harry Darbee, and Harry gave me my initial lessons in fly tying. Rather full of myself, I remember saying, "Gee, Harry, I'll bet I'm going to tie better flies than you do." Harry replied, "I hope you do, I hope you do." I suddenly felt very small.

In 1966, I co-founded, with Dom Pirone—a retired biology professor at Manhattan College—the Hudson River Fishermen's Association, later renamed Riverkeeper, an organization dedicated to preserving the Hudson River.

It was Dom who told me about Bob Abplanalp, the aerosol king who loved to fish. The Abplanalp story, as the journalistic cliche goes, had "legs on it." Watergate broke after the piece about him appeared in *SI*, and the media wanted to interview him because he was one of Richard Nixon's two closest pals (the other was Bebe Rebozo). Abplanalp refused to give interviews, and the media had to resort to mining the *SI* profile. A few years later, Abplanalp again popped up in the news when F. Sherwood (Sherry) Rowland and Mario Molina at the University of California, Irvine, warned that CFCs, chlorofluorocarbons, could devastate the stratospheric ozone layer. The public began boycotting aerosol spray cans, and Abplanalp, the biggest aerosol-spray manufacturer in the world, publicly lambasted the two scientists. In 1978, the United States, Canada, Norway and Sweden, banned CFC-aerosol sprays, and in 1987, the U.S. and 23 other nations formally agreed to cut back on CFC use.

I'm probably one of the few people in the world, maybe the only one, who has interviewed both Sherry Rowland and Bob Abplanalp, and so in 1989 while I was writing a book, *Dead Heat, The Race Against the Greenhouse Effect,* with Michael Oppenheimer of the Environmental Defense Fund, I called Abplanalp to ask him what he was thinking about, just what was he doing while he was lambasting Rowland and Molina. I got an interesting answer. He said that he was very quietly searching for a substitute propellant, and when the 1978 ban went into effect he was ready with Aquasol, a nonflammable solution of water and butane.

"This gave us a hell of an edge," he said. "Maybe I did call Molina an asshole, but he did a lot for us. Business has been fantastic." It's gotten even more so, and so have the size of the accommodations and prices at Walkers Key, although Abplanalp is now out of the tropical fish business. As for Sherry Rowland and Molina, well, in 1995 they won the Nobel Prize in Chemistry.

When Eric Leiser had his fly shop Rivergate in Cold Spring, a great gathering place for sundry characters, he introduced me to Paul Schmookler and Art (the Black Ghost) Broadie. Eric also told me about another character, Boston cabbie and flytyer named Jack Gartside. Broadie winters in Florida, and I've recently seen Jack at fly-fishing shows selling flies and his self-published books. Paul Schmookler has given up embalming aquatic insects in plastic and has moved from the Bronx to Massachusetts where he and Ingrid Sils, the love of his life—they met when they happened to see one another turning over rocks in a stream—have written, illustrated and produced several stunningly beautiful heavyweight books themselves, starting with *Rare and Unusual Fly Tying Materials: A Natural History.* Eric put me on to Lefty Kreh, who remains as ebullient as ever. Lefty's Deceiver is even on a U.S. postage stamp.

I forget how I heard about Donal O'Brien, but he is now the Chairman of the National Audubon Society. I first heard about Dr. Herbert R. Axelrod in an aquarium store, and I only got to interview him because he said that I was a nut, too. No longer with TFH, he is living in New Jersey where he has an "unlisted phone at the customer's request." When I last spoke to him some years ago he exulted, "I have genera named after me! That means everything in the genus has my name!"

I met Ken Gerhardt, now deep jigging off Cape Cod, fishing for striped bass in the Croton River, I went to Trinity with Joe Hyde, and I met Seth Rosenbaum, who became my bass fishing buddy, at a meeting of the American Littoral Society in 1963. Alas, Seth died in the summer of 2000 after selling his plug collection some years previous. I ran across John Betts tying his synthetic flies at an outdoor show. The first time I stopped at his booth, I thought this guy's crazy, and walked on. Then I said wait a minute to myself, this guy's a hell of a story and went back to talk to him. John now lives in Denver where he forges his own 17th-century-style hooks and makes his own tapered fly lines out of multi-strand monofilament core placed inside Dacron backing. Impregnated with a floatant, he says that the line "floats all the way to the tip and doesn't rot like silk." I knew about William E. Ricker, still living in British Columbia at this writing, by reputation and from reading his stonefly papers, and the same goes for Ken Stewart, a leading nymphmaniac, now a regents research professor at the University of North Texas and busy revising *Plecoptera Nymphs of North America.* Serge Doroshov, a world authority on sturgeon and professor of Animal Science at UC, Davis, told me about Bill Casper, an object lesson of what one fisherman can accomplish and a winner of the *Outdoor Life* Conservation award. In July 2001, Bill was instrumental in holding an international sturgeon symposium that drew more than 380 scientists from 22 countries in North America and Eurasia to Oshkosh, by gosh.

And finally there is Joe DeFalco, Famous Hunter. I heard about Joe DeFalco from Jim Brady, retired Treasury agent, fishing friend, and outdoor writer who wrote one of the first books on turkey hunting. Joe DeFalco is still putting on his Annual Joe DeFalco Hunting Expo, his how to dress a deer show. Joe DeFalco's last one, in the year 2000 at the Vanderbilt, a night club on Long Island, drew 5,000 people, and Joe DeFalco's book, *The Complete Deer Hunt,* sells 100,000 to 150,000 copies a year. Joe DeFalco owns 1,700 acres of land in the Catskills, including two and a half miles on the Delaware River. Joe DeFalco has won 204 lawsuits in a row battling politicians, and Joe DeFalco has a stable of 10 race horses. (Joe DeFalco has his own website, Joe DeFalco.com.) When the Riverkeeper organization launched the Riverkeeper boat in 1983, we didn't have enough money for an engine. Joe DeFalco got us one, a Mariner, but he never got to go out on the boat. Joe DeFalco, I hope this book makes up for that omission.

—NOVEMBER 2001

Permissions Acknowledgments

You Spigotty Anglease?" appeared in an abbreviated form in the *New York Times* (July 23, 2000).

All other articles originally appeared in *Sports Illustrated*. "No Fly-by-Night Cabbie Is Jack" (September 13, 1982); "Gotcha! Hook, Line and Lingerie" (May 1, 1981); "He Deftly Ties the World's Fanciest Flies" (August 21, 1963); "Spare the Rod(s), Spoil the Cast" (April 7, 1980); "Shhh! It's the Black Ghost" (December 8, 1980); "The Man Who Lived Two Lives in One" (August 29, 1968); "He's Got a Very Fishy Look" (September 3, 1979); "A Warm Spot for a Very Cold Sport" (February 15, 1988); "The Strange Fish and Stranger Times of Dr. Herbert R. Axelrod" (May 13, 1965); "With a Quack, Quack Here" (September 27, 1971); "The Obsessions of a Late Bloomer" (August 18, 1969); "'Hey, You Wanna Deer?'" (January 10, 1983); "Step in and Enjoy the Turmoil" (June 13, 1977); "An Absence of Wood Nymphs" (September 14, 1959); "Trick or Truite" (November 8, 1971); "Yep, Another Nymphmaniac" (August 18, 1980); "Spitmouth Puffers in the Living Room" (December 8, 1969); "*Nomen Piscis est Morone Saxatilis*—And It Is Best Not to Argue About It" (October, 27, 1975); "'I'm a Bit of a

Fanatic'" (October 21, 1963); "The Man's Hooked on Plugs" (July 14, 1975); "Salmon & Stoneflies from a Darwin Who Does Math" (November 12, 1984); "Friends of a Living Fossil" (April 3, 1996); "The Creature from the Aquarium" (April 22, 1991).

Reprinted courtesy of *Sports Illustrated* © 1959, 1963, 1964, 1965, 1968, 1969, 1971, 1975, 1977, 1979, 1980, 1981, 1982, 1983, 1984, 1988, 1991, 1996.